Right Time, Right Place

ALSO BY RICHARD BROOKHISER

The Outside Story:
How Democrats and Republicans Re-Elected Reagan

The Way of the WASP:
How It Made America, and How It Can Save It . . . So to Speak

Founding Father: Rediscovering George Washington

Rules of Civility: The 110 Precepts That Guided
Our First President in War and Peace

Alexander Hamilton, American

America's First Dynasty: The Adamses 1735–1918

Gentleman Revolutionary:
Gouverneur Morris, The Rake Who Wrote the Constitution

What Would the Founders Do? (Our Questions, Their Answers)

George Washington on Leadership

Right Time, Right Place

Coming of Age with William F. Buckley Jr. and the Conservative Movement

RICHARD BROOKHISER

BASIC
BOOKS

A Member of the Perseus Books Group
New York

Published by Basic Books,
A Member of the Perseus Books Group

Books published by Basic Books are available at special discounts for bulk purchases in the United States by corporations, institutions, and other organizations. For more information, please contact the Special Markets Department at the Perseus Books Group, 2300 Chestnut Street, Suite 200, Philadelphia, PA 19103, or call (800) 810-4145, ext. 5000, or e-mail special.markets@perseusbooks.com.

Designed by Brent Wilcox

Library of Congress Cataloging-in-Publication Data
Brookhiser, Richard.
    Right time, right place : my coming of age with William F. Buckley Jr. and the conservative movement / Richard Brookhiser.
        p.   cm.
    Includes index.
    ISBN 978-0-465-01355-5 (alk. paper)
    1. Brookhiser, Richard.   2. Buckley, William F. (William Frank), 1925–2008—Friends and associates.   3. Conservatism—United States. 4. Journalists—United States—Biography.   I. Title.
    PN4874.B725A33 2009
    070.92—dc22
    [B]
                                                            2009003073

10 9 8 7 6 5 4 3 2 1

FOR
Terry Teachout

Bliss was it in that dawn to be alive,
But to be young was very Heaven!
WILLIAM WORDSWORTH

Never glad confident morning again!
ROBERT BROWNING

Acknowledgments

Lou Cannon refreshed my memory of the 1984 cycle.

I would like to thank my editor, Lara Heimert, and my agent, Michael Carlisle.

My wife, Jeanne Safer, urged me to dig deeper, as she always does.

INTRODUCTION

WILLIAM F. BUCKLEY JR. (1925–2008) changed the world. I was at his side during the years the world noticed it. George Will once said, "Without Buckley, no *National Review* [the magazine he edited for twenty-five years]; without *National Review*, no conservative takeover of the Republican party; without that, no Reagan; without Reagan, no victory in the Cold War." I came into Bill Buckley's life in 1969, halfway through that march of accomplishments. I came of age, and middle age, along with the conservative movement that he midwifed. He was my boss and my mentor. He discovered me, tapped me as his heir—and then changed his mind. I had to find a new voice, as a writer and a historian, while both of us reconfigured our relationship, and while the world changed again, in ways nobody had predicted.

This is my story of a remarkable man. Bill Buckley was a famous man—at the top of his game, he was at the top of the world. His television show aired in a hundred markets, his syndicated column ran in hundreds of newspapers, his books appeared regularly on the best-seller list. Presidents and movie stars hobnobbed with him, world-famous musicians performed in his living room, comics imitated him. Much of that slipped away as he aged and tired, but when he died he was treated as a fallen head of state. "If I'm still famous," he had instructed his son about his funeral, "ask the cardinal to hold it in St. Patrick's; otherwise, tuck me away in Sharon," the family's Connecticut home. The memorial mass was in St. Patrick's, with 2,200 mourners.

He was also vital. What he liked he loved, and what he loved he had to share with colleagues, friends, and casual acquaintances. His delight was a boy's, even when the taste was a connoisseur's and the judgment a man's. At the end of one of his books about sailing, the onboard representative of the owner of the yacht he has rented tells him there is some weakness in the mast, he should let up on the last leg. Bill's attitude is, that's the owner's problem; I rented the boat, we're in the Atlantic Ocean with a good wind, let her rip. He brought that avidity of appreciation to ideas, words, music, food, gadgets; to his friendships.

THIS IS ALSO my story of the conservative movement, and of the world in which it came to power, with the potential for accomplishments and the certainty of failure that power entails. In the age of Obama, conservatism is in retreat—though perhaps its retreat began with Bill Clinton, or the Bushes, father and son—but it will be back, and its ups and downs are of interest to conservatives, their enemies, and ordinary Americans. When I met Bill Buckley, there were still Soviet troops in Berlin. Ten years later, they were in Afghanistan. Ten years after that, the Berlin Wall collapsed. Twelve years after that, the World Trade Towers collapsed. The conservative movement helped elect presidents, from Richard Nixon to Ronald Reagan to George W. Bush. Like a typhoon, the turn of the millennium threw amazing sea creatures on the beach: prophets (Aleksandr Solzhenitsyn), freaks (Monica Lewinsky), monsters (Pol Pot). Working for Bill Buckley at *National Review*, I covered these and many other figures and events. I shook Castro's hand; Reagan laughed at one of my jokes, and Margaret Thatcher repeated it. One of my friends got anthrax after 9/11. You *had* to be interested in history from 1969 to 2008; to borrow a line from Christopher Hitchens, it was interested in you.

THIS IS, FINALLY, my story of a relationship. Bill was a generous and devoted man; he was also willful, capricious, impulsive. The former qualities generally prevailed over eruptions of the latter, but the latter could give you a wild ride. I went on a number. One fine day he announced that I would succeed him; another, he announced that I would not (there were other little surprises in store besides those). I was the more susceptible because I was thirty years younger than he was, because I was looking for someone to look up to, because it took me thirty years to realize that friendship is one of the few solid things you can have in this world, and rare enough.

The story includes the teller of the story. When I met Bill Buckley I was a teenager—a young man from the provinces. In forty years I have fallen in love many times—with writing, with Bill and his magazine, with my wife, with a man who has been dead for two hundred years (though he is still alive). I am unusually impressionable, and I keep better-than-average track of my impressions. They are the substance of my life, and the medium of this book.

This story is especially for the young. Those who are too young to remember Buckley will meet an arresting and significant figure; they may also learn, from the evolutions of my career, some points of use for their own. My life has not been quite what I expected it to be, but then nothing ever is; we make the best of new opportunities. Finding your own place in the world is a neat trick. I offer my experiences as stimulus and guidance.

CHAPTER 1

I MET BILL Buckley by writing for him.

I grew up in Irondequoit, New York, a suburb of Rochester, a midsize upstate city, with my parents and my older brother, Bob. We lived in a ranch house on a half-acre lot in a tract of other post-war houses that had been developed in a former peach orchard. Dad worked, Mom was the mother, Bob and I were smart—that was the family division of labor.

In the fall of 1969 I was a freshman in the local public high school (I didn't know anybody who went to private ones); my brother was a junior at Yale. Every weekend of the school year since he had gone away to college I wrote him, on a small black metal typewriter that had belonged to Mom, a letter rehearsing the events of the week—basketball games, school plays, little triumphs, tiny disasters, bulletins of adolescence dramatized and ironized. I wrote to inform him: He knew many of the repeating characters—parents, teachers, friends of mine who were younger siblings of friends of his. But mostly I wrote to portray myself, to Bob, and to my parents, to whom I read the letters aloud (like an out-of-town preview) before mailing them off.

One week the news barged into this home theater. Opponents of the Vietnam War had called for a nationwide moratorium, or day of protests, on October 15. The moratorium looked to be a big thing on college campuses, where teach-ins and boycotts of classes were planned. Some kids in my high school decided to join in. I thought they were wrong; I also thought there was something phony about the exercise, simultaneously preening and copycat. The moratorium's supporters at Irondequoit High presented themselves as dissidents, but they were tagging along with a national movement, mimicking their elders.

I decided to put counterposters, antiprotest protests, on the school walls. I imagined myself as a latter-day Martin Luther, taping rather than hammering up criticisms of orthodoxy for all to see. I generated my posters by typing them out, over and over, on the black typewriter, using carbon paper to produce four copies at a time (I had only twelve contentious theses, not Luther's ninety-five). The bottom copy of each batch was pretty fuzzy, and when I put the carbon paper in backward for one batch I got a set of mirror-image duds. After a night's work I had made thirty-three posters, and I gave them to the world on the fifteenth.

All my efforts, and the more organized protests of Moratorium Day that I hoped to deflate, went into that weekend's letter to my brother. It made for a longer story than usual, and in his next letter home he said he had enjoyed it. Then my father said, Why don't you send it to *National Review*?

No one in my family knew anything about journalism. We knew William F. Buckley Jr. from television, and we had been subscribing to his magazine for half a year. Perhaps that would be entrée enough. I took "Dear Bob" off the beginning of my letter, added a conclusion, and sent it away.

Months passed without a word from *National Review*. I assumed they had not liked the submission and thrown it away, and that this was standard procedure in journalism. Then, after the New Year, I got a letter from C. H. Simonds, assistant managing editor.

Dear Mr. Brookhiser:
Please forgive our slowness in dealing with your manuscript. It somehow got buried on my desk. [This, I would learn, actually was standard procedure in journalism.] *Miss Buckley* [Priscilla Buckley,

Bill's older sister and managing editor], *Mr. Buckley and I have read it, and are eager to publish it.*

He added, "We do receive manuscripts from people your age; but I'm sure this will be the first we've ever published."

Anyone who submits something for the approval of the world expects, in some corner of his mind, that he will be approved. This expectation is stronger in the ignorant, who don't know the system or the odds, strongest maybe in a teenager with encouraging parents (doting, in the case of my mother) whose admiration, he assumes, will be widely shared as soon as the world takes notice. But when approval actually came, it was startling. The world of public events, which included the media that reported on them, was "out there." Now someone from out there had signaled back.

More surprises followed. When my article appeared, in the issue dated February 24, 1970, one day after my fifteenth birthday, it was the cover story. The cover image was a sepia-tone photograph of a boy wearing a buttoned-down shirt, open at the neck, and a jacket covered with political buttons. The boy was a son of the magazine's art director, but by chance, he looked rather like me (dark hair, half sideburns, wavy bang, snub nose). *MORATORIUM DAY AT IRONDEQUOIT HIGH*, said the headline, *by RICK BROOKHISER, student.*

The next surprise, a few weeks later, was a check for $180. The question of money had given me some anxiety. It must cost something, I thought, to print magazines and distribute them; perhaps I would be asked to contribute, to help defray expenses. The idea that I might be paid, in addition to being published, was icing on the cake.

About the time the check arrived, I began getting letters from readers. Some came from other young writers who said they were like me, and sent their writings to prove it: a science fiction magazine from Saskatchewan; a mimeographed medieval fanzine from somewhere in the South. Most of the letter writers praised, gawked, or did both at once. There were twenty in all, which would be a piddling response in the days of e-mail and texting, but in 1969 when each of these communications had to be sealed, stamped, and dropped in a mailbox, it seemed impressive, all the more to someone who had never gotten a letter from anyone he did not know.

There were media aftershocks. *The Rochester Times-Union* took my picture for a profile of the local boy who had made good. Two academics asked to reprint the article in a book called *Student Dissent in the Schools* (I was to be the token right-winger). A teacher at a local college interviewed me for a piece she hoped to write for *Esquire*. *Esquire* did not bite; the magazine that sent Jean Genet to cover the Chicago convention was not interested in Irondequoit High. But the newspaper article and the book appeared as planned. That, plus the original article, made three more appearances in the world out there than I could realistically have expected to make.

What was the article like? If I got it as an editor now, would I publish it? It had its bitchy moments—I criticized the moratorium supporters for using "such words as 'leafletting.'" It had its light moments—I recorded all the elaborate labor of the carbon paper. I banged away in high dudgeon. When supporters of the moratorium stood on the high school lawn and read a list of soldiers who had died in Vietnam, I took the mangling of a name to be a sign that it was all for show; if they really cared, they would have pronounced the dead man's name correctly. There was a lot of showing going on, but honest people also make slips of the tongue; having sent my thoughts to *National Review,* I was not innocent of showing them off myself. Even as a teenager I saw one thing that opponents of the war denied or fudged: Withdrawing from Vietnam would leave it "open to Communist subjugation."

I know why the assistant managing editor, Miss Buckley, and Mr. Buckley published it. I was a dog walking on its hind legs: Fifteen-year-old speaks! I was also dog bites man. There were plenty of young people even in the late sixties who were conservative, or simply not liberal. When eighteen- to twenty-one-year-olds voted in the 1972 election, as many of them voted for Richard Nixon as for George McGovern. But they were not the young people you saw on television, or in most newspapers and magazines. The archetypal young people of the major media, whether admired or feared, were idealistic liberals, hairy radicals, or copulating druggies: heroes, rebels, or freaks. Here, said the editors of *National Review*, was a kid, a high school freshman no less, who speaks for the unseen.

There was one more reaction to the piece, the most important of all: a blue three-by-five card, with *National Review*'s name and address in bold, and an italicized identifier, *Wm. F. Buckley Jr., Editor*. Below that, in spindly red ink, a message, something like, "Richard: Nice going. Congratulations" or "Rick: Very nice. Thanks." In time I would learn that every contributor to every issue of *National Review* got such a card from Wm. F. Buckley Jr., which did not diminish its value. Rather, the reverse; the cards were a courtesy in a profession that often skipped courtesies. Over the years I saved many such cards, a fraction of all the ones I was sent. Since they are undated, I can't tell now which one came first. No matter; it was—they were—a beam of attention from the top.

MY FIRST ENCOUNTER with Bill Buckley was as fortuitous as a lightning strike. But the material for the fire had been piling up for years.

I first saw him, as many people did, on his TV show, *Firing Line*. It went on the air in 1966. When my family started watching it, it was (as it remained for most of its thirty-three-year run) an hour of discussion, mostly political, moderated by Buckley.

The world of media and the world of political talk were much smaller then. There was, of course, no Internet, and no talk radio (except for Paul Harvey in the Midwest). There were three TV networks, plus public television, which was making its transition from state college professors giving extension courses to British imports. Commercial television consisted of entertainment, sports, and news, in that order. The boundaries of taste were set by comfortable, mainstream figures. David Brinkley and Johnny Carson were witty; Walter Cronkite was authoritative.

Firing Line seemed to come from a different planet. The show was epitomized by the theme song—the trumpet fanfare from the third movement of the Second Brandenburg Concerto. The perky little instrument that played it was a baroque trumpet, bright and high-voiced, an instrument that had been a museum piece since the days of Bach and Handel. If you were not a classical music buff, the only other time you had heard one was in "Penny Lane." The theme promised a show that would be quick, sharp, light, serious, and cool.

The set was simple: two chairs, three if there were two guests; little side tables for glasses of water. The spareness highlighted Buckley's posture and mannerisms. He took the show very seriously—he sat with a clipboard that held the capsule biographies he had written as introductions for his guests and quotations of theirs that he intended to confront them with. The clipboard also supported a stopwatch, so he could keep track of the time.

But Buckley was determined to be comfortable while he talked. Comfort for him required motion. He swiveled, leaned, and slouched. He never bothered about his clothes—his wife, Pat, picked them all—but they were good quality. He was handsome, not in a movie star way, neither All-American nor Method Ethnic, but with a look that, if he had been short, would have been elfin.

Comics who included Buckley among their impressions focused on his tongue. That was obvious; he had a way of licking his lips—licking his chops—when he was about to make a point; Robin Williams turned him into a monitor lizard. But the most striking thing about Buckley on TV was the way his eyes widened, to signal amusement, mock bafflement, or the imminent destruction of an interlocutor. The eyes were heat-seeking—and pleasure-seeking—sensors. They were quick, too—the winks and stares flashed by like semaphore.

His accent struck most people, including me, as British. There was something transatlantic in it—he had spent a few years at a Catholic private school in England—but the base paint was southern: His father was an oil man from Texas, his mother a New Orleans belle. Many people disliked his accent, thinking that it was a snobbish affectation; I liked it for the same reason, in the way that deferential Americans embraced tony Brits from the Avengers to Alistair Cooke.

Firing Line would be inconceivable now. Jesus would not get an hour on television if He came back. Years later I would meet an old left-wing man who asked me to thank Mr. Buckley for giving the Left its only forum in the late sixties. He meant, the only opportunity for leftists to state their views at length (they were covered, if not quoted, by the news). Buckley gave them this opportunity only to try to beat them up. But he did give them the opportunity (honor comes only from victory over worthy opponents). One of my favorite clips of *Firing Line* shows Bill and a young, slim Allen Ginsberg, who is holding something on his lap. The poet asks if can sing a song in praise of Lord Krishna. Bill says generously, "Go right ahead." Ginsberg's object turns out to be a harmonium, which he plays while singing, badly but passionately, a long chant. When he finishes, Bill says, "That's the most unhurried Krishna I've ever heard." He joked, but he let Ginsberg sing it first.

But what most struck me about Buckley on *Firing Line* as a new viewer was the beating up. In this sense he was the ancestor, legitimate if distant, of 24/7 contention, all yelling all the time. I remember an encounter with the radical lawyer William Kunstler. Kunstler's hair looked like stuffing from a sofa. His manner was both familiar and overbearing, a combination of *haimish* and obnoxious. Buckley gripped him like a terrier and would not let him go. He maintained the formalities, giving each guest his *Mr.* or her *Mrs.*, to a degree that was unusual in first-name/nickname America. But he would not give their beliefs a respite, if they were enemies of America, my family, or me.

AFTER WATCHING BUCKLEY on television I read him. My father came home one day with a paperback he had found in the rack at the drugstore: *Up from Liberalism*, by William F. Buckley Jr. This was a reissue of his third book, first published in 1959. No one seems to have noticed—or did they?—that, in the cover shot, the hand propped against his right cheek is giving the finger.

The book was an amalgam of controversial bits and pieces he had written over several years. It showed two of his favorite literary methods at work: Each episode was a counterpunch, taking a public figure—Eleanor Roosevelt, Dwight Eisenhower, John Kenneth

Galbraith—and picking apart something she or he had said or done; the episodes were brought together in a montage, mixed up and bounced off each other. When the techniques worked, it was like riffling a deck of pictures that show you a running man.

One image went straight to my memory. Buckley was talking about interest group politics in the modern welfare state. Subway riders in New York City do not want the fare to be raised (when he wrote it was fifteen cents). To appease them politicians running for governor promise to keep it low, but that can be done only by raising taxes statewide. In time, apple pickers in Cayuga County will ask for benefits of their own, which must come, in part, from subway riders. "Keep this up, you will readily see, and the skies are black with crisscrossing dollars. A dispassionate accountant, viewing the purposeless pell-mell, would surely wonder, What on earth is this all about? It is liberalism on the wing." The passage explained a political process, but what sold me was the jingle of "purposeless pell-mell," and the dollars, transformed Disney-style into migrating birds, then transformed once again into liberalism itself.

Buckley had a theme, which held his book together and overrode its weaker subarguments (he talked a lot about Joe McCarthy, who was unknown to me; he also favored keeping blacks in the South from voting, which struck me as un-American—I did not yet know how American it was). His title played off *Up from Slavery*, by Booker T. Washington; Buckley asserted that liberalism was a form, however mild or well-intentioned, of bondage. But why would Americans submit to such a thing? Liberalism prevailed, Buckley said, because it was socially acceptable. He therefore wanted to lift taboos on thought and discussion; once that happened, elections would take care of themselves.

Up from Liberalism was less a book about politics or policy than about manners, presented in a style that was simultaneously well-mannered (elegant, articulate) and ill-mannered (impudent, aggressive).

A word about his words. It was obvious that Buckley loved big ones, often drawn from rhetoric—*paralepsis, apopemptic*—and foreign ones, usually Latin—*mutatis mutandis*. But the tingle of his style owed as much to odd phrases composed of ordinary words—*over against*, *than which*. He picked up an additional tingle by swinging from fancy materials and scaffolding into colloquialisms. His ear ruled everything. He defended both the arcane words and the slangy words on the grounds that they were just the right words, even though they had to be hauled from the armoire or the garage. But their rightness was as much a matter of timing as meaning. The effect, at its best, was a lively rattle, like someone playing a harpsichord or a washboard.

AFTER DISCOVERING HIS TV show and his book my family and I subscribed to his magazine, *National Review*. (In heaven Jim McFadden, circulation manager at the time, is smiling.) It came out fortnightly, as Buckley (and Buckley alone) said. The covers of the late '60s were touched by the Day-Glo of the era. Mine with the sepia boy and the buttons would be on the sedate side; there was one about druggies going to Goa to die that could have been used by the Grateful Dead.

The drill bit of every issue was its editorial section, called "The Week," a title held over from the earliest days of the magazine when it had been a weekly. The section consisted of single paragraphs, some as short as one-liners, followed by mini-essays with titles, all unsigned, except for the notably gracious obits.

The body of the magazine consisted of columns, articles, and reviews. The columnists—James Burnham, Russell Kirk, Frank Meyer, Erik von Kuehnelt-Leddihn—were men in the homestretch of long careers, of whom I had never heard. Reading them once or twice a month, though, I quickly became attuned to their frequencies.

The column format is easy on readers, who appreciate familiarity; for *National Review* it was a way to use writers who disagreed with, and sometimes disliked, each other. There was a lot of polemic for small government in the magazine, on both economic and political grounds, as foreshadowed by Buckley's riff on crisscrossing dollars. There was also a lot of fondness (from Russell Kirk, keening) for old ways. Frank Meyer pushed a synthesis, which he called fusionism, whereby capitalism and liberty were sustained by traditional morals and habits—an idea that the magazine as a whole tacitly endorsed. Burnham, off to the side, wrote about the cold war, which he called the Third World War.

Buckley bracketed the magazine: "Notes & Asides," a selection of his correspondence, with replies, ran at the end of "The Week." It was a polemicist's batting practice. Three of his syndicated columns—he wrote three a week—followed the book reviews at the end.

Buckley's beliefs, his concerns, his personality pervaded the whole magazine. If *National Review* wrote about religion it was usually his (Roman Catholicism). If it reviewed music, the music was classical. If it mentioned sports, they were the kind of sports he played (no teams, individual efforts only; a two-page ad offering to rent his yacht, the *Cyrano*, ran almost fortnightly). British politics was well covered; some of the editorial cartoons were picked up from *Punch*. Other Buckleys pitched in to help. Priscilla L. Buckley, sister, was on the masthead as managing editor. Aloise Buckley Heath, a sister who had died, was remembered each Christmas with one of the humorous pieces she had written about family life. If *National Review* was not Buckley's shadow—the columnists were too oddly bright for that—it was his baby. The only other magazine that was so personal was Hugh Hefner's *Playboy*.

WHEN I FOUND Bill Buckley in the late sixties, he had just reached the plateau of his career. He had been getting there for almost twenty years, starting in college. After World War II the Ivy League began moving from caste to meritocracy, which instead of dissipating its power only entrenched it. The doings of selected twenty-year-olds could have national resonance. Buckley earned his notoriety by flaying the establishment of which he was a part. He won the big campus prizes—chairman of the *Yale Daily News*; election, along with the Bushes, the Wise Men, and Dink Stover, to Skull and Bones. But he told Yale, in speeches and editorials, that it was running a con. It took the sons of Christian capitalists, and filled their heads with skepticism and socialism. He made this the thesis of his first book, and first best-seller, *God and Man at Yale*, published in 1951. For a few years after that he was an acolyte of Joe McCarthy—a dead end, in several ways (Bill told me once that he lost a fortune by following McCarthy's stock tips). After McCarthy destroyed himself Buckley decided that the cold war was to be won not by exposing communists in government and public life but by countering fallacious ideas. Hunting moles was work for gumshoes. Winning arguments required a debater and a performer; changing cultural fashions—a task implied by *Up from Liberalism*: How else could one end the liberal fashion?—required someone who was very cool. *National Review*, which he launched in 1955, helped him perform all three tasks, reinforced by the talents he brought together. Buckley offered Evelyn Waugh $5,000 a year to be a columnist, not only because he would say the right things but because he could not write an ugly sentence. Waugh didn't take him up on his offer—"until you get much richer (which I hope will be soon) or I get much poorer (which I fear may be sooner) I am unable to accept"—though he did contribute several pieces. No snob, Buckley looked for brightness in obscure places: John Leonard was hired after dropping out of Harvard, Garry Wills after leaving a Jesuit seminary.

Buckley's 1965 run for mayor of New York City was the solo performance that ended his apprenticeship, his masterpiece. Buckley's opponents were Democrat Abraham Beame, a decent, dull liberal, and Republican John Lindsay, a tall, handsome, ever-so-slightly wooden liberal (Buckley ran on the line of the Conservative Party). The race produced one of his best books, *The Unmaking of a Mayor*, the title a send-up of Theodore White's earnest accounts of presidential elections. It also produced one of his most quoted, and overquoted lines: When asked what he would do if he won, he said, "Demand a recount." (Bill called the crack his c-sharp-minor prelude, a reference to the warhorse Rachmaninoff tired of playing.)

The cultural and political changes Buckley hoped for had mostly not happened by the end of the sixties. Barry Goldwater, conservatism's ideal politician, had been buried in the 1964 presidential election; Buckley won only 13 percent of the vote in his mayoral race, which Lindsay, the opponent he least liked, won. In 1968, Richard Nixon became president, narrowly. *National Review* had endorsed him, without real enthusiasm; it wasn't just liberals who found him tricky. Buckley had happened, though; he had made himself a provocateur who was also a serious man.

WHY WAS I attracted to such a man?

My parents came from small towns in central New York near where Theodore Dreiser set *An American Tragedy*. When I read Dreiser I had the accidental satisfaction of ticking off places I had known for years from visiting relatives.

My mother's family, the Starks, owned a dry goods store in Johnstown (one of Dreiser's characters sees it as he glances down a street). Her father died when she was six months old; her mother lived to be ninety-six, and remembered Geronimo as a retired public figure. My mother, Elizabeth, was one of those people who learned musical instruments at will, and could play the piano by ear. Her Beethoven, her Grieg, her sheet music—"Claire de Lune," "Rustle of Spring," "The Glow-Worm"—went with her all her life.

My mother must have looked good on the stool of her family's upright. In later years, my wife and I were looking through an old photo album of hers. I was pleased to see my twenty-year-old father, standing next to her, wearing a pair of two-toned shoes. "He looks sharp," I said. "Rick," my wife answered seriously, "your mother was *gorgeous*." I knew it, but I was so close to my mother emotionally that I never expressed such truths.

My mother was as forceful and intelligent as she was striking. The pet of her family—she had two older sisters, both quite plain—she was used to being right, and to getting her way. (Bill Buckley had the same qualities; I must have recognized them, through the differences in sex and class.) My mother went to Mount Holyoke, where she majored in math, and was recruited to be a code breaker during World War II. But by then she had already married my father; her skills went unused for the rest of her life. The belated repository of her talents, and her ambitions, would be me.

My father Robert's accounts of his boyhood in Fonda were small-town pastoral: sliding into a cave whose walls were covered with bats, learning the hook shot (then a new move) from seeing it done on newsreels. Only over years, and bit by bit, did he reveal and I understand that he came from destitution. His two-toned shoes must have been cheap; otherwise, he could not have owned them.

His father was a signal man for the New York Central Railroad who was crippled by multiple sclerosis; his mother lost her mind when he was a boy and was institutionalized for the rest of her life. Coming home one morning after camping in the woods with friends, he found the Brookhiser house burned down to the chimney; a cinder from the engine of a branch-line train had ignited it.

My father was a bright boy, whose teachers wanted him to learn Latin. He refused; that was for the college bound, and he wasn't going to college, so why bother?

Marriage to my mother changed his prospects (Johnstown and Fonda were close enough and small enough that everybody almost did know everybody else). My mother's sisters were spinsters; no doubt her husband could have taken over the Stark store.

My father's family objected to the match on religious grounds: The Brookhisers were Catholic; the Starks belonged to the Presbyterian church. My mother would not convert, or raise Catholic children; my father didn't mind. After he was drafted in early 1941, his family arranged for him to be seen by his Catholic chaplain, who warned him he would go to hell if he persisted. My father said he would see him there, and went ahead with his marriage.

He served in the Army Air Corps as a flight instructor. Once, he was assigned to fly a B-25 from Columbia, South Carolina, to Rome, New York. On the last leg of the trip he decided to pass Fonda. He thought of flying under the bridge that crossed the Mohawk River there, thought better of it, and buzzed the town. It was my image of his great success—escaping. He was a genial man, but that was superficial; his strategies for survival were stubbornness and silence.

I was my mother's darling; I always felt awkward around my father. But in my passivity and willfulness I was more like him than I knew.

My father went to college after all, thanks to the G.I. Bill, then worked for Eastman Kodak, the largest employer in Rochester, New York; Irondequoit was one of the bedroom communities. Memories, dim but warm, and photographs, clear but faded, show small houses, neat yards, trick-or-treaters dressed in the odds and ends of their young parents' closets. Eugene Genovese, who had taught at the University of Rochester, once told me, in the argot of his Marxist youth, that "the big bourgeoisie" ran the city well. Maybe they did, but I rarely went there, except to take piano lessons at the Eastman School of Music.

Life was among the lawns: the world of school (classes, chorus, plays—girls were still on deck); one television in the living room; a neighbor's swimming pool, which they let us use; bicycles, one-speed, then three-speed; transistor radios (when I first heard Simon and Garfunkel's "7 O'clock News/Silent Night" I twiddled the dial, trying to get away from the newscast, until I realized that stapling the world's horrors onto the Christmas carol was the point).

In the summer I went with my Scout troop to the Adirondacks for loons and constellations; for Thanksgiving the family went to Johnstown. Sometimes we took vacations farther afield, always by car: New York City; Florida; California (the Corn Palace, geysers, Chinatown). The rest of my life I spent in Irondequoit.

I spent much of it in books. I read anything. My grandmother had a copy of *Harold: The Last of the Saxon Kings*, by Edward Bulwer-Lytton—medieval melodrama. I read it. My brother had a copy of *Nausea*, by Jean-Paul Sartre—existentialist melodrama. I read that too. I read obsessively; I read *Cyrano de Bergerac* (in the Brian Hooker translation) and *The Lord of the Rings* twenty times each. Once I picked them up, I felt impelled to begin again and read them through. Returning to such favorites showed a taste for drama, sweep, and melancholy, if not tragedy.

My attraction to another book showed these tastes in a different way: *The Gathering Storm* by Winston S. Churchill. This was a first printing of the hardcover, given to me by a neighbor who was done with it (he had left some of the pages uncut). The first of Churchill's six volumes of war memoirs, it recounts the run-up to World War

II, and ends with his becoming prime minister in May 1940. This was history, but recent history; my father had served in the war it described. It also seemed to be history trying not to repeat itself in my lifetime. Churchill's message to his postwar readers was stated on page ix, in ragged lines like an inscription:

THEME OF THE VOLUME
How the English-speaking peoples
through their unwisdom,
carelessness, and good nature
allowed the wicked
to rearm

Communism had never rearmed, having never disarmed; what was the cold war except an attempt to prevent the wicked of our time from trying to dominate us?

I had a twin compulsion to put myself on paper. Before I could read and write I drew wordless cartoons. As soon as I learned two-finger typing, I wrote "books"—ten-page stories that began, as real books did, with a table of contents; I then had to write chapters that fleshed out what I had projected. Over time they grew; the last "book," never finished, opened with a sixty-page single-spaced account of a basketball game. This tireless wheel-spinning occurred in a void. My father was bemused by it; my mother admired it, uncritically. Though they were both smart, they had not turned their minds in such directions. I was acquiring skills without any guidance, or any idea what to do with them.

My parents were profoundly conservative without being especially political. My mother was a Republican by birthright, and my father became one readily enough (the migration of men like him into the postwar GOP is the story of the death of the New Deal coalition). The first presidential election I remember was 1960, when I was five. Mom and Dad both voted for Nixon. When he lost, I was mildly surprised that the country had defied them. But it was a contest without passion, or (seemingly) consequences. Kennedy's murder three years later was a shock; I was sent home, with no explanation, from third grade, to find my mother weeping. Yet even this was a tragedy on television, out there.

Politics began to come home in two ways. In 1964 Rochester had a race riot. The big bourgeoisie had not done so well, it seemed. Irondequoit was all white; I did not know a single Negro, as they were then called. Our back-door neighbors put a little sticker on their house declaring that they would sell to black people; this was an advertisement of do-goodism, not of a house for sale.

Black people lived in Rochester, in the dilapidated three-story wooden houses we passed driving to and from piano lessons. They belonged to a different civilization. Once when we went to a store downtown, the black man minding it told my mother that the owner was "yonder." I had never heard the word spoken before (I have not heard it spoken, except by actors, since). In July 1964 those houses burned in a riot. Four people were killed, hundreds of stores were looted; the governor called out the National Guard. The worst of urban violence—Watts, Newark, Detroit—was still to come, but Rochester had a preview of it. Our black people voted (one assumed); what was going on?

Soon thereafter the counterculture began its march through the American mind. Present-day twenty-year-olds, baffled by the artifacts of aged baby boomers thrust at them like Greek at sullen English schoolboys, can scarcely imagine a time when these things were new or exciting. The counterculture entered our house only in the form of music. My parents, my mother in particular, detested rock and roll. My brother and I could not help inhabiting it. Rochester had two rock stations. I remember one tense drive in the car when "Get Off of My Cloud" was braying through the static of the radio: *'n th' MAWnin' th' PAHKin' tickets wuh jus-like-a FLAG own MAH WANdow SCREEN.* My fed-up mother stabbed one of the buttons of the radio, preset to all the local stations, anything to get rid of it, but she hit the button that pulled in the other rock station, which was also playing "Get Off of My Cloud," at about the same measure. There was no escape.

My taste of the counterculture stopped there, at least then (I did not get stoned until college), but it was in the air, like an incoming front. The media conveyed an image of it that was lurid and alluring. The coverage that was not hostile was voyeuristic. Who picked the pictures of naked hippie chicks that illustrated stories about Woodstock? Hippies themselves? Even hippie boys? No—leering adult photo editors. The counterculture, to the extent it was serious (always a question), carried a lot of political baggage. It did not care about the gathering storm, and it had no love for neat lawns.

I had already made my own approach to politics, as a hobby and a sport. Since I was not athletic, elections became my box scores. They were a body of organized historical knowledge, with winners and losers. I not only learned the names of all the presidents, I memorized all the also-rans (down to Rufus King and Winfield Scott Hancock—1816 and 1880, of course).

Contemporary elections were equally engrossing. The same neighbor who gave me his Churchill subscribed to *U.S. News & World Report*, which during the 1964 election published electoral maps of the states each candidate hoped to win (Goldwater obviously fell far short of his projected total). These were as absorbing to me as a stamp collection—Kansans here, Floridians there. I had already watched both conventions on television, typing up everything that happened, or at least everything that Walter Cronkite and Huntley/Brinkley said happened. I learned the rituals, how in every roll call New Mexico identified itself as the "Land of Enchantment," and Guam said it was "where America's day begins" (both in slight accents). These were box scores being made, and you could see it.

The 1968 election had a more elaborate statistical profile, since it included a third party led by George Wallace. With its riots and murders it burst the neat bounds of sport; the most intrusive disaster, thanks to the luck of news gathering, was the second Kennedy assassination, the shaken radio reporter in the hotel pantry in Los Angeles telling bodyguard Rafer Johnson to "get the gun" of Sirhan Sirhan, over and over on his tape, then his tape being repeated over and over on our radio, as we ate breakfast in the kitchen before school.

But even that election, chaotic and distressing as it was, could be written about; I had never read a novel by Norman Mailer, but I read *Miami and the Siege of Chicago*, the paperback edition of his 1968 convention coverage for *Harper's*, as soon as it came out.

So even at age fourteen, politics was both a pastime and a force in my world; reading and writing were equally compelling. Who could be a better model than William F. Buckley Jr.? He understood freedom and the forces that threatened it, from foolish policies (crisscrossing dollars) to anarchy (in songs, or in the streets). He understood the gravest threat of all, communism. He understood words—words that confused plain thinking, and words that made everything clear. Almost miraculously, he understood my words. What my parents only indulged or praised automatically, he knew from the inside.

AT FORTY-FOUR, Bill's age when he accepted my article, he was conscious of the passage of time. Before the New York mayoral race, William Rickenbacker, a younger colleague, sat in on one of his interviews. Bill was in fine form, like a Jet with a switchblade. The reporter saved his toughest question for walking out the door; Bill smartly knocked it aside. When the door closed, he turned to Rickenbacker and grinned, "I can keep this shit up until I'm forty." He kept it up much longer, but even an *enfant terrible* senses when he is no longer literally an *enfant*. Out of the blue, here came a kid pulling the same stunts he had pulled in college—only he was doing it in high school. Bill may have thought, even then, Maybe I have found another me.

CHAPTER 2

THE SEVENTIES—MY adolescence, and *National Review*'s—began under the star of Richard Nixon, the almost accidental president, who had won with just over 43 percent of the vote but grew more potent over the course of his presidency, until he believed he might set the agenda for a decade.

He did not owe his success to a vision of what America should be at home. He thought the country didn't need a president for domestic affairs; cabinet secretaries could handle all that. Politics was a matter of keeping competing factions off balance, or in his corner, often both.

One of the factions he sought to manage, with a mixture of policies, rhetoric, and blandishments, was the conservative movement. He deployed Pat Buchanan, a young Jesuit-educated journalist, as his conservative speechwriter (he had two others, one liberal, Ray Price, and one in-between, Bill Safire). He invited our contributor Russell Kirk, the traditionalist essayist, to the White House. Kirk was a nicer man than Henry Adams, but the occasion must have been even odder than the old gargoyle's dinners with Theodore Roosevelt. Kirk told the president to read *Notes Toward a Definition of Culture*, by T. S. Eliot. "I could read about it in your book on Eliot, couldn't I?" Nixon asked. Kirk assured him that the Eliot book was quite short.

Nixon tacitly backed a Buckley in the 1970 Senate race in New York. Nixon's support had to be tacit, since there was already a

Republican in the race—the incumbent senator, Charles Goodell, a former congressman who had been appointed to fill Robert Kennedy's seat, and then moved left. The Democrats nominated one of their congressmen, Richard Ottinger. Bill Buckley had considered a second run for office on the Conservative Party line if he could run against Kennedy in 1970; it was Bobby's iconic status, and the desire to chip it, that attracted him, as much as the prospect of a Senate seat. Kennedy was one of the few public figures who declined to appear on *Firing Line* (when asked why Kennedy demurred, Bill answered, "Why does baloney reject the grinder?"). Bill's older brother, James, vice president of the Buckley family oil business, ran in the Kennedy-less election instead. Nixon tipped his almost invisible hand by sending his vice president, Spiro Agnew, into the state and arranging for the Secret Service to part ranks so that a crowd of Buckley supporters with signs could swarm into a photograph with the veep. Jim eked out an even narrower victory than Nixon's.

Did Bill Buckley ever replay that election in his mind? In 1971, he was a guest on *Rowan and Martin's Laugh-In*, the TV comedy show that featured Goldie Hawn as a go-go girl. Bill got off a nice line, no less good for being borrowed (theft is one of the arts): He agreed to go on the show, he said, when the producers offered to fly him to the taping in a plane with two right wings. This performance brought an angry letter to Senator Buckley from a constituent who thought *he* had been the guest, thus committing "an affront to the dignity of the Senate." Jim sent the letter to Bill, who ran it in "Notes & Asides," with a double revelation: Jim was indeed the Buckley who had appeared on *Laugh-In*, but his constituent should not worry, since Bill was the Buckley who had been elected senator. Regrets? Or was it better joking about being a senator than being one?

Politics was the air Richard Nixon breathed, but his mind was intent on the world. His strategic instrument was his national security adviser, then secretary of state, Henry Kissinger, who happened to be a friend of Bill Buckley's. Buckley and Kissinger had met in the early sixties when the Harvard professor invited the conservative to address some seminars he was leading; their relationship would last four decades. Buckley liked liberals for two reasons: Either they wrote well (the columnist Murray Kempton), or they treated him and his ideas with respect. He wrung such respect from economist John Kenneth Galbraith; Kissinger, another Ivy League insider, gave it freely. Kissinger cultivated Buckley for reasons of prudence—in the great game of ambition it might be good to have a conservative you could call on the phone—and indeed it was Buckley who introduced him to Nixon's circle.

Nixon's design was to manage both the Vietnam War and the cold war by playing the Soviet Union and Communist China off against each other. Exploiting their rivalry would give America room to maneuver, and to scale back her commitments in Vietnam. But playing China would mean first dealing with China, something the United States had not done since the Communists took over the mainland in 1949.

Thus Nixon the Machiavellian. But he was also stirred by a vision of himself, making the big trip, the grand gesture. My second piece for *National Review* ran in the fall of 1971 when I was a junior in high school, and I labeled him and it romantic. I had no experience to offer in this piece; it was a thumb sucker, cobbled together from comparisons of Nixon to peacemakers like Woodrow Wilson (whom he admired) and Czar Alexander I (of whom he may never have thought, but about whom I had read in *War and Peace*). The magazine ran it as a young conservative's take on Nixon. But I was right about Nixon's romanticism. He wanted to be a towering figure, a power player but also a seer. Journalists and now historians have spent many years sifting all the things Nixon was, but romantic was truly one of them.

NIXON WENT TO China in February 1972, and Bill Buckley was one of the journalists who went along to cover the trip. *National Review* was an old enemy of Communist China, and a supporter of the Nationalist remnant on Taiwan. Marvin Liebman, a good friend of the magazine, ran the Committee of One Million, ostensibly 1 million supporters of Taiwan, in fact Marvin and his mailing list. Like most American media then, *National Review* used the old Wade-Giles transliteration of Chinese, not the pinyin devised by Beijing; some of the editors (not Buckley) went a step further, writing *Peking* as *Peiping*, because the latter form denoted a provincial capital, which, they argued, was what Peiping was so long as China's legitimate rulers were lodged in Taipei.

That was the perspective of the magazine, and the movement—the perspective of right-world.

Buckley's dispatches from China, collected in *National Review*, are among his finest hours. On the spot with Nixon in China, Buckley was inflamed by the atmospherics of the voyage: "We have lost—irretrievably—any remaining sense of moral mission in the world. Mr. Nixon's appetite for a summit conference in Peking transformed the affair from a meeting of diplomatic technicians . . . into a pageant of moral togetherness." Mao and his colleagues were the worst murderers of the century—worse than Hitler, worse than Stalin. History might dictate new policies, but we should call things by their right names. Instead, Nixon "managed to give the impression that he was consorting with Marian Anderson, Billy Graham and Albert Schweitzer." That was tart, but this, on the repeated toasts Nixon offered his hosts at a grand ceremonial banquet, was brutal: "I would not have been surprised, that night, if he had lurched into a toast of Alger Hiss." Hiss was the communist spy whose exposure had launched Nixon's national career; *lurched* suggested Nixon's infatuation, even intoxication. This was telling the truth about gangsters, and their new best friend, the president of the United States.

A handful of conservatives, including Buckley, had staged a forlorn little revolt against Nixon earlier in the year, supporting Rep. John Ashbrook of Ohio in the New Hampshire primary as a conservative protest candidate. Ashbrook won only 10 percent of the vote, and dropped out. Nixon was unstoppable. All Republicans rallied to him, and many Democrats. His 1972 victory over George McGovern was a historic wipeout (we mavens knew the parallels—

Johnson/Goldwater, Roosevelt/Landon, Harding/Cox). Nixon said later that he intended to remake the GOP on "new majority" lines, though what those might have been, beyond adventures abroad and opportunism at home, was not clear.

Then, suddenly, it slid away. The imperial presidency fell to a pair of reporters; the "-gate" suffix entered American life. Senator Buckley, encouraged by brother Bill, called for Nixon's resignation in May 1974. I happened to be in his office the afternoon of this announcement. I was a freshman in college, having followed my brother to Yale, and my singing group was passing through D.C. for spring break. Another freshman, a courtly Virginian, suggested we call on his good family friend Justice Lewis Powell. The justice greeted us in his chambers. All I could think to match that was a trip to the office of my idol's brother. Senator Buckley was not in, but I could hear the phones ringing off the hooks, mostly from conservative constituents angry that he was joining the liberal hyenas circling Nixon. The ongoing revelations put almost everyone on the side of the hyenas.

I learned later, via *National Review*'s publisher, Bill Rusher, that when a delegation of congressional Republicans, led by Barry Goldwater, went to the White House after the release of the smoking-gun tape in August to tell Nixon that the game was up, they found the soon-to-be-ex-president perfectly at ease, at a point of weightlessness, all effort spent, the descent still to come.

Nixon fared better than the world he left behind. The fighting standoff he had arranged with Hanoi, Beijing, and Moscow worked only so long as America supported South Vietnam with aid, if not its full military might. A newly liberal Congress settled that. Saigon fell in April 1975, the spring of my sophomore year. That night Yalies painted jubilant slogans on campus construction sites; some of us went out later to paint them over. The two sides ran into each other, and doused each other with paint.

I had sense enough not to write this up for *National Review*. Two conservative Yalies I knew had volunteered to serve in the military during the Vietnam years: One went into the marines; one of our paint throwers had come from the navy. I obeyed the laws; I had a medium-low draft number. But I did not want it to come up, and I did not volunteer. I was a mouth warrior only. Better not to talk about campus paint wars when there was real fighting going on.

By 1975 the war's opponents accepted communist victory. They thought of the communists as nationalists and socialists, hence not so bad, even admirable. Democracy as practiced by Asians led to corruption and coups; why bother with it? The devastation of the war and any misbehavior by the victors could be blamed on American resistance. Events would test these assumptions.

DURING THE EARLY '70s I led a double life. In one I went through high school and college, a bright conservative kid.

You're not serious when you're seventeen, said Rimbaud. Or you're nothing but. Ivy League kids today are supposed to be a bland careerist bunch, intent on accumulating status markers that will help them land good jobs in the overclass. The trend was beginning, perhaps, as early as the seventies, but I missed it. At Yale I took courses because I was interested in them. I majored in English and steered clear of theory; I read William Wordsworth, not Harold Bloom. I joined groups without giving thought to my résumé. I sang in the Duke's Men, a small all-male group that specialized in emeritus popular music. I looked good in tails, I had a pleasant baritone voice, I arranged "Lullaby of Birdland" and "Goody Goody"; in time I became the pitch pipe, or conductor. I also joined the Party of the Right of the Political Union. The POR touched all the impulses of the conservative movement, in the manner of college students, flamboyantly. The Chairman's toast was the scaffold speech of Charles I, blessed king and martyr, and one of the debate topics my freshman year was "Resolved: Heroin Should Be Sold in Vending Machines" (the resolution passed). I rose to the top in this group too, becoming Chairman.

I had the disappointments that young men usually have with young women (and that young women have with us). But the first check to my progress came at the end of my junior year, when I was not tapped for the Whiffenpoofs. They were the oldest small male singing group in the Ivy League, all seniors; every year they picked the best of the best for the next group. I had wanted to be one since I first heard them, when my brother was a freshman, and I fully expected—when had I been frustrated before?—that they would want me. But they didn't. Bummer. So I joined the Russian Chorus instead. One bitter New Haven night, as I was slipping across the ice of Cross Campus with a friend who spoke Russian, I said, "*Muy dolgo molcha otstupali*" (*We retreated through the snows*), a line from an old Russian army song about the battle of Borodino. He loved it. I sang for the pleasure of it and read what I liked.

One of the writers I read was Aleksandr Solzhenitsyn. I read only a little of him, but it was enough to know that this was a great man. In my freshman year, one of my suite mates was Paul Rudnick, who listened to Bette Midler and the Pointer Sisters and said things like, "Leslie Gore—she was a *goddess*." I didn't know what to make of it. I put a picture of Solzhenitsyn on my door; he didn't know what to make of that. Each of us, in his way, was ahead of the curve.

Years later, after the fall of the Soviet Union, obituarists discussed who had done the most to bring it down: Mikhail Gorbachev? Boris Yeltsin? Ronald Reagan? John Paul II? Solzhenitsyn was braver than all of them. The other Russians were insiders; Reagan led a superpower; the pope led a church. Solzhenitsyn was a writer with a few friends. What he did, which was as significant as anything the others did, was introduce one word into the world's vocabulary: *gulag* (Russians knew it already). Before Solzhenitsyn, all the iconography of modern despotism was Nazi: If you wanted to talk about extermination, you thought of Auschwitz; if you wanted to talk about killers, or even the cop who gave you a ticket, you thought of the Gestapo. Solzhenitsyn said, communism means the gulag, which is also bad, and this is why; and this, and this, and this.

Another writer I met in college was Evelyn Waugh. One day, after exams, I picked up a library copy of *Mr. Scott-King's Modern Europe*. Scott-King is an English schoolteacher who visits a Mediterranean country plagued by misgovernment and intrigue. "I suppose they were desperate fellows," says one character of two men who were just arrested. "Spies, bimetallists, who can say?" *Brideshead Revisited* would become Waugh's pop hit, thanks to the BBC serialization (introduced on PBS by Bill Buckley). It wasn't the best of his works to bring before the general public. Love and memory are lovingly evoked, but the religious plot is a failure. Scott-King and the African novels, *Scoop* and *Black Mischief*, with their coldhearted clatter of human baseness, made more of an impression on me.

That was my daily life. In my parallel life, I was already a professional journalist. One article is an event; two are a career. Throughout high school and college I kept sending pieces to *National Review*, one or two a year, and most of them kept being published. *National Review* suggested I send a humor piece to the *Alternative*, a monthly in Bloomington, Indiana; its tone was simultaneously meaner, and more fey, and they became the second place to run me. While I was in Irondequoit High I cudgeled my brain for subjects; at Yale it was easier, since more of what happened there intersected with the real world. An instructor in the Russian Department turned out to have a Nazi past; he was fired. But when the communist historian Herbert Aptheker was invited to lecture, that was no problem. I made the censorious contrast.

My second life was public, and professional. I was writing for a national magazine, albeit one of small circulation, and learning, still for the most part unconsciously, the tricks of the trade: how to propose an idea; what it is like to be edited; how not to cling to what Daniel Oliver, one of *National Review*'s contributors, called "every goddamn golden syllable." But the most important aspect of my second life was the special pipeline to William F. Buckley Jr. The connection was special because it ran two ways. I admired Buckley and yearned for his praise, but he made me believe that I performed services for him that he appreciated.

I had first met my editor face-to-face when I was still in high school and he came to the University of Rochester for a debate. I barely remember what I saw and heard from my remote seat; the TV screen suited Buckley better. In any case the point was to see him afterward. I remember his courtesy, his smile, and his tiredness, as if he had just played four quarters. Performing is work. I saw him a second time three or four years later after another debate, before the Yale Political Union—a favorite venue of his, where he had shone as an undergraduate, and to which he regularly returned. I got him to come to a postdebate reception hosted by the Party of the Right. Students swarmed around him like koi. "They should let him breathe," my girlfriend exclaimed, out of sheer empathy. Empathy would not have stopped me from charging in with the rest; the reason I could afford to give him room was because I felt I already had a connection.

At Yale for the first time I met other people who had their own connections with him. Lloyd Grove, the future gossip writer, who was in a writing class with me, was a friend of Buckley's son, Chris, and thus a frequent houseguest of the family. Irondequoit had appeared not to have a class system; at Yale I began to discover the existence of one, the old school ties that tied more strongly when they were more than simply going to the same school. One of my friends, Eugene Meyer, had another kind of connection. Gene was the son of Frank Meyer, the *National Review* columnist; he knew Bill as his father's colleague. When Bill visited the Meyer home in Woodstock, New York, he brought young Gene chocolate cigarettes. (Since the Meyers were nocturnal, Bill had to come for their breakfast, his dinner.) Another friend, Greg Hyatt, corresponded with Buckley. I would learn about Buckley's correspondence later, when I helped him write it. To Greg he was civil, encouraging, helpful; he recommended Greg for a fellowship after he graduated, and offered to let him spend his honeymoon in Buckley's Swiss chalet. That was another kind of connection. We all got something from Buckley—hospitality, kindness, interest in our doings, borrowed glamour. But unlike the others, I was giving something back.

While I was at Yale I discovered one more possible way of relating to Buckley: as a renegade, one who had taken things from him and given things to him, but now only took and gave grief. Garry Wills was a professor at Johns Hopkins, but in the spring of 1974 he taught a seminar at Yale. Wills had met Bill almost a decade earlier. He had left the seminary, shy of ordination, and sent articles to four magazines. *National Review* was the first to write back, and Bill hired him. For a while Wills was Bill's official biographer—a convenient shield against the curious, Bill readily admitted, who could be shunted to Wills.

But the civil rights movement and the Vietnam War pulled Wills sharply to the left. One of his best books, *Nixon Agonistes*, on the 1968 election, was written just after his political conversion; the ruins of his former ideological self are still visible beneath the clean-as-glass reporting and writing—though he deplores Nixon, he feels considerable sympathy for him. It was clear to me as a reader of *National Review* that Wills had been an important figure at the magazine, if only because the magazine continued to needle him. One cover pasted Wills's head on a famous image of Black Panther Huey Newton, enthroned with spear and shotgun on his wicker chair; on Wills's head was pasted a papal tiara. Radical Garry, *urbi et orbi.*

I was curious to see what he was like. His seminar was by application only, because enrollment was limited; an interview was part of the process. When I went to meet the professor, he asked me a few questions, then we played a game of Ping-Pong (there was a table in the college basement near the seminar room). He had noticed on my application that I had written for *National Review*. "That's a bad place to start," he said portentously. I was only witty enough to say, "So it seems," after I had left. But he accepted me for his course. He was an excellent teacher. He was getting ready to write his first book on the founders, *Inventing America*, about Thomas Jefferson, and we got the foam of what he was thinking and learning. He liked Jefferson, portraying him as intelligent and quirky. But from time to time he also introduced George Washington, generally as a stick to beat Jefferson with (gently). He clearly loved and honored Washington. If Wills (it is hard for me to call him anything but Professor Wills) has a vice as a writer it is pride, knowing better than his subjects. But he never held himself up as better than Washington. I hoped to learn something from him, however oblique, about Bill Buckley, and I didn't, but I did begin to learn something.

WHATEVER YOU GAVE back to Bill he always topped you in return. The same term I was learning about Jefferson and Washington, the Political Union withdrew an invitation they had extended to William Shockley, the Nobel Prize–winning physicist and crackpot geneticist. Shockley, coinventor of the solid-state transistor, had won a second name for himself preaching the dysgenic effects of overbreeding by stupid people; according to his calculations, black people tended to be more stupid than whites. The Political Union had invited him looking for a little controversy; when they got a lot, they backed off.

Greg Hyatt and Gene Meyer decided to bring Shockley to Yale, under the auspices of dormant conservative campus groups, revived for the occasion, to debate William Rusher, *National Review*'s publisher. They wanted to establish the principle of free speech, and they wanted to attack Shockley from the right. *National Review* had abandoned the segregationist views expressed in *Up from Liberalism*; even then, Buckley had said that the danger of black voting came from blacks' lower educational level, not from any innate inferiority; in his ideal southern world, some blacks would be allowed to vote and some whites wouldn't. Such notions, fantastic even at the time—no one was interested in enforcing a color-blind education-based franchise—had been blown away by the sixties.

Rusher proposed to rebut Shockley by arguing that intelligence tests are a dim light for viewing human beings, and irrelevant to their rights. He never got the chance. When the debate finally came off, in May, the participants were inundated by ninety minutes of shouting. When the demonstrators augmented their din by smuggling a bullhorn into the hall through a window, the university police called the show off.

I wrote a letter to Buckley describing the goings-on (he had taken my brother's place as an at least occasional correspondent). The debate was "like a high school basketball game with one side, no game, and only the refs to boo. . . . Outside, an ice cream truck had parked in front of [the] hall and was making a killing. I learned that the Young Christian Fellowship had been out too, singing hymns. 'Whose side were they on?' Someone shrugged. 'God's.' . . . I saw 500 people, supposedly the brightest in my generation, panicked by an idea. . . . [If] 'the public' isn't mature enough to hear Shockley debated and refuted, then all the more reason why the elite should be absolutely clear about their convictions—and that comes only from having them challenged and debated." So I wrote in the flush of contentiousness, while my friends were arguing about heroin in vending machines.

Bill Buckley did not answer my letter. Instead, he published it in his syndicated column. "Is there a greater joy on earth than the 19-year-old who sees things as they are, writes about them with the quiet authority of a professional, and seasons his commentary with the wit and urbanity of a humanist? The following came in as a letter from a sophomore at Yale University. I commend it to all who despair of American youth, and the author, Richard Brookhiser, to editors looking for writers from the Class of 1976."

Buckley had given no advance warning of this favor (he never did); I learned of his column when my brother called from Boston, where he had read it in the *Globe*. It was a surprise attack of generosity, and like the first one four and a half years earlier it was overwhelming. There were two mistakes in Buckley's intro: I was a freshman in the class of 1977; and there *is* a greater joy on earth than the nineteen-year-old who sees things as they are—the almost-fifty-year-old who sees you as you might be and hauls you before the readers of 350 newspapers. Could I be professional enough for this man?

———

IN 1976, WHEN I was twenty-one years old, I went to work for *National Review* as a summer intern. In-house, the internships were called Miss Buckley's Finishing School for Young Ladies and Gentlemen. Vicki Marani, a Yalie a few years ahead of me, was one of the ladies who had recently passed through it; she told me about the position and urged me to apply for it. I got the nod, and after Memorial Day my parents drove me to the city and installed me at a midtown YMCA.

National Review's offices were on East Thirty-fifth Street, on the southeast slope of Murray Hill, a neighborhood that was a staid mix of apartment buildings and brownstones, hotels and clubs. Up the street was a Swedenborgian church with rose of Sharon in its front yard. *National Review* occupied several floors of a prewar building mostly converted to offices. The apartment-style layout made its premises crabbed and eccentric (the flattering term was *Dickensian*). Bill Buckley valued the unusually high number of bathrooms; he said he didn't want to "cross a proscenium" to relieve himself.

My first day was an editorial Monday, the beginning of the end of the biweekly production cycle. The cover was done, all the articles, columns, and reviews set in type. Only "The Week" remained to be assigned and written. I arrived wearing a light-blue polyester summer suit, and was given a desk in the main editorial office on the second floor, then followed everyone to the third for the editorial conference.

On the way we passed Bill's office, a dark den with a red carpet. An enormous illuminated globe sat in one corner. The flat surfaces were stacked with papers and books, the walls covered with plaques he had been awarded and cartoons of which he was the subject. A metal gizmo on his desk waved three small flags when you turned the crank. He typically sat in the window in a swivel chair, in the angle between his desk and a small table that supported his typewriter. When he was on the phone with a friend he stuck his legs up and leaned back happily. There was a dumbwaiter in the corner behind him that went down to Priscilla's office on the floor below; when she had copy to send up to him, she would ring a bell by pressing the head of a small bronze turtle. Even hurrying past on day one, I registered a few of these details avidly.

The editorial conference was held in the library, lined with built-in shelves and almost filled by a heavy black rectangular table. I sat at the bottom. Some of the people I knew; I had met Bill and William Rusher and corresponded with Priscilla. A few of the others I recognized by name, particularly James Burnham, who sat near the head of the table next to Bill. The names of the rest passed in a blur. The purpose of the conference was to decide what the magazine should cover in its unsigned, corporate voice in "The Week." Bill Rusher, at Bill's left, made a few terse suggestions and departed. Then everyone else gave his ideas, starting with Burnham on Bill's right, and moving counterclockwise. I quickly learned that everyone more or less showed off for Bill, except Burnham and Priscilla, who didn't have to, and Rusher, who had made a separate peace. When we finished Bill assigned each topic to a writer, consulting the scratchings—he frequently asked Priscilla what it was that he had written—of his notes. To me he assigned a labor union matter, items on Chile and Cambodia, and the obituary of a historian I had never heard of. He ended the meeting by lightly slapping the table and saying, "*Entonces*" (Spanish for "*Well, then*"). We returned to our desks to start writing.

The editorial staff worked on the second floor. At each desk there was a Royal Standard manual typewriter, gray, serious, and solid, noble Industrial Age artifacts; the patter of the keys striking the cylinder made anything written on them seem urgent, even a thank-you note; you could have thrown one out the second-floor window onto the sidewalk, and it would still have pecked away. I was told I would be getting clips from the research library, a three-man staff in yet another office: articles cut from the major newspapers, the *New York Times*, *Washington Post*, and *Wall Street Journal*. But before I had set to work, I was asked to lunch.

The writers and editors, led by Bill, walked around the corner to Nicola Paone's. My notions of fine dining were defined at that point by nineteenth-century inns in the countryside around Rochester where we drove for Sunday dinners after church. This was a fancy meal in the middle of a workday, an unheard-of extravagance—unheard of by me, at any rate. We were seated at a large round table in the main room by Franco, the gray-suited maître d' with a gold wrist chain. Mr. Paone, older, courtlier, more ethnic, described his specials as if he were reciting poetry; he described his desserts like lovers. He had given the regular dishes on his menu whimsical names—Nightgown, Boom-boom—which my colleagues all seemed to know. Even in 1976, Paone's was old-fashioned. All the elements of the meal supported each other like acrobats in a pyramid; the wine lubricated the food, dessert topped it off, coffee cut the dessert and the wine. Bill presided, never letting the conversation flag (a skill, I would discover, that is not common). The process took an hour and a half. I was back at my Royal Standard in midafternoon, without having turned to Chile or the late historian.

Then one of my new colleagues, Joe Sobran, strolled into my office and gave me something else to think about. Joe was a dark-haired, bearish young man with a deep voice and a sweet smile; he was probably smoking one of the short cigars he was so fond of. I knew his byline well—he had written the critique of Garry Wills that accompanied the papal Huey Newton cover—and many other pieces besides. He had been assigned to go to Yankee Stadium that night to see if there was anything interesting in a rally of the Unification Church, but couldn't make it. Would I like to go in his stead? He loaned me his press card and gave me directions.

I had not been on a subway since I had taken the Flushing Line to the 1964 World's Fair with my parents; happily, Yankee Stadium was a straight shot north from Grand Central. The Unification Church, which was just making a splash in the United States, was a pseudo-Christian religion built around its founder, the Reverend Sun Myung Moon, a Korean evangelist who claimed to be the Messiah (Jesus had failed; Moon would get it right). The Moonies were accused of brainwashing their converts. They wanted a big-deal rally to show how mainstream they were; their enemies seized on the occasion to condemn them. The Moonies had taken over a moribund orchestra, the New York City Symphony, which sat on the infield playing classical repertoire. There were speeches, almost incomprehensible through the sound system and the Korean accent. At one point anti-Moonies broke through security and scuffled with the crowd in the seats.

Coming and going, I found myself in a religious Reichstag of protesters—evangelicals insisting that Jesus was Lord, Catholics who believed that the Virgin Mary had appeared in Bayside. I took copious notes, and wrote up the story when I got back to my YMCA cubicle, on my own portable typewriter. I supplied background by reading the leaflets pro and con that had been thrust at me, and the clips supplied by the research library; I wrote the story by opening my eyes. The next day Priscilla told me they could slip the account into the magazine as a one-page article.

I made a hash of the historian; Bill ended up writing the obit himself, since he had actually known the man. But the editorial on Cambodia worked. A French Jesuit, Fr. François Ponchaud, based in Cambodia, had reported the first accounts of refugees fleeing the Khmer Rouge; the victorious Communists, it appeared, had murdered several hundred thousand people. Father Ponchaud's estimates turned out to be on the low side. All I did was retell the story; the thing spoke for itself. Years later, the soundman on a documentary I was hosting came to a shoot wearing a remarkable T-shirt: It showed the cartoon character Tintin creeping through jungle vines toward a pile of skulls. The caption read: "Tintin's Adventure in the Cambodian Forest." I asked where he had gotten such a monstrous thing. In Cambodia itself, he said; sick jokes were the only way the people could deal with what they had been through, and with the presence, even after the fall of the Khmer Rouge, of the perpetrators, living freely among them.

"The Week" went to bed at five o'clock on Wednesday afternoon. Attendance was not mandatory at the closing, but it too was a public occasion, this time a performance by Bill, with some help from his sister. Bill believed in overassigning, so he always had twice as much copy as there was space to fill. That was fine, because it gave him leeway to select and shape. All the editorials were gathered in a sheaf; the paragraphs were spread out, page by page, on the conference room table and the counters of the bookshelves. Priscilla told him how many lines were available for "The Week." Bill marked the total on his adding machine, a Swiss contraption that looked like a black pepper shaker. He made a final cut of the editorials, arranging them in order—foreign, domestic, offbeat—and noting the line count. Then he prowled the room, eliminating paragraphs by turning them facedown. Priscilla, who also had the power to kill a paragraph, did the same, calling out the length of each victim. As the losers fell by the wayside, Bill kept a running tally on his pepper shaker of how close he was to the final target. When he was within a line or two, he arranged the surviving paragraphs in the same order as the editorials, asking himself, "Where's my lead?" as he did so. The lead paragraph had to be funny, sharp, startling; it was often written by Joe. The whole show, maybe fifteen minutes long, was performance art, laying mosaic at the speed of hit-and-run. When he was done, he handed the batch to Priscilla and joined us for drinks, which appeared from a cabinet in the corner, or went off to his next gig.

Every magazine and newspaper holds conferences, and all of them edit, but I couldn't imagine any doing it with such panache.

THE PEOPLE I met that summer would be in my life for many years, as colleagues or memories. James Burnham, more than seventy years old, was from another time. A wealthy young philosophy professor in the 1930s, he had chosen to become a revolutionary. The communists recruited him, but at that moment they were calling for an independent black nation in the American South, which struck even young Burnham as unrealistic. Instead, he became a Trotskyist (Trotskyite, he let us know, was a hostile communist locution).

Burnham's two best books appeared during World War II, after he had broken with Trotsky (and after Stalin had completed their own break). *The Managerial Revolution* predicted a world of endless conflict between postcapitalist, postsocialist empires; George Orwell, who was both repelled and impressed by it, borrowed the geopolitical framework for *1984*. (I was impressed that a man everyone had read in high school—"Four legs good, two legs better"; "He loved Big Brother"—had read the man in the room down the hall; I read Orwell's criticisms of my colleague in the four-volume paperback set of Orwell's journalism, colored like children's blocks, that sat on the

National Review library shelf.) *The Machiavellians,* a favorable account of Machiavelli and his way of thinking, taught the chilling
moral that all ideologies, even "good" ones, are masks of elites fighting to retain or acquire power; in the course of these struggles
crumbs of freedom sometimes fall to the rest of us, which we must be
alert to scoop up.

Burnham's manner was polite, cool. He treated a half-century-
younger colleague like me as a possibly promising student. When I
used some term out of Spartan history, he asked, "Why don't we
look it up in the dictionary?" I knew before I turned the pages that
I had blundered.

Jeffrey Hart was a few years younger than Bill. He had a ruddy
face, and a raucous, infectious laugh. He loved jokes, and had the
rare knack of making his pleasure in his own amusing. He was a student of Lionel Trilling's who had become a professor of English at
Dartmouth. I could see that he must be a great teacher; he loved his
subjects—Fitzgerald, Hemingway, the eighteenth century—and he
loved discussing them, especially with young people. He had the imp
of mischief that holds attention. He had written speeches for both
Richard Nixon and Ronald Reagan, the prince of darkness and the
beau ideal, and saw no anomaly in that. His view of politics was cut-
and-dried; you did what you had to do to win. He greatly admired
Nixon's political demographer Kevin Phillips, then still a right-winger.

Chilton Williamson, Linda Bridges, and Joe were closer to my
own age. Chilton, the book review editor, would move to Wyoming
and become a cowboy, but when I met him he was an urban fashion
plate. He once was having lunch with Tom Wolfe and Timothy Dickinson, an eccentric Englishman who supplied writers with quotations
from Alexander Kinglake, the Victorian historian. Chilton was in a
quandary. If he wore his white three-piece suit, Wolfe would think he
was putting him on, but if he wore his black pinstripe—Dickinson's
uniform—Timothy would think the same. I don't remember what he
did; seersucker?

Linda Bridges was short and bespectacled, and wore her hair long
and straight (later she put it up in a bun). She had intervened, by

mail, in a dispute between Bill and the literary critic Hugh Kenner over the lead sentence of one of Bill's columns. Kenner, who spent his professional life explaining Pound's *Cantos*, thought Bill's sentence was invertebrate. Bill defended himself and, being Bill, published their correspondence in "Notes & Asides." The Miss Bridges who joined in, taking Bill's side, turned out to be a French major at USC. Bill published her letter too, and called her up to ask if she wouldn't like to work for *National Review*. She came east with her literary sensibility and her eye for detail. She would edit copy not only for sense and for typos but also for appearance, alert for "rivers" of type, angled chains of *y*'s, *f*'s, and *g*'s that coursed through printed paragraphs like watermarks. I believe she encouraged them.

Linda's visual sense appeared to desert her when it came to her surroundings. Looking into her office, you would have said it was a mess: Her desk was buried in piles of manuscripts, newspapers, and magazines; so was the floor. But you would have been wrong, for Linda knew where everything was, and could retrieve anything, with only a few minutes' digging.

Joe's office was a mess. If he had ever arranged anything in piles, they had long ago toppled and slid. His chair legs rested on a lava flow of paper. There were old Coke cans in there, loose cigars, un-paid bills, and uncashed checks. Jack Fowler, from the publishing side, once found a check from the *Wanderer*, a conservative Catholic paper, for fifty dollars (I did not know the *Wanderer* paid quarterly). It was a miracle that Joe did not combust, like the pawnbroker in *Bleak House*. He took better care of his books. He brought me on one lunch break that summer to the Strand, the huge used-book store below Union Square, where I bought Golding's translation of Ovid's *Metamorphoses*, which I still have, and still have to read. His first love was Shakespeare. I rode with him once in his van; he had a com-plete Shakespeare sitting on the dashboard, I suppose in case he wanted to look something up before the light changed. He knew *Hamlet* by heart. He loved the great actors, and was an excellent mimic. He could begin some soliloquy—"Now is the winter of our discontent"—as Olivier; I would call out *Gielgud, Burton*, and he would change voices like gears. He read critics the way other people read mysteries or romances, always moving on to the next one. Later in life he decided that the works of Shakespeare had been written by Edward de Vere, the seventeenth Earl of Oxford, an old crackpot notion; he hoped to popularize it by arguing that Oxford was gay: "He's here, he's queer, he's Edward de Vere." I thought part of his motivation was simply the desire to shuffle the beloved deck one more time. His second favorite author was Dr. Johnson, whom he admired for his personality, his rhetoric, his attitude. He savored the explosions of temper as much as the wisdom. When Johnson declared that his mother should have whipped him for a burst of boyhood skepticism, Joe approved.

The office of Bill Rusher was separate from the editorial offices, and separate from Bill Buckley's. There all was neatness and order. Rusher's hair, his neckties, and his pronunciation were trim, almost severe. A few years older than Buckley, he had once dated Bill's sister Maureen. Analytical and self-analytical, Rusher knew that Buckley was a bird of paradise, and that he was not. He prided himself on his own proper skills, which were political. In 1961 Rusher, along with F. Clifton White, a longtime Republican operative, and John Ashbrook, a young congressman from Ohio, formed the Draft Goldwater Committee that captured the Republican nomination for him three years later. Bill Rusher spotted Ronald Reagan early on, and hoped he would win the 1968 nomination instead of Nixon, whom Rusher never liked—until the moment Nixon began to fall, when Rusher became a fierce partisan. One of Nixon's last loyal boosters at the end of his endgame was an Orthodox rabbi, Baruch Korff; Rusher ruefully called himself "Rabbi Korff's Rabbi Korff." He had a tropism for causes even more unpopular than ordinary conservatism, sticking up for white South Africa, and the Moonies. (For all three defendants, Nixon, Afrikanerdom, and the Reverend Moon, he acted as a trial lawyer: My client was not there, and if he was he didn't shoot, and if he did it was self-defense.) Beneath his somewhat forbidding exterior, Rusher was a generous, hospitable man, who enjoyed lunches and dinners out; he was on the wine committee of the University Club, and he liked the restaurant Le Perigord, only apologizing for its location: "Because we're near the UN," he said the first time he took me there, "we do get a lot of riffraff." Most surprising, he did not think an occasion complete without poetry. His favorites were Swinburne, Housman, and Santayana; he responded to the passion in all three, florid in Swinburne, and to the sadness and restraint of the last two.

Some people became a part of my life at long distance. Russell Kirk's oblique relation to the world most of us call real was epitomized by two items of his bibliography: He wrote ghost stories, and he had written an admiring biography of the crazy nineteenth-century congressman John Randolph of Roanoke. Ghosts were less paranormal than John Randolph. Kirk sent his column in from his home in rural Michigan. I never got there; I met him in Chicago at a meeting of the Philadelphia Society, an annual conservative pow-wow. In one night, I saw Kirk accosted by a streetwalker and pinned against the wall of a hotel corridor by a haranguing Russian émigré. He refused the one and endured the other graciously.

Erik von Kuehnelt-Leddihn made more of an impression on me, because editing him took so much effort. Erik sent us bulletins on Europe, European culture, and anything else that interested him (much did). He lived in the Austrian Tyrol, dirt poor. He went to Switzerland once by train to meet Bill, who asked him why he had come second class. "Because there is no third class," Erik explained. Erik had general ideas—Catholicism, monarchism, antinationalism—but one read him for his details. Turkish was one of the many languages he spoke, and he noticed that he could use it to converse with Azerbaijanis; in a town square in Guatemala he was bemused to see statues of a saint, and of Rufino Barrios, a murderous dictator. He wrote his aperçus in impenetrable, anti-idiomatic English, stippled with parentheses and exclamation points. My favorite: ". . . the Balkans (where many wars have begun—World War I, for instance!)." Editing him took two people, one to begin, the other to save the first.

I also met the dead, who lived on in the magazine's lore. Frank Meyer had died in 1972. He had been a senior editor and the magazine's book review editor since almost the beginning. Everybody loved him, particularly his reviewers, and the college students he drew to his Woodstock aerie, but he was a difficult man. In the early sixties Meyer had schemed against James Burnham, trying to spread the rumor that he was senile. Bill put a stop to that. Burnham for his part needled Meyer by suggesting that Meyer's precious book reviews be shortened, to make them more like the reviews in the *Economist*. Priscilla told Frank that Jim did this only to get his goat. Meyer saw it, but seeing it made no difference; Burnham got his goat anyway. Their dislike was as old as their revolutionary past, for Meyer had been a communist. It seemed to me, viewing the split from psychic miles away, that communists thought they were more realistic, while Trotskyites thought they were more intelligent. Perhaps apostates felt the same.

Willmoore Kendall, another deceased senior editor, led a wispier posthumous existence. He had been one of Bill's professors at Yale, and wrote and spoke in an eccentric style that had influenced Bill's. He had an original mind, arguing that Rousseau at his best believed in simple democracy, and that he was right to do so; Willmoore thought liberal elites gummed it up. But in 1976 he was remembered for the brown leather couch, still sitting, after two moves, in one of our offices, on which he had been caught *in flagrante delicto* with a colleague one morning, much to the dismay of the colleague who caught them. Bill and his former professor walked around the block and came to a gentleman's agreement: Bill would not ask him not to do it again, but Willmoore would not do it again.

Mightiest of the dead, in Bill's mind, was still another senior editor, Whittaker Chambers, poet, journalist, and communist spymaster who told the world that State Department functionary Alger Hiss had been one of his minions. Today only the enabling friends of Hiss's son, Tony, deny that Hiss was what Chambers said he was, a Soviet spy. But the struggle to prove it, in congressional testimony, two trials, and the court of public opinion, was black and exhausting. Chambers had a dark view of the world, quite apart from Hiss. Despair over modern America made Chambers join the Communist Party; he rejected communism, but not despair, convinced that he was moving from the winning to the losing side. "It is idle to speak of saving western civilization," he wrote Bill. "It is a wreck from within." Bill wrote of him often, and always quoted him whenever he wrote of him. No man was busier or more lively than Bill; if these things presume hope, no man was more hopeful. But Chambers's voice was like an organ tone resounding in his head.

All these characters, living and dead, present and absent, were enhanced and enlarged by *National Review*'s raconteurs. For the world at large, we were committed to print; withindoors, we feasted on talk. Because all our talkers were also writers, they wrote their stories down, then told them again and again. Jeff Hart had a great one about W. H. Auden speaking at Dartmouth, and being so drunk that he could not put his notes in order after dropping them on the way to the lectern. So he swept them up and read them anyhow as the pages appeared. Interesting insights, said Jeff's colleagues, but a little disjointed. A week or two after Jeff recalled the story, I read it in one of the red-bound volumes of back issues, in a review Jeff had written years earlier.

Our champion raconteur was Priscilla. She told us about ourselves: how John Leonard, latterly a hotshot columnist for the *New York Times*, but once a fledgling *National Review* writer even younger than I now was, had been asked at the editorial conference to write about gold. Minutes later he poked his head into Priscilla's office and asked, "What do we think of gold?" Shortly thereafter, the magazine sent him to newly Communist Cuba to report on the fate of an anti-Castro journalist. No question what the Communists thought of *National Review*'s correspondent: John got a call one morning from the British Embassy telling him he must leave Havana, now, or he would be—arrested? rubbed out? Nothing good.

Priscilla also told us about the world of mainstream journalism, for she was the only in-house editor who had any experience of it, having worked for United Press in New York and Paris. She saw the sultan of Morocco reconciled with a rebellious subject, the pasha of Marrakech, in a French palace. The pasha threw himself at the sultan's feet, but the sultan graciously raised him up. Next week, *Time* reported that the sultan's chamberlain had grabbed the repentant pasha's head and pressed it onto his master's foot. Priscilla called the *Time* correspondent in Paris, a friend of hers, and told him, "That's not what I saw." "That's not what I wrote," he answered.

My summer was bounded by work and reading and writing. I hardly lived in New York; I inhabited the rut from the YMCA to *National Review*. But the magazine had associated places, like overseas territories, which I visited. Seeing them was another glimpse behind the curtain at how things that I had known for years worked. One was the printing plant. We wrote on typewriters; our copy was set on Linotype machines in Connecticut. Two employees would drive to the plant to deliver the copy and bring back the proofs, long typeset strips of off-white paper. Linotype machines were Rube Goldberg constructions, eight or ten feet tall. Pressing a single key sprang a half-dozen moving parts into action; since the touch of the keyboard was so light, the Linotypists could make the place rock. Today this is as remote as the broughams and phaetons that drive through Thackeray and Jane Austen, but that is how things were done at the end of the Gutenberg era.

The other home away from home was the studio on East Twenty-third Street in which *Firing Line* was shot. This was ruled by the producer Warren Steibel, tall, stout, wavy haired, with a thick New York accent like Mel Brooks putting it on or Harvey Fierstein talking normally. Warren had directed a feature film, *The Honeymoon Killers*, which was a lurid cult classic. A gay Jewish liberal, he was nevertheless devoted to *Firing Line*, not only because of Bill's talents but because he believed "the *oth*uh side might know something, youknow? YouknowwhatI'm *say*ing?" When I sat in the control room I saw beyond the window the set I knew from our living room television: the plain backdrop, the spartan chairs, Bill lounging. Inside the control room Warren fumed. "Camera 1," he shouted, then louder, "*Camera 1!*" Camera 1 took its cue, Bill wrapped it up, the baroque trumpet sounded, and another show was in the can.

There was a final aspect of *National Review* that was almost like a foreign country: its Catholicism. Bill Rusher was not a Catholic, and neither was I; there may have been a few others. But Catholicism drenched the magazine. A few years later, Joe Sobran brought three priests to editorial drinks. David Brooks (Jewish) leaned in toward me (Methodist) and said, "I haven't been with so many Catholics since lunch." The Catholicism came out in religious metaphors (anathematize), in Latin phrases quoted as one quotes pop songs (*ex cathedra*), even in the anticlericalism of cradle Catholics. In the mid-sixties, *National Review* had called *Pacem in Terris*, a papal encyclical it disagreed with, "a venture in triviality."

The eighth floor of our building held yet another cluster of the magazine's offices, the domain of the assistant publisher, Jim McFadden, where he presided over circulation and conducted polemics against abortion (*Roe v. Wade* had been handed down three years earlier). There Catholicism flourished in its second- and third-generation Irish American form. That summer Kevin Lynch, the articles editor, proposed to Josephine Gallagher, Jim's secretary, and Jim threw them a party. It was louder than a typical office party, and there was more beer, but what made it stand out was the aged man playing the fiddle. McFadden pressed a sweating bottle into my hand, and said, through his ever-present pipe, "Isn't this is a *great National Review* party?"

My Methodism was a wan thing; I had had the usual struggles with morality and mortality, I remembered the hymns of the Wesley brothers, and on the rare occasions when I thought of God I thought in the Revised Standard Version. The pressure of so many Catholics made me hold on to Protestantism like a passport—an ID and a carapace.

Day in and day out, I wrote copy, edited copy, sorted the mail. There was a lot of time to read. I read all of Orwell's journalism, not just his reactions to Burnham. Some of it, from the early days of World War II, recalled Churchill. I disagreed with his socialism, but as a conservative of my generation, who defined himself as being in the minority, I rolled with the punches and read on. I pondered "Politics and the English Language," and its advice to writers. Orwell said good writing was simple. But his writing was also infused with a tone of authority. He turned that tone on itself, asking where in English life—Eton, the lower upper middle class—it had come from. But he never foreswore it.

I also read some of the conservative thinkers whose names appeared in our pages, and whose books sat on our shelves. Michael Oakeshott, the English philosopher, had spoken at our twentieth-anniversary celebration the year before (at great length, Jeff and Linda reported, and inaudibily). His writing was polished, intelligent, and inedible. He preached opportunism on stilts; no principles, please, we're British! Richard Weaver's essays on Abraham Lincoln and Edmund Burke were the antidote to Oakeshott: Only those who, like Lincoln and unlike Burke, think long and hard and know what they think can do anything in this sad world.

I read a lot of pernicious rubbish. I developed a taste for it, as others do for H. P. Lovecraft. There are a lot of crazy people in America, I discovered, and they spent much of their time sending their thoughts to us. Two newsletters that showed up in our mail were *Attack* and *Thunderbolt*. One was Klan, one Nazi. Jimmy Carter was in the process of winning the Democratic nomination, and he drove both nuts. One said he was a Jew; the other said he was black (look at those lips). How would subscribers to both, I wondered, reconcile the two theories?

Someone sent in a copy of a book, *The Naked Capitalist*, by W. Cleon Skousen (great name). The most popular right-wing conspiracy theory of the early sixties had been promulgated by the John Birch Society: Everyone who counted was a communist. Bill and *National Review* had performed a service by reading the Birchers out of the movement; Russell Kirk had come up with the best rejoinder to their frantic exegeses—Eisenhower was not a communist; he was a golfer. W. Cleon Skousen breathed a more austere atmosphere. Other people's bugaboos—communists, Jews, Masons—were epiphenomena to him. The real wire-pullers of history were the insiders: businessmen and their strategists who sponsored revolutions and wars to fatten their wallets. The *ur*-insider turned out to be an aide to Woodrow Wilson, Col. Edwin House; a novel he had written,

Philippe Dru: Administrator, explained all later history. It was funny in its way, except that we would all see Skousenism and its many descendants again.

We paid to get one brutish publication, the *Daily Worker*. Its cartoons were the only place apart from Get Out of Jail Free cards in Monopoly that still depicted rich men in cutaways and toppers. Priscilla read every issue and was sometimes rewarded with material for offbeat items, such as offers of the complete works of Leonid Brezhnev.

MY SUMMER AT *National Review* would have been compelling any year, but beyond us and obsessing us that summer was the election. Burnham, Rusher, and Hart were piqued by Jimmy Carter, a southern Democrat who seemed apart from his party's liberal establishment. But the drama was on the Republican side, our side.

Gerald Ford, Nixon's successor, was by nature a conservative man, with a skeptical eye for Washington business-as-usual. During his presidency, a bill to regulate the trucking industry landed on his desk. "If X [chairman of a relevant congressional committee] likes it, and if Y [a leading Teamster] likes it, and if Z [a major trucking executive] likes it, then it must be a bad bill," he said, before vetoing it. But by the mid-seventies, there was a conservative movement, which might loosely be defined as Bill Buckley's admirers and *National Review*'s readers, self-aware, ideological, which Ford had never been part of. When he made what the movement considered to be mistakes, he did not know how to repair them, maybe did not know that he ought to repair them, and had no credit to draw on. We especially disliked Ford's continuing practice of Nixon's foreign policy, as represented by Henry Kissinger, still secretary of state—after the fall of Saigon, it lacked even the patina of success.

Our unhappiness opened the way for Ronald Reagan. Reagan's life had three acts: small-town happy-go-luckiness, banishing any dark thoughts he may have had of straitened means and a drunken father; escape to success on the radio, and spectacular success in Hollywood; then transformation into a conservative politician. Nixon once told Bill Buckley scornfully that Americans would never put a former actor in the White House. But Californians put Reagan into the governor's mansion twice. Years later, when Reagan was about to be awarded a French decoration, he asked aide Mike Deaver what was coming. Deaver mistakenly said it was the *Croix de Guerre*. But that is for military valor, Reagan said; he didn't deserve it. Reagan's ambassador to France, Van Galbraith, interjected that the award was to be the *Legion d'Honneur*, which is given for statesmanship. Reagan gave a little cinch to the knot of his tie and smiled. "I can play that."

Reagan's challenge to Gerald Ford for the 1976 presidential nomination was the first moment since the Goldwater campaign when the whole movement knew what to do. Barry Goldwater himself endorsed Ford, but he was clearly jealous of his followers' new darling. Everyone else felt the same tingling in their antennae, like ants. The early primaries—New Hampshire, Florida, Illinois—added an element of drama to the struggle as Reagan was shut out and seemingly doomed, until a surprise win in North Carolina at the end of March saved him to fight on through the spring and summer.

A friend of mine from the Party of the Right worked for the Reagan campaign as a gofer; she had just broken up with her boyfriend, whom I hoped to replace, but she went for a fellow campaigner instead. Every day at lunchtime I went down to the sidewalk with a pocket full of coins, fed them into a pay phone (I didn't feel I could use *National Review*'s nickel for such calls), and got her view of the contest. Hers was no clearer than what I read in the newspapers. The Ford-Reagan fight was as slow and pitiless as Obama-Clinton in 2008. Reagan's last gambit as he finally fell short was to pick a running mate in advance of the Kansas City convention, hoping to force Ford to do the same. The man he picked was Richard Schweiker, a liberalish senator from Pennsylvania. Bill got an advance briefing from Reagan himself on Schweiker, which he passed glumly on to us: The senator was prolife and progun, the rest slim pickings. The gambit failed, either to make Ford tip his hand or to shake his lead. At the convention the Texas delegation, unanimous for Reagan, led their soul mates in cheers of *Viva—olé!* until they were hoarse. In vain. I heard it all on my YMCA-room TV.

Bill Rusher had a plan B. He had hoped for Reagan's victory, but expected defeat. Rusher had concluded that the GOP was a lost cause, wedded to bad habits. He thought there were populist stirrings in the land, which could find a proper home only in a conservative third party. He had written a book, *The Making of the New Majority Party*, as a manifesto for this idea, and hoped, before the 1976 cycle began in earnest, that the effort might be led by Reagan himself.

Bill Buckley thought Rusher was crazy. He was ambivalent about populism. His style was elite, and, for his nonelite fans, aspirational. On the other hand (prompted perhaps by memories of Kendall), he often found more sense in ordinary people than in their betters. He famously said he would rather be governed by the first two thousand names in the Boston phone book than by the faculty of Harvard University.

Buckley's opinions on third parties were clear. He had run for mayor as a candidate of the Conservative Party of New York, but he embraced it only as a pressure group, not as an effort to supplant the GOP. Rusher ignored him. He thought his own political judgment was far better than Buckley's: Buckley's notion of how Goldwater might win the 1964 election had been to tap Dwight Eisenhower as his running mate.

A Reagan-less third party was holding its convention in Chicago in September. During a lunchtime traffic jam on Park Avenue, between backseat driving the cabbie, Rusher explained to me his hopes for the gathering: There were enough delegates who were not dolts or kooks to pick someone who could run a decent holding operation. Rusher did not express himself that harshly; he should have. The man the delegates picked was Lester Maddox, the racist former governor of Georgia. Rusher came back to *National Review* to do the honorable thing, denouncing candidate and party, and Buckley did the honorable thing, letting him write the anathema without any I-told-you-sos. It was a lesson in the futility of the politics of purity.

Ford went on to lose, narrowly. James Buckley went down too. It looked as if New York's Democrats might help him out by nominating Bella Abzug, an old Stalinist congresswoman. But they picked instead Daniel Patrick Moynihan. Like Jim, Moynihan was an Irish Catholic; unlike him, he had a gift of gab; and he supported enough conservative positions—federal aid to parochial schools—to rope in his coreligionists. Bill was torn. Moynihan was a respectful liberal intellectual, of the kind whose respect Bill craved; he was also a friend. Bill did not want to appear to be succumbing to nepotism. In the home stretch, *National Review* devoted a cover story to Jim, but nothing would have saved him in 1976. The Nixon years ended in dust and ashes.

By election day I was back in my first life, well into my last year of school.

CHAPTER 3

IN MY FINAL year of college I had to give some thought, however unwilling and distracted, to what I would do not just the year after but for the next forty. What would I be? The train tracks of classes and activities were ending. Where should I go next, and how? I was an English major, but literature was no way to make a living. The default choice for humanities majors in the seventies was to put the choice off by going to law school. I had no bent for the law, but I dutifully took the LSAT and sent out applications. I shared these halfhearted plans with Priscilla Buckley, who suggested I put the choice off more productively by coming to work for *National Review* for a year. Yale Law School deferred my admission, and in August 1977 I went back again to East Thirty-fifth Street.

My father and I drove down to the city early in the summer to look for an apartment. We had the real estate listings from the *New York Times* (newspapers made a fortune from listings in those days). We looked at a great block of nothing in Queens, and many offerings in Manhattan; a downpour filled the gutters with floating bottles. We found a studio a block from Gramercy Park, in an old building that had been the headquarters of a charity. The room looked on the courtyard and was spackled with God knows what, probably asbestos. It rented for $275 a month. A couple months later my parents and I drove down in a car loaded with furniture that had migrated to the basement and the glassed-in sunporch, and the typewriter that had got me here.

Living in an apartment, in the cash nexus, was different from home, even from dorms. Dogs barking at night across the courtyard seemed at first like the suburbs, therefore comforting, but they went on longer, with harsher echoes. People copulating in the next room were never comforting. The city opened itself slowly, especially to me, who was slow to examine it. I carried all the prejudices of upstate. New York City was an alien place; it was full of welfare cheats who sucked our taxes. I thought only of the greedy subway riders, not of the Cayuga County apple pickers.

In fact, the city was in a bad way. It had gone bankrupt, rescued only by the federal government. Everything that was fray-able had frayed, habits worst of all. No one picked up dog waste; no one paid much attention to human waste (derelicts were about to be rechristened "the homeless," and turned into sacred totems and an intractable problem). Boom boxes serenaded all and sundry (cheap earphones and portable CD players had not been invented yet).

A few blocks from my apartment was Union Square. The carcass of Klein's, a bargain department store, anchored one corner. The park itself was grassless and dusty; unsavory types lounged on the benches or in the bushes. When you walked past, they muttered, "Smokes, smokes." I missed the blackout in July, which was accompanied by a free-for-all. But I was in the city the next month for the arrest of Son of Sam, the serial killer who claimed to take orders from a Satanic dog. Rupert Murdoch had bought the *New York Post* less than a year earlier. I remembered the old *Post*, liberal and solemn, from my internship. Murdoch had not yet begun to change its politics, but he changed its style to match the moment. The letters of the headline announcing the Son of Sam's arrest were three inches tall, in red. Days later, the *Post* kept the pot boiling with a photograph of the killer, dozing on a jail cot, under the screamer: SAM SLEEPS. I read these messages from the collective unconscious in the steaming stations of the Lexington Avenue Line, the train cars glowing with graffiti, the platforms mottled with black flattened gum wads.

Slowly I changed, and the city changed for me. Gramercy Park showed me what a city park could be. In the suburbs there were lawns, golf courses, woods with runaway vines. The city had to be more selective. The park straddled a block, breaking the street grid. Its trees looked down like sentinels on traffic, passersby, and its own benches and birds. I spent weekends sitting on the low stone wall that ran around its edge, reading a biography of John L. Lewis that I was reviewing for *National Review*. Occasionally, people with keys (the park was fenced and locked, hence its state of preservation) passed in or out. I have coveted many things, but this was the only privilege of wealth I coveted.

But Gramercy Park was not my eye-opener; it was too close to be first. First came the Empire State Building. Anybody could tell the Chrysler Building was a jewel, with its gleaming tip and lightning-bolt patterns: It was the future of the past, assertive as tail fins. The Empire State Building was plainer; it needed a third and fourth look. But when you bothered you saw how it shot up. The fussing at the base launched a clean shaft, ending in a few last steps and the dirigible mast. Once I saw it, I began seeing other buildings. Even the dowdy World Trade Towers looked good twice a day, at dawn and dusk, when they took on a fleeting air of insubstantiality.

Meeting my future wife helped. Two Party of the Right friends lived in the East Village, where he managed a building and she sang in a group. The Renaissance Street Singers, who still perform, sang religious music of the Renaissance, from green premusic to glories of God; Bach and Beethoven are bigger and deeper, not more perfect. The group sang every Sunday for three hours, for free; when listeners dropped money in the director's music folder, he stopped conducting to give it back. No venue was too small, from a church in the Bronx to a community group in East New York. But the group's favorite spots were the crossroads, like the Staten Island Ferry and Grand Central Terminal. My friend said the group needed basses. It turned out that one of the sopranos and I wanted each other.

Jeanne Safer was a psychoanalyst who had been living in the city for eight years. She is a liberal Democrat; during the Clinton years,

I would tell her he was her problem, even as Nixon had been mine. I liked to shock her; after she greeted one beetling man in the receiving line at a *National Review* function, I informed her that she had just shaken hands with the inventor of the H-bomb.

After Jeanne became a writer, we cowrote many pieces about the dynamics of our bipolitical relationship. Two of the bridges across our ideological divide were that Jeanne thought most politicians were rascals or idiots, a rather conservative insight, and she practiced psychoanalysis, an old-fashioned if not dying art. Now the science heads and the insurance companies give us hierarchies and pills to make us free and happy.

Jeanne had loved the city all her life, dreaming of moving there from her suburbia, and she led me further in, to Szechuan restaurants, coffeehouses with pressed-tin ceilings, street fairs on Bedford Street when they were still good, belly dance clubs.

One peculiarity of the city in 1977 and for some years thereafter must be mentioned: the popularity and prominence of Jews. Jeanne gave me a window into this, for she is Jewish. But the fact was inescapable. In November 1977, the first Jewish mayor of New York, Abraham Beame, gave way to the second, Edward Koch. Woody Allen was moving from being a comic to being a filmmaker (unfortunately, a "serious filmmaker"). His lifestyle, he living in an apartment on one flank of Central Park, his lover and mother of his children, Mia Farrow, living in an apartment on the other, would become a topic of general discussion and envy. Saul Bellow had just won the Nobel Prize for Literature. He was a Chicago boy, but some of his novels were set in New York and many of his boosters lived and wrote here; his fans compared his Nobel speech to Faulkner's. Some Jews felt beleaguered (some Jews always do) by the animosity that fights in the New York public school system—black activists and parents versus Jewish principals and teachers—had exposed. But that seemed to be a local matter merely. Even being part of a problem did not necessarily feel bad to New York's Jews, because then they could be part of the discussion of the problem. I had had Jewish friends in high school, enough to learn a few simple in-jokes.

There was one about King Arthur's court whose punch line was a line from the Passover seder: Why is this (k)night different from all other (k)nights? (Having it explained drained what little humor it possessed.) But New York was different. It was Zion, and Jews were at home in it. Who knew it was doomed?

One day as I was hurrying up Fifth Avenue, I wrote one verse of a song, with chorus. In my head it was sung by Mick Jagger, circa "Honky-Tonk Woman"/"Brown Sugar."

I was on Fifth Avenue
When I ran into you.
You were going somewhere in your car.
You didn't look at me,
But babe you better believe
When I start cooking, you won't be looking far.

And there were towers of steel
And girls in high heels
And there were old men making money
And young men playing their games.
And there were block-long Rolls-Royces
And a crowd with a million voices
Saying, "In a year, everyone here
's gonna know your name."

I never revealed this song, ardent and preposterous, to anyone. It was my wedding song to New York, and to my second life, which seemed to have fused with my first.

———

AFTER ALL THESE years I began to enter Bill Buckley's life. Writing for him from Irondequoit or New Haven, even writing from a desk at *National Review* as an intern, had been contributions to his enterprises. But now I moved in his slipstream.

Bill had described a week of his life in a book, *Cruising Speed* (1971). It starts with the beginning of a workday, as he gets into his limo in Connecticut, while trying to keep his King Charles spaniel out of it, and walks through that day and the next six, moving back in time when necessary to explain acquaintances or set up events. Bill gave a fly-on-the-wall look at a celebrity and public intellectual in action. Today it might be done as a reality show, if a reality show could have wit and speed, and could swear off grossness and humiliation. At the end of it all he asked himself a big question: What did his many activities amount to? Bill was haunted off and on by an unwritten book, which would have applied Ortega y Gassett's *Revolt of the Masses* to mid-twentieth-century America. Willmoore Kendall had urged the project on him, but it never got done. Bill was a journalist, which, translated literally from the original French, means a daily-ist. The missing book was no loss: *Revolt of the Masses* is a thumb sucker that would have been better as an essay; the world did not need an American version. In *Cruising Speed*, Bill asked himself a larger question: Was the speed of his life too fast, the pace too hectic? "What are my *reserves*? How will I satisfy them, who listen to me today, *tomorrow*? Hell, how will I satisfy *myself* tomorrow?" He gave no answer, except the book itself, and the life it depicted: This is what I am, and these are the things I have to do now, and the next day, and the day after.

I became acquainted with Bill's limos. They weren't block-long Rolls-Royces, but they were plenty big, stretch jobs with a lot of legroom and jump seats on the back of the driver's seat. He owned one at a time; over the years they seemed to get longer. For all their roominess, they were not comfortable; you felt yourself bouncing around in them, as if you were a marble in a kid's pencil box. But the limo served its function as an on-the-road office. Bill had two homes, a maisonette on East Seventy-third Street and a house on the Sound in Stamford. Whichever one he was en route to or from, he could curl up in the backseat, flipping on the reading light if it was dark, and go through his briefcase of letters and manuscripts.

Bill's own manuscripts had begun to include fiction. His first spy novel, *Saving the Queen*, had appeared the year before. Bill intended it as an alternative to the nihilism of John Le Carré, who wrote about the cold war as if it were a battle between indistinguishable dinosaurs. His hero was a playful alter ego, Blackford Oakes, a Yalie recruited into the CIA (Bill had been in the CIA briefly after leaving Yale; his spymaster was Howard Hunt, who went on to spy on the Democrats at the Watergate). Bill had been anxious about trying a new genre; he shared his puzzlements about writing, usually momentary, with everyone. He was careful to call *Saving the Queen* an "entertainment," as a preemptive defense against criticism. He told all of us the advice that Hugh Kenner had given him: Since you must not count on good reviews (reviewers may want to trip you up outside your home turf), you have to have a plot twist that can pass by word of mouth, in one sentence. Bill's twist was: American spy screws the queen of England (not Elizabeth II, but a fictional Caroline). John Kenneth Galbraith remarked that Bill had been writing fiction for years, now he was open about it, but this was praise lightly disguised as sniping, making a shtick of their ideological rivalry. Bill happily used it as a blurb.

I avoided reading *Saving the Queen*. I suffered from English-major snobbery: I was supposed to go from *The Good Soldier* to this? I also felt rivalry: I was in the process of writing my first (and last) novel in my spare time. My subject was college love. What else did I have to write about? (I had this, though I didn't know it at the time.) At a deeper and hidden level, I feared for Bill's literary judgment. He did his journalism so well; why try something else? If his judgment could be mistaken, suppose he had made a mistake about me? Bill need not have worried about the reviews; they were friendly, and his novel was a success. By the fall of 1977 he had already finished the next one. I still put off reading them.

TWO OF THE most important people in Bill's professional life were women. I had already worked with Priscilla, his sister. As an employee of the magazine, I began to work with his secretary and assistant, Frances Bronson. Her office adjoined the red den; she was the organizer, the dispatcher, the crowd controller of his life. She was a Jewish cockney who wore gypsy turbans and had a lustrous voice. I asked her once how the pub dialogue in "The Waste Land" should be pronounced, and she talked me through it: *I = uh; make = mike; teeth = teeff; others = ovvers.* She had an offer to join the D'Oyly Carte company when she was young. But instead of going onstage she ended up working with a performer.

Bill drove her furiously; one of her favorite stories was of a long phone call, Bill ticking off eight or ten assignments and asking, at the end, if the first had been done already. Like Warren Steibel, she kept her cool by being on perpetual simmer. The only time she lost it was because of another of Bill's phone calls, this one from Switzerland, asking her to find a tuning fork and hit a concert A so that he could tune his harpsichord. There was a tuning fork in the chalet somewhere, but he calculated it would take less time (and time was always of the essence) to call New York and get the A from her. After giving him his pitch, she gave a "He's driving me mad" soliloquy to the editorial staff, which was just closing an issue. As revenge, they pasted a bogus page into Bill's copy of "The Week," filled with everything he forbade: bad grammar, botched Latin quotations, lewd jokes, gross physical smears (they wrote of Justice William O. Douglas's "motorized old ticker"). Bill, reading it, thought his beloved magazine had collapsed before his eyes. He was (only just) relieved to be told it had all been a joke.

The Swiss edition happened several years before I came to *National Review*, and the story of it was an in-house staple, but no one learned from it. Bill did not change his behavior, because he could not. Frances loved the challenge of keeping him going.

ONE OF MY assignments now that I was on staff was to handle, via Frances, a portion of Bill's mail. This was not the magazine's mail, the letters to the editor and the dozens of newsletters, racist and otherwise, that flowed in over the transom, but the correspondence specifically addressed to Bill. There was a mass of it, and I was only one of his devils; another sister, Jane Buckley Smith, also bore a heavy load. Bill signed off on everything we wrote, and took many letters on himself. The best of them went to his *National Review* column "Notes & Asides"; at the end of his life, the best of the best were collected in a volume whose title came from one of his replies: *Cancel Your Own Goddam Subscription*. The best of these winners was an exchange with Arthur Schlesinger Jr., who had referred in passing to "*National Review*, or the *National Enquirer*, or whatever you call your magazine." Bill asked how Schlesinger would like it if he wrote, "Dear Arthur, or Dear Barfer, or whatever you call yourself." This was the perfect answer: telling the great man that he was behaving like a five-year-old, and showing him how for good measure.

The letters that were not from Pulitzer Prize winners presented their own challenges. The most insistent correspondents were prisoners. Bill had come to their attention by lobbying throughout the late sixties for the retrial of Edgar Smith, a man awaiting execution in New Jersey for murdering a fifteen-year-old girl. Smith came to Bill's attention the same way I had, by writing well. With Bill's unflagging support, Smith succeeded in persuading a court that there had been errors in his conviction. He was released in 1971, and after a few years tried to murder another victim, fortunately not successfully, and went back to jail where he belonged. Bill wrote a piece about the debacle for *Life* magazine, which was about as honest as it could be under the circumstances. Warren Steibel, whose own imaginative life was much taken with sex and death, never believed Smith for a moment. He attributed Bill's credulity to denial: "If you're uncomfortable with your *own* violence . . ." I thought (guiltily?) that Bill was too comfortable with good prose.

In prisons across America, inmates hoped to be the next Smith. They were disconcertingly eloquent, though all of them struck me as guilty. The one letter I pursued was from a man who had been convicted of burning down his house, killing his wife and daughter. The prosecution said that he had shut off the gas valve outside, lit fires before every outlet in the house, then turned the outside valve back on. He said this could not have caused a blaze: All the gas would have dissipated through the first outlet. He mourned pitiably for his dead dear ones. Since our house in Irondequoit had not been heated by gas, I did know from my own experience the likelihood of his defense, but I called up ConEd, the local utility, and got someone who patiently explained that of course enough gas would go down the line, just as it does when the outlets are in use. I wrote the sad prisoner to tell him that he was guilty.

Worst were the mad. Bill was a famous man; Bill was on television. Surely he could solve their problems? One appeal was accompanied by a thick stack of photocopied letters. The letter on top was addressed to U Thant, secretary-general of the United Nations. The next was addressed to the president of the United States. Down and down the letters went, through the levels of authority, until they reached a college somewhere, and finally a department within the college, where it seemed to me that the aggrieved letter writer had in fact long ago been wronged. But he had not been able to shrug it off, and so it consumed him. Worst ever was a day I was subbing for Frances, and one of the letter writers came to the office. She was a distracted middle-aged woman; I could see she had been quite pretty once. The CIA was sending messages to her through her television, and she hoped Bill and Teddy Kennedy could stop it. She brought her children, two boys, who stood by awkwardly, saying nothing, but old enough to know that something was wrong with Mother. There was no way to help. The best I could do was do no harm.

After a year of helping with the correspondence, Bill sent me a note:

Dear Rick:
At the risk of supererogation, I must tell you what a fine job you continue to do in the matter of what I call my delicate correspondence. . . . It is an extremely important crucible—I use that inflated word with awe, but with precision. I observe most keenly what you do, my impressions of your value are confirmed by the polish of your thought, courtesy, and craftsmanship. I seek with this brief communication to advise you that in my judgment there is nothing you do

that is of greater value to the magazine, and I even encourage you to
believe, that for all the tedium involved, it may prove that there is
nothing you do that contributes more intensively to your education
viewed whole.
   Gratefully,
   Bill

If I made an answer, I have lost it. No doubt I accepted Bill's letter gratefully at the time; it was, after all, praise. What to make of it
now? I have certainly not followed in Bill's footsteps. Not being a
famous man, I get one hundredth of his correspondence. Anything I
answer I do by hand, which keeps answers short. Anything that is
abusive or combative or demanding I throw away. The Barfers of
the world will have to pass through it uninstructed by me. Bill's double-
breasted prose—*supererogation, inflated word*—tried to make romance out of scut work. I was helping him with an onerous chore,
which he chose, for reasons of his own, to take on.

But he had his reasons (this was one thing his letter was telling
me). When you live at cruising speed, in public, and when you are
trying to change your country and the world, you are always on.

I DID MY work in the magazine's smallest office, a bee's cell off the
third-floor hallway to Bill's. It was filled with filing cabinets and
dusty books, and looked out on the air shaft. At the summer solstice
a bar of light touched the desk for a half hour. Whittaker Chambers
had occupied that office when he came up from his Maryland farm
to write in-house. The advantage of the office was its proximity to
Frances and Bill. Everyone who came and went passed by. One night
Bill's wife, Pat, passed by with David Niven, who looked just like
himself. Pat was carrying an armful of stuff, including a pair of shoes
that slithered to the floor. David Niven did what he would have done
on-screen, graciously picking them up.

I met Pat at the *National Review* Christmas party that first year.
The door to her and Bill's street-level apartment on East Seventy-
third Street gave on a short, narrow hallway that opened into a foyer,

with a curving staircase to the second floor. The dining room was to the left, the living room and library to the right. The public rooms were redecorated at least once in the time I knew them, becoming even darker, richer, and more *fin de siècle*. In December 1977 it was full of stuff, drenched in red; the lamps had little bronze leaves growing out of their finials. The paintings on the walls, soups of red and blue, were lit with spots. In a corner of the living room was Pat's piano, a Bosendorfer, a Germanic grand. All I saw at first coming through the front door, besides the crush of fellow partygoers, were the black and white tiles of the floor, which struck the eye like the piccolo solo in "The Stars and Stripes Forever."

I had no idea what to wear to such a party. I owned a set of tails I had bought secondhand from a tuxedo rental place, for fancy Yale singing gigs, and a girlfriend in college had given me a cane, seeing in me a desire to step out, however far I was from being able to pull it off. Pat took in my costume and asked if I had an injury.

"No," I said brightly. "This is an affectation."

"Well—" (not pleased) "will you please leave your affectation in the hall?"

Pat was from a rich Vancouver family. As a young woman, she had been movie-star beautiful, though perhaps a bit exotic, a bit wild-looking for the actual studio system. She was a most impressive woman, tall, imperious. She first met Van Galbraith, one of Bill's college chums, at a lunch he threw for her at the Fence Club when she was Bill's new fiancée. "Bill tells me," she announced, loudly enough for the whole room to hear, "you're drunk half the time." "Oh, no," Van said, "we drink twice as much as that."

Pat was anxious about her education: What we learned in Vancouver was to ride and to shoot, she often said. She had gone to Vassar, where she met Bill, but had not graduated. To protect herself in the presence of Bill's acquaintances, political or literary or wonky, she developed an iron exterior. She need not have worried; she could hold her own in any company (after sitting next to her at a party, Chip McGrath, the veteran journalistic infielder, concluded that Chris Buckley's humor owed much more to Pat's than to Bill's). I need not have worried, because the crust was penetrable. Not on the first night, though.

At the Christmas party I was introduced to Keith Mano, the novelist who wrote "The Gimlet Eye," an impressionistic column that ran in the back of the magazine. He looked up from his drink, with a grin and a gleam in his eye—amused, amusing, a little feral, ready to rumble. I am six-foot-four; he was short and mindful of it. "You're a big prick, aren't you?" he began. Keith started a friendship like he started a column, with a strong lede. "The Gimlet Eye" was the best writing that was ever done for the magazine. Great writers wrote for us occasionally—Waugh, John Dos Passos, Chambers. No one was better than Bill at his best, but he took so many at bats that it depressed his average. Issue after issue, Keith hit the sign to win the free suit. Meeting him was a high point of any party.

There were parts of Bill's life that he shared with many friends, though not with me. If I had been athletic, I might have seen more of him at play. I sailed with him only once, on an overnight trip from Stamford to Long Island—a far cry from his transoceanic sails. He enjoyed even this little jaunt, happily cooking dinner and dumping a stick of butter in the French fries. But I am a landlubber. I have never skied, and never saw him ski. His socialite friend Taki Theodoracopulos called him "a strong skier, braver than he was good." Bill skied in a fisherman's cap and an old coat; he was a daredevil, and insisted on taking the lead down the slopes. One year Jeff Hart and his family joined him in Switzerland, and one of Jeff's young sons shot ahead. Bill remembered it; a year later, when the Harts returned, he asked if Speedy Gonzales wished to precede him again. I missed him in Gstaad and mid-Pacific, but I was at home in his home base.

Bill worked and lived like a rich man, which made his life bright and glamorous. The cars, the knickknacks, the whirl were a long way from Irondequoit. But they were not the point of my attraction, for though I was consumed with snobbery, it was focused on politics, journalism, and writing. The appurtenances were like wrapping paper on Christmas morning, bright, ripped off and thrown aside to get to the presents. Being in Bill's presence was status as I measured it. What he gave me that I had never had before (besides national exposure) was an attitude. My parents, with their beliefs and their experience of Depression Johnstown and Fonda, lived carefully. Bill lived brashly. His sharing and his showing off were the same.

WE WERE NOT yet sure what the Carter years meant. Bill Rusher, balked of his third party, wondered if the Democrats might become a vehicle of the new populism; he tried to give advice to an old Georgia crony of Carter's, Bert Lance; then Lance vanished in a squall of scandal. Carter saw Soviet dissident Vladimir Bukovsky in the White House, something both Nixon and Ford would have scotched as contrary to the etiquette of détente. But Carter already gave a hint, in his first energy speech, of his fondness for unconvincing lectures—fussy, preachy, and ineffectual.

I had come back to New York with some story ideas. One was about a woman in my hometown who was trying to operate her own private letter-delivery service, with her own postage stamps (they showed a U.S. Mail plane of World War I vintage, crashed in a tree). This was a libertarian five-finger exercise. The law securing the federal government's monopoly of first-class mail was clear, but why should it be? It made a nice little piece.

But Bill had his own idea.

He asked me to meet him in the conference room one afternoon. He arrived with a manuscript in a ring binder and lounged in his accustomed chair. The Republicans, he said, had been in the White House for eight years. Now that they were out, they would be able to talk freely. I should talk to "them" (he did not say precisely whom) and find out why Washington does not work. The ring binder held the draft of a forthcoming book by Bill Simon, treasury secretary for Nixon and Ford, which would surely have interesting things in it. I should write a series of pieces, he said, with a total length of 30,000 words. And then he left.

I sat a moment, then did what John Leonard had done when the question was gold, and asked Priscilla for advice. She gave me the names and phone numbers of three friends of the magazine in Washington: George Will had been our book review editor briefly after the death of Frank Meyer; he was at the beginning of his eminence, writing for *Newsweek*, soon to write for the *Washington Post*. John Coyne, a former associate editor, had written speeches for Spiro Agnew. Aram Bakshian was a frequent contributor who had written speeches for everybody in the GOP. I called each man and explained my assignment, got his views, then asked who else I should speak to. Then I called every person they suggested and repeated the process. I did this all fall, with trips to Washington to meet some people in person. I read Bill Simon's book, and several others. By the end of the year I had interviewed seventy-five people.

I cast a wide net. I met David Gergen, who believed in doing what was possible, and would go on to careers in journalism, television, and the Reagan and Clinton White Houses. I met Paul Weyrich, who believed in changing the boundaries of what was possible. Then in his mid-thirties, he dressed and acted like an older man from an older time, wearing suspenders, speaking as if out of a Bakelite radio. He had helped found the Heritage Foundation, which had become Washington's main conservative think tank, four years earlier, and he would help found the Moral Majority two years later. I quickly formed a composite image of the people I was interviewing that persisted even when I was speaking to them on the phone: men in their thirties to early fifties, of middling rank. I was thrown off my stride when someone who had been in the Labor Department suggested I call John Dunlop. Mr. Dunlop (born 1914) turned out to have been the former secretary; he began his response to my chipper opening spiel by saying, "Having served in every administration since Roosevelt's . . ." (Nowadays Wikipedia would have warned me to show more respect.) I made all my phone calls on *National Review*'s nickels, a lot of them; they went through our switchboard, a thing out of old movies with cords that plugged into sockets, guarded by a dragonish operator; if "Mr. Buckley" or "Mr. Rusher" wanted the line, I got disconnected. When I told Buckley and Rusher this, they deplored the inconvenience and said of course I should finish my calls, though that would have required me to tell that to the operator.

The funniest thing I learned had to do with the Family Assistance Plan, a version of Milton Friedman's negative income tax, which sought to replace welfare with cash payments to poor people. Daniel Patrick Moynihan had sold the idea to a suspicious Richard Nixon by saying it would get rid of bureaucrats. Nixon's heart was briefly stirred. But the plan had been first outlined by a pair of bureaucrats who were so dubious of success that they gave their proposed legislation a joke title, "The Christian Working Man's Anti-Communist National Defense Rivers and Harbors Act of 1969."

The most interesting thing I read was the unpublished memoir of a career civil servant. He made the maneuvers and rituals of his milieu interesting, in a Gogol/Kafka sort of way, only nicer (this was America, after all). It was he who introduced me to the broom-closet technique, which he had both used and suffered: If you want to get rid of someone with job security, move his desk to the broom closet, or, in extreme cases, the hall.

About the time of the Christmas party I decided to stop listening and start writing, which I did all winter. Kevin Lynch joked that I would follow the threads to San Clemente, where Nixon himself would reveal all. It wasn't that kind of a project. Much of it was a structural analysis of stasis—how the executive, the legislature, and the interests (civil servants, congressional staff, and lobbyists) keep things the same, whatever officeholders and voters may want. That was a very Washington, D.C., insight, even a hackneyed one, expressed by intelligent civil servants, staffers, and lobbyists themselves. But I placed it in a political context, which Weyrich more than anyone else guided me to: Unless you know what you want, and want it hard, Washington will roll you over. He said ultraliberals in Washington will roll you over, but anyone would agree he was right about the undertow of things as they are. Such a state of affairs called for a certain kind of politician—a conviction politician, not Gerald Ford, not Richard Nixon (where domestic affairs were concerned), not Edmund Burke as depicted by Richard Weaver. To help such politicians, when and if they appeared, I ended the piece with a suggestion that was followed, not because I made it but because it was the way things were already going: Conservatives would have to make careers in Washington, rather than in business or the academy, if they wanted political change. This is what conservatives increasingly did, which was a mixed blessing; change came, but some of the changes happened to us, and some of them would be bad.

I wrote 20,000 words. I imagine Bill half-hoped that if I wrote as many as thirty, they might make a short book, maybe *God and Man in the Nixon White House*. Twenty thousand words made two long articles in *National Review* in the fall of 1978, both cover stories: my first cover stories since my first piece in 1970. Twenty-three years old, and I had my first comeback.

I was happy with what I had done, and when Bill asked me to lunch at Paone's, I expected that he would be happy too, perhaps propose another idea. He did have another idea, but it was not what I expected.

We sat, we ordered. Bill came to the point. He had decided, he said, that I would succeed him as editor in chief of *National Review*, when it came time for him to retire. Bill owned all the stock of the magazine; that would then become mine. He would roll the news out gradually. I would have to become a senior editor, in a year or so; later I would serve as managing editor.

If I do not remember many details of this lunch, it is because I was overwhelmed (Jeanne remembers, from my having told her, the part about owning the stock of the magazine; I had forgotten it). I did ask Bill why he had not turned to one of my colleagues. I suspected, from the state of Joe's office, that however gifted he was as a writer he was not made for editorial administration; if he had received my first manuscript instead of Chris Simonds, it would still be lost. But there was Jeff Hart—an Ivy League professor, the man who ran the editorial conferences when Bill was out of town on his annual winter vacation in Switzerland, or for any other reason. Bill's control of the magazine in the midst of his celebrity-activist lifestyle was the product of ceaseless attention, but it also depended on the day-to-day presence of Priscilla, his flesh and blood, who shared his ideas and tastes and deferred to his judgment, and on Jeff holding the fort of "The Week" in his absence. Bill told me that when he made his first transoceanic sail, he had arranged that Jeff would take over in the event that he sank. But that would not apply to the future.

Bill was fifty-two the day we had lunch (a year younger than I am now as I write this). If he stepped down when he was sixty-five, he would run the magazine through 1990. Now was on the early side to start thinking of successors, though not absurdly so. What was incredible was that he should think of a twenty-three year old, ten months out of college.

There was a Machiavellian element to his announcement. I had a slot waiting for me at law school next fall. I might decide to stay instead at *National Review*; probably I would have—what else had I been preparing to do for a third of my life? But Bill wanted to make sure he kept me at his side. Since *National Review* could not offer the usual employer's inducements—good money—he could close the deal by offering the future.

But the offer was also sincere. Bill cared about two things. One was talent, as he defined it. ("We are lucky," Bill Rusher once said, "the *Communist Manifesto* is not better written.") Bill would look for talent almost anywhere, and go to almost any lengths to grab a piece of it. The other thing he cared about was youth. When he started the magazine, at age twenty-nine, he was a young man among elders—Burnham, Kendall, Kirk, Erik in the Tyrol; very soon, Chambers and Meyer. He charmed them by playing on the difference in their ages, tacitly offering himself as the protégé of each. When these older men discovered that he was in fact his own man, some of them reacted very badly. Willmoore Kendall, Bill's old teacher, had gone off in a rage; Rusher pointed out shrewdly that Kendall, unlike many of the others, had no actual son of his own. Now Bill was past that point in his life. But to hell with his peers, or near peers; he would reach for youth again—mine, and his own, which he still inhabited spiritually.

Jeanne's training as a psychoanalyst was Freudian. But early in her career she had worked at the Jung Institute in New York, so she was familiar with their lingo. One of Jung's archetypes, the templates that he believed underlie personality and myth, was the *puer eternus*, the eternal youth. Hermes/Mercury represented this type in classical religion. The *puer* is quick, clever, verbal, sometimes shifty. Bill was unquestionably a *puer eternus*. He would always be on the lookout for others. He had found a number of bright young writers already—John Leonard, Garry Wills, Joe Sobran—and there would be more in the years that I knew him. But I was the one he tapped in the spring of 1978.

His sincerity did not make his offer any less manipulative. I was certainly young, and I wrote well. But suppose I was not otherwise like him? Suppose I did not want to be like him? That hadn't come up at our lunch. It couldn't. I was too much in his thrall. I had trouble dealing with the switchboard operator; how could I have it out with him?

I felt the weight of responsibility. I knew how important *National Review* was to me—a combination pastime, religion, and secret society. I also believed it might be important to the world. The state of things, according to our ideas, was bad (it was about to get even worse). Things changed politically, we believed, only through the force of ideas, and ideas got their dry runs in places like *National Review*. Bill, who had been carrying this burden of change for twenty-three years, now held it out to me. I was free from normal pride—I had much more pride than normal, and every childish and adolescent day- and night dream seemed to have been fulfilled by my career so far (barring the Whiffenpoofs). But Bill's offer took adult ambition out of the falling-asleep world of home runs, heroic self-sacrifice, and unfailing sexual success, and made it real.

BILL BELIEVED IN the big gesture. When he persuaded Whittaker Chambers to write for the magazine, he rented an airplane and flew down to Maryland to shake hands on the deal; Chambers told him the only other editor to arrive in such style had been Henry Luce.

Perhaps he felt the lunch had not been big enough, for a little more than a year later Bill told me that we were going to Mexico.

Since the succession was a profound secret, and was designed to be so for years—at that point, probably only Priscilla knew—he could not say we were going to discuss my heir apparent–ship. He spun some story even to Frances. At JFK he thrust a wad of pesos into my hand: petty cash. In Miami, where we changed planes, a fan recognized him as we stood in line. He answered the man politely, but briefly, then monosyllabically. This, he whispered, was a necessary skill: how to shake off admirers in public.

He warned me as we approached Mexico City that city and airport sat in a bowl formed by a ring of mountains, and were perennially enveloped in smog. But it was crystal clear when we landed; the snowcapped volcano that looms in the distance was perfectly visible. So were the remains of a DC-10 that had cracked up on the tarmac the day before. We picked up a car and drove south.

As we cleared the mountains, we stopped at an old roadside place for a beer and a bathroom break. The Virgin of Guadalupe presided over the bar (she was not yet ubiquitous in New York, or other American cities outside the Southwest). The urinal was the side of an old oil tank out back. We went on into dusk, then night. Dinner was in Cuernevaca, at some high-end alfresco place, but we had farther to go. Our headlights occasionally picked out a cow. We came into Taxco, a colonial silver-mining town, very late, and had a nightcap on the balcony of a restaurant that overlooked the baroque square, hung with ornaments and doodads as if sprayed from a can. But there was still farther yet to go to our destination, a hotel in the hills overlooking the town. Bill had stayed there with his son, Chris, and he remembered not only the place but the particular rooms they had occupied, two suites connected by a terrace. By the time we arrived everyone was asleep. We had to rouse the night porter, an Indian in a wool cap. The hotel was artfully laid out on uneven ground; to get around, you had to clamber up and down. The porter did not know what rooms Bill was talking about; we tried a few, and kept having to try others. The moon blazed, lighting up walls, covering the paths in ink. Finally, we found something that was something like Bill's memory.

The next day we worked on a batch of correspondence he had brought along, though we could have done that in New York, or me in New York and him in Timbuktu. We had come to Mexico, it seemed, so he could say, This is the life, live it; see what I do for you, do what I want.

We went back to Mexico City after two nights in Taxco. Bill took me to the basilica where the Virgin of Guadalupe's image, imprinted on a sixteenth-century Indian's cloak, is displayed. The ugly modern building was packed; Mexicans moved down the aisles toward the image on their knees. If I believed it was what they believed it was, I would certainly have approached it on my knees, if at all. I went to Sanborn's, an old department store, and bought Jeanne a small silver box. The night before we were to fly home, Bill gave me a silver plate, inlaid with turquoise, as his memento for Jeanne. He had gotten several of them as gifts, including one for Frances. Jeanne said she liked my gift better, and since she tells me quite frankly when she doesn't like my gifts, I believed her. But I was distressed nevertheless because Bill's gift had been fancier.

At our last dinner, Bill finally came out with the one new thing he had to say: I should step into my future role more, be more assertive. That I could do, unless he meant I should be more like him. That I might not be able to do.

CHAPTER 4

THE CARTER ADMINISTRATION sent one problem right to Bill Buckley's lap: the treaties giving the Panama Canal to Panama. They had been in the works for years, and conservatives had been opposing them for years: One of Reagan's best applause lines in his race against Ford had been about the canal. "We bought it, we paid for it, it's ours, and we're going to keep it." But now Bill decided that we should give it up. It would be impossible to defend against an incorrigible Panama, and Panamanians had legitimate reasons for wanting it back.

There was nothing coy about the rollout of this idea. Bill came into an editorial conference in August 1977, and announced what the magazine's position would be. Jeff Hart, rapping his pipe into an ashtray, tried to demur, arguing that surrendering the canal would be "bad poetry." Bill cut him off. Bill Rusher declared that he would be opposing the treaties; fine, he was Rusher.

The magazine ran a long three-part editorial calling on conservatives to be realistic, and Bill orchestrated other features in that issue to support it: He asked Priscilla to arrange "For the Record," a page of brief news items (like a start-up menu or a news crawl today), so that the reactions of conservative figures might suggest "movement." There was movement all right—overwhelmingly negative. The canal was bound up with Theodore Roosevelt, the conquest of malaria, and heroic engineering. I visited one of the locks seven years later while following Jesse Jackson on a tour of Central America; he was asked if he would like to open it. He turned a plump dial on a control panel, like the dials of a bathtub in an old hotel. Below the control-room window, the lock doors smoothly parted, releasing tons of water. Are you going to computerize the controls? I asked the staff. No, they said, it would probably not work as well. This was what our diplomats, and Bill, proposed to surrender. Post-Vietnam, it seemed to be a gratuitous insult, the farce after the tragedy. Angry letters, many of them CMS (cancel my subscription), rolled into *National Review*.

In January 1978 Bill and *Firing Line* staged an intramural debate on the treaties at the University of South Carolina. The pro team consisted of almost every conservative who backed the treaties—Jim Burnham and George Will. The antis included Pat Buchanan and Adm. John McCain Jr. But the stars of the debate were the principals, Bill, pro, and Ronald Reagan, con. Reagan was earnest, and detail oriented, having a superior grasp of the issues. (This was an aspect of Reagan that hardly anyone, friend or foe, appreciated during his lifetime, though it has gotten its due with the publication of his letters and diaries.) Bill tried to distract him and the audience with debater's thrusts and swirling capes of rhetoric. When Bill asked a question, and Reagan paused, in his old man's way, Bill pounced: "Take your time answering that" (*smile*).

Bill appealed to national pride—Panama's, and ours, invoking the Revolution, whose bicentennial had been celebrated just a year and a half earlier. "For our own self-esteem, we are big enough to grant little people what we ourselves fought for two hundred years ago." Bill's feel for Mexico, personal and familial, may have prepared him to make such an argument. He had no respect for the Mexican Revolution, or for subsequent Mexican governments. But he did like, and in some ways admire, Mexicans. Perhaps he extended that empathy to Panamanians.

I was as unhappy with the treaties as any of our letter writers, and unhappier to see Bill relying on short-winded debater's points and weak arguments. Life on the firing line, it seemed, involved a lot of both. Bill persuaded almost no one in right-world; the treaties passed with Democratic and liberal support.

Then they became a *fait accompli*. Reagan made no effort to undo them once he became president. George H. W. Bush invaded Panama in 1989 and arrested its dictator for drug trafficking, but never thought to take the canal back. The issue simply died, along with conservative sentiment about it, although since the company that manages the canal now is owned by China, it may stir again.

ON THE WAY back from South Carolina, Jim Burnham, seventy-three years old, had a stroke. He would live until 1987, but his mind took a disabling hit, and his working life was over. One of the essential props of Bill's conception of the magazine had crumpled. A column-based magazine without its major surviving columnist was weakened.

Even as *National Review* was changing, so the Right was changing around it, taking on new recruits. The Reverend Jerry Falwell, pastor of a megachurch in Lynchburg, Virginia, began to mobilize and politicize evangelicals. Everyone thought they had disappeared after the Scopes trial; *Inherit the Wind*, that treacly favorite of high school drama departments, said so. But Paul Weyrich appeared to have discovered millions of them. Weyrich feared that the name Moral Majority was too combative for the group that he and Falwell founded, but Falwell liked it just fine.

Bill defended the evangelicals against their cultured despisers, even though they were a new thing in his experience. The religion of the Right, especially his part of it, had been Catholicism. At the high end of polemics, Catholics drew on Waugh and G. K. Chesterton, ultimately on Aquinas. At the low end, they engaged in trench warfare. Some old Jewish man, I think it was Nathan Glazer, told me once that life had been very simple in the New York of his youth: Whatever Francis Cardinal Spellman, the local archbishop, supported, was wrong. The newly politicized evangelicals liked to mix it up, but their whole relation to ideas was different from that of argumentative Catholics, being anchored in biblical exegesis. *National Review* was discovering whole new tracts of America, even as they were discovering the conservative movement.

At the same time, intellectuals like Glazer who wondered whether the modern welfare state was counterproductive, or who hated the caution and confusion of post-Vietnam foreign policy, began moving right. *Neoconservative* was originally a term of abuse that, like *Whig*, *Tory*, and *Methodist*, the victims learned to accept. All but a handful of neoconservatives were Jews; they would wheel out Daniel Patrick Moynihan to show their catholicity. Bill respected the neocons for their intelligence, their academic chops, and their lingering aura as former liberals.

I found evangelicals alien but interesting, roots music for white Protestants. Neoconservatives struck me as forbidding, unfunny, and too apt to take credit for thoughts that we at *National Review* had thought years earlier (long before "I" was one of "us"; but with a group personality comes a group memory).

The new recruits who most engaged my attention were supply-side economists. The notion that rising marginal tax rates at some point drive down revenue by discouraging work and rewarding chicanery had come to a pair of economists, Arthur Laffer and Robert Mundell. The man who saw the potential political gains for conservativism and who proclaimed them far and wide was Bob Bartley, editor of the *Wall Street Journal*'s editorial page. Bartley was a resourceful and tireless campaigner, and everyone who worked for him liked him. But he had the manner and accent of a midwestern pharmacist, and outside his shop, he was so colorless as to be invisible. The day after some big function I could not remember whether I had spoken to Bartley in the crush. "Then you spoke to him," said David Brooks.

The public face of supply-side economics was one of Bartley's hires, Jude Wanniski. Wanniski had written a book about it, *The Way the World Works*; Jude's father, a Marxist, had wanted his son to write a great book like *Das Kapital*, and Jude believed that he had. Jude explained, or explained away, everything. The Roman emperor Commodus raised Europe's tax rates in the second century, and Napoleon cut them in the early nineteenth; that made the intervening eon a featureless bog as far as Jude was concerned. Jude had an insinuating voice and the sunny smile of one who possesses universal knowledge. He was an autodidact and a monomaniac; I don't mind such people, but you have to sit back and let them do the talking. They will do it anyway, but it will go better for you if you surrender preemptively.

One of Wanniski's converts was a former employee of *National Review*, Jeff Bell. In 1978 Bell challenged four-term New Jersey senator Clifford Case in the Republican primary, and I covered the campaign. Bell based his claim to rule not on his youth and energy—he was thirty-four, Case seventy-four—or even on his conservatism, so much as on his superior understanding of tax rates. His headquarters had a pile of Wanniski's book stacked like hymnals. Bell was contemptuous of most other conservative politicians. Ronald Reagan, Bell's press secretary told me over dinner, wants to take power by picking liberals to be his running mates (a slap at the Schweiker gambit). Phil Crane, a popular Illinois congressman, wants to take power by electing his family (Phil's brother Dan was also running for Congress that year). There was a better way, said Bell's aide: Jack Kemp, former quarterback for the Buffalo Bills, now a congressman from upstate New York, wanted to take power by understanding tax cuts, as Bell himself did, and showing the voters how they would benefit from them. It worked for Bell, up to a point; he beat Case in the primary, but lost to former Knicks forward Bill Bradley in November.

For all their bumptiousness, I thought the supply-siders were right in principle—government shouldn't be a vacuum cleaner of taxes—and right politically, since those who made the first point were bound to benefit at the polls. *National Review* embraced the supply-side case, though the brunt of the argument, day in and day out, was borne by the *Wall Street Journal*.

The movement experienced defections. Frank Meyer's fusionist scheme of things was like a pair of lungs: Libertarians took care of economics and political science, while traditionalists taught us how to behave. As the seventies ran out, more and more libertarians became unhappy with this division of labor, especially as abortion, gay rights, and drug use became political issues. One of my friends from college, Wally Olson, came to New York to work for a new aggressively libertarian journal, *Libertarian Review*. Wally was deeply traditional in his tastes and habits. He once shamed a boy who had jumped a turnstile in the subway into dropping a token in the slot. He savored old cocktail recipes, and their elaborate, corny names. He liked the novels of Jane Austen, but he loved those of Mrs. Gaskell. Yet Wally was a principled libertarian. In college he entertained us with public readings of Lysander Spooner, a nineteenth-century abolitionist who argued that the Constitution bound only the thirty-nine men who had signed it, and their descendants. Wally never went quite so far as Spooner, or his *Libertarian Review* colleagues, who were among other things soft on communism. This is a common destination for antiwar libertarians and pacifists generally. If the state at war is the worst thing in the world, then the enemies of the state at any given moment can't be so bad, even if they are Nazis, communists, or al-Qaeda. Logically it makes no sense, but emotionally it is a necessity.

National Review assailed the new libertarians with a long article by Ernest van den Haag. Ernest was a professor of psychology and social sciences, with a slashing, polemical style. But he was not the ideal man to settle a matter of principle. Ernest's manner could fairly be called reptilian. I think he would admire the designation; the serpent is seductive. Joe Sobran once said, in a birthday toast to him, that reading Bill was first love; reading Ernest was S&M. When Ernest first arrived in New York—he had a thick *mitteleuropaisch* accent—Sidney Hook asked him if he was Jewish. When Ernest said no, Hook said, "That's all right, everyone will think you are." He had the academic credentials and the rigor to write for *Commentary*, though he once fought with editor Norman Podhoretz over a joke: Ernest wanted it, but *Commentary* frowned on jokes; they compromised by putting it in a footnote. In a manner not unlike Burnham, Ernest used the tools of skepticism to decapitate ideas he did not like. He arraigned libertarianism as rigid, impractical, and unworldly.

National Review was ecumenical up to a point, but it also had a long history of excluding and expelling, going back to the John Birch Society. The new libertarians, who already felt outside the conservative movement, simply continued on their way.

During this period there were also changes of status within our ranks, and in the world's perception of us. In 1977 George Will won the Pulitzer Prize for Commentary for his biweekly column for *Newsweek*. He deserved a Pulitzer. But so did Bill, who never won it. Will could scatter anecdotes and quotations like flower petals, or grip a point or an opponent like cleats. He augmented his talents with his persona, not flamboyant like Bill's, but droll, almost academic (he had taught political philosophy). He posed in one ad reading *The Times* of London (pre-Murdoch). He seemed to have grown beyond the sordid struggles that preoccupied the rest of us. Joe, who watched his rise with fascination, coined a one-word epigram: George was "equidistant." Bill laughed when Joe told him, though he never failed to praise Will's work, or be grateful on the occasions when he wrote for us.

IN 1978, BILL came up with a second big assignment for me. He wanted an entire issue devoted to nuclear power, and asked me to edit it. I had never given nuclear power a thought, but after spending a few months on it, it became one of my hobbyhorses. There had been one energy crisis already in the early seventies, and we were heading for another. Oil and politics were the causes of the bottleneck; nuclear power by itself could not break the bottle—we did not then have electric cars—but it could relieve some of the pressure. Our expert witness for nuclear power was Bernard L. Cohen, a professor of physics at the University of Pittsburgh. Cohen had the personality, sweet and slightly unearthly, of many academics in math and the hard sciences. But he had a flair for polemics. When Ralph Nader called plutonium, a fuel for reactors, the most dangerous substance known to man, Cohen offered to eat as much plutonium as Nader would eat caffeine, knowing that Nader would sicken before he did. Nader did not take him up on it. Cohen bristled with comparisons: The extra radiation you would get by moving next door to a nuclear power plant was less than you would get by moving from New Orleans to Manhattan (New Orleans rests on mud; Manhattan bedrock is full of granite, which contains traces of radioactivity). I flew out to Pittsburgh and did a mammoth interview with him.

The issue appeared in February 1979. One month later, there was an accident at the Three Mile Island reactor near Harrisburg, Pennsylvania. Bill asked for a rapid response from Cohen, "if he is not in East Berlin." Cohen responded with an able analysis. There were no deaths or injuries at Three Mile Island (the Soviets would show us how that was done at Chernobyl). But the accident made nuclear power a hopeless cause. The *Village Voice* reported a glowing fish in the Susquehanna; the *New York Post* ran with the headline A CLOUD MOVES CLOSER. *The China Syndrome*, a thriller about the evil nuclear power industry, would be nominated for four Oscars. The work *National Review* did was true and important, but futile. So we stumble along; only the collapse of the world financial system can drive the price of oil below a hundred dollars a barrel.

The nuclear power issue carried an item of news in the last paragraph of "Notes & Asides." "The editing of this issue is substantially the diligent and ingenious work of Richard Brookhiser, who wrote his first article for *National Review* in 1970. He was then 14 years old." My precocity followed me like my shadow. "The editors of *National Review* take great pride and pleasure in announcing his election as a Senior Editor. At age 23, he considers himself a late-achiever.—WFB."

———

JIMMY CARTER IS the worst ex-president in history, but he was also, after an erratic start, a very bad president: small-minded, moralizing, and incompetent. He achieved almost none of his goals, and he seemed buffeted by the events the world presented him. In November 1978 a mob seized the American Embassy in Tehran. Next month the Soviet army invaded Afghanistan. Communists and radicals moved about the world as free agents. Southeast Asia was their school yard; the cause of good government in Cambodia was represented by Vietnamese invaders. Cubans policed the former Portuguese empire in Africa. Nicaragua's dictator was deposed by left-wing rebels; Grenadian leftists followed suit when the prime minister was off-island, lecturing the United Nations about UFOs. (One day at *National Review* I answered my phone to find myself speaking with "Sir Eric Gairy, the legitimate prime minister of Grenada." In exile the man didn't even have a flunky to make his phone calls.) Reality was made yet darker by fears. Maybe even Britain would go down the tubes: The country seemed paralyzed by its labor unions, many of which were dominated by small cadres of radicals. Here and there were countertrends: The Catholic Church got a Polish pope, and Britain elected a Tory government as the decade dwindled. But what would happen in America?

The glow of sentiment surrounding Ronald Reagan obscures the fact that the conservative movement was less united behind him as 1980 approached than it had been when he challenged Gerald Ford. History and age were Reagan's great enemies. This was his third try for the presidency, counting his flirtation in 1968, and three is an unlucky number in presidential politics, associated with recidivist losers—Henry Clay, William Jennings Bryan. If he won, he would be the oldest president in history, almost seventy; the man who then held that distinction, William Henry Harrison, had died a month after his inauguration. The conservative movement was now large enough to attract many aspirants, and a posse of other candidates gathered in case Reagan stumbled. John Connally, whom Nixon had wooed from the Democratic Party, offered himself as the candidate of manly will; his hard, handsome features, like a face on a coin, made his case for him. Strom Thurmond, old enough to be Connally's father but still vigorous himself, testified that Connally was a "firm, tough mayn." Phil Crane offered himself as Reagan, only younger; he had been born in 1930, to Reagan's 1911. George H. W. Bush (there was no need to distinguish him with initials yet) had a somewhat amorphous record—two terms in the House, director of Central Intelligence, assorted diplomatic posts—and a somewhat amorphous political profile: Was he against abortion? For guns? No one could say quickly. He too offered himself as a relative youth, "up for the eighties." He would be fifty-six on election day, but he seemed younger, thanks to his physique (he had played baseball in college), his enthusiasm, and his malapropisms.

This field divided conservative activists and *National Review* in various ways. Jeff Hart was hot for Connally. Connally, said Keith Mano, "spent $10 million on his campaign [then a huge sum] and only got Jeff; I would have backed him for half that." Weyrich and a handful of other Washington operatives were for Crane, until they jumped ship to Connally, only weeks before he sank.

Bill Buckley also had his reservations about Reagan's third run, despite a friendship that went back years. Bill loved to tell the story of their first meeting in the early sixties. They were scheduled to speak at a school auditorium in Los Angeles, Reagan to make the introduction, Bill to give the main talk, but the sound system was down and the door to the second-floor control room was locked. Reagan, acting as his own stuntman, opened the window of an adjoining room, sidled along the ledge, broke a pane of the control-room window, and let himself in. Bill was philosophical about their disagreement over the Panama Canal; during their debate he called Reagan "the politician in America I admire most," which was debater's blarney, but also true. Bill enjoyed Reagan's sense of humor, which was not unlike his own, and acknowledged his skill as a communicator, which was nothing like his own: Both men sought to convince, but Bill did it by dazzling, Reagan by establishing a bond.

Bill, however, admired all his friends, and one of them was George H. W. Bush. They been at Yale together in the huge post–World War II class designed to accommodate veterans. Bill liked the all-American Ivy League type, which he wasn't, quite. Van Galbraith was such a person; so was Blackford Oakes; so was Bush. The traits of the type were simplicity, fun, spirit, and courage (Bill was too ornate, at least on the surface, to be the first). Chris Buckley, who shared his father's esteem for Bush, made a neat defense of him in later years when cartoonist Garry Trudeau began to mock him. Chris referred to a Banana Republic catalogue in which Trudeau was quoted praising the company's World War II bomber jackets—the very jacket Bush had worn as a navy lieutenant, while he was winning the Distinguished Flying Cross. Whose jacket, Chris asked, is the real one?

Bill had another candidate in the 1980 race, however briefly. One night after work, when the office had emptied out, he talked up Pat Moynihan. Not to me: I overheard his end of a phone call, floating from his office down the hall to mine in the post–five o'clock quiet. I don't recommend eavesdropping as a habit, but no political junkie could close his ears to talk of that kind. The Moynihan talk was a measure of Bill's urgency; the state of the world was such that he would back a still fairly liberal Democrat with only four years in the Senate, if he was the best chance of stopping the Soviets.

THE 1980 RACE gave me one of the best assignments of my life. *National Review*'s election coverage for the last few cycles had been the domain of James Jackson Kilpatrick, longtime Virginia journalist, now a syndicated columnist. Norman Mailer was my first exposure to political writing, but *Miami and the Siege of Chicago*, however brilliant, was a one-shot. Kilpatrick showed me how it might be done brightly and regularly, like a four-year comet. Every election year in winter and spring, he traveled with each major candidate, assembling a profile from background knowledge and observation; in the summer, he did the same for the two conventions. Kilpatrick was both efficient and beautiful; he told you what you needed to know, and he made it memorable. I had one of his convention vignettes— of John McCormack, eighty-year-old former Speaker—by heart: "He stood at the rostrum like an aged heron on a cypress stump, white-haired, gaunt-eyed."

I wanted to be able to write things like that. Now I got my chance, for Bill and Priscilla gave the 1980 campaign to me. Bill wanted the first profile to be about Reagan, assuming that he would come to grief early and drop out. ("Don't you think so?" he asked

Priscilla, for confirmation.) Carter, the incumbent, did not need fresh treatment, so I did five pieces, on Reagan, Bush, Connally, Ted Kennedy, and John Anderson, the Republican who became liberalism's heartthrob. (In every cycle there is a candidate reporters and liberals fall in love with whom they do not call liberal but call instead fresh or new or independent or a laughter-loving Aphrodite.) My pieces all came out in a caffeinated present tense. Naturally; I was present, at the great sorting out. My approach was impressionistic. If I listened and looked hard enough, the story would tell itself, and if I wrote well enough, I could make you see and hear it too.

I made exceptions for one category of nonsensory information—the story that shone a light into a candidate's psyche. In a memoir, *Where's the Rest of Me?* written on the eve of his first run for governor of California, Reagan told a story of finding his alcoholic father passed out on the front porch, in a snowfall out of Frank Capra. "I could feel no resentment," Reagan wrote. Of course he could, and did—if not at that moment, then at earlier ones. The revelation of the story is that Reagan chose to turn his anger aside—a strategy for his life, and one of the secrets of his optimism and his appeal (whatever consequences it wreaked on those around him). I told that story not to show him up or run him down, but to explain how he had decided, as we all do in our different ways, to navigate the world.

I used the old school tie to get one interview. The father of the young man with whom I had called on Justice Powell was working for George H. W. Bush, and through him I interviewed the candidate. I asked him a number of obvious questions, plus one about his membership in Skull and Bones, which had briefly come up as an issue among the wilder brethren of the GOP, who believed it to be a sinister organization (Skousenism, alive and well). He asked politely if I was a member—no indeed—then scoffed at the story. I found him earnest and likable, but I wasn't sure of his principles. I repaid his courtesy by having some fun with his speaking style. "He drops awkward pauses in the middle of sentences like moving men leaving a piano on the landing of the stairs." He was no Patrick Henry, but he surprised everyone by winning the Iowa caucuses.

Reagan had steamed into the race as the front-runner. Bill and others in the conservative movement might be doubters, but conservative voters and much of the party establishment Reagan had defied four years earlier had accepted him. Then came Iowa. It seemed like 1976 and the stumbling early primaries all over again.

I passionately wanted Reagan to win. It was my first experience of devotion to a politician (there would be one other). He incarnated the model we all believed in: Rally a movement; match it with a leader; put that man in the White House. He had been saying the right things for years, and he was even saying new right things, for he had taken up the supply-side argument. I was not bothered by questions of age or distracted by the pursuit of alternatives; if you have put your money down, keep it there. I felt, in addition, the tug of Reagan's public personality. I followed him from Miami to someplace in the woods of South Carolina to Minneapolis, and in each venue I had an experience that would be repeated every other time I heard him speak. He already had the reputation of a great speaker, which would only grow over the years. Yet as soon as he began, I felt flooded with disappointment. He would bobble words; he would give that little shake of the head; he seemed subdued. Who was this guy? His art was not to grab the spotlight, the center of attention that hovers over every lectern, but to hang back from it, which pulled you forward, toward him. By the time he finished, you were on his side.

Reagan won New Hampshire, and *National Review* endorsed him afterward, warmly, though too late to have done him any good. It didn't matter; he won six of the next seven primaries, which showed that conservatives were on his side, despite the doubts of a handful of leaders. Bush soldiered on, with a determination that struck Reagan as bitterness, managing to win two late primaries in Pennsylvania and Michigan. Bill sent Bush congratulatory telegrams, but the Republican race was over.

Bill covered the Republican convention in Detroit for the magazine; I went to Madison Square Garden to watch the Democrats. Teddy Kennedy made a vain fight (in both senses of the adjective) for himself and for pure liberalism, but the battered liberalism of President Carter prevailed. Carter was a vague irritating presence, a ghost at his own banquet. He ignominiously mangled the name of the late Hubert Humphrey, calling him Hubert Horatio Hornblower. When Kennedy joined him after his acceptance speech in a gesture of unity, Carter pursued him around the podium before Kennedy deigned to shake his hand.

Bill Rusher joined me one evening to watch a new politician, first-term Arkansas governor Bill Clinton. The Democrats, said Rusher, think this man is going places; look at the podium time they have given him. He seemed pleasant and well put together, mindful of his opportunity.

Between the conventions and the election, workers in the Gdansk shipyards in Poland struck for an independent labor union and were not mowed down by the army, at least not right away, though there was always the Soviet army to consider. The strike was hopeful but, in the fourth lap of the Carter administration, unsettling as well. I happened to buy in a used-book store an H. G. Wells novel, *Mr. Britling Sees It Through*, in which scenes of intellectual and gentry life in the English countryside are intercut, heavy-handedly, with the Balkan events that cause World War I. World War II had begun in Poland. Could World War III also begin there?

JEANNE AND I were married in New York in September. Finding a place was a chore. I went to no church, and Jeanne had not belonged to a temple since she was a teenager. We found a judge who turned out to have been an old rival of Bill Rusher's in the New York Young Republicans. Thanks to Marvin Liebman, we were able to use the library of the Union League Club. The Union League Club had been founded to support the Union during the Civil War; portraits of Ulysses Grant and other bearded generals looked down from its walls. The black waiters were the haughtiest men on earth; you could not misbehave in their presence. Marvin had started out in life as a communist and a gunrunner for the Irgun; after one lunch in the Union League Club, Rusher saw him lingering at a window. Thirty years ago, Marvin gestured at the sidewalk, I was out there, shouting "Plutocrats!" In 1980 Marvin had just joined the Catholic Church. When Jeanne and I took him to lunch to thank him for sponsoring our wedding, he merrily described his confirmation, among a cohort of Hispanic girls.

Religion made a bigger problem than where to get married. My parents, particularly my mother, did not want me to marry Jeanne. Ideally, my mother would not have wanted me to marry anyone, not even a younger replica of herself (such a woman would have been too strong willed), but Jeanne's Jewishness was certainly a bad part of the mix. My father had encountered similar opposition himself, but as he always did in family matters he supported the policy of the administration, which was set by my mother. He never said anything against Jeanne, but he let my mother give the evil eye unchallenged.

We had coordinated the date of our wedding with Frances so that Bill could attend. He gave us a party beforehand at East Seventy-third Street. I don't know how much Bill knew of the unpleasant dynamics—I was too angry and ashamed to tell him—but Frances got the lay of the land as soon as she walked into the room. I see what is going on, she told Jeanne; don't worry—I will make things easier. She did this by encouraging my father to take many, many pictures, which kept everyone, even possibly my mother, distracted. At the wedding Bill Rusher read 1 Corinthians 13. A quartet from the Street Singers sang love songs from centuries past. The day after my father, unbending a bit, gave us brunch at the Windows on the World.

I got to thank Bill by inviting him and Pat to have dinner at our apartment. Jeanne and I had moved into a two-bedroom in a white-brick sixties building on Third Avenue, in an anomalous stretch between midtown and the Bowery. Bill and Pat's arrival gave us cred with our doorman that lasted for decades. Jeanne made a full-court press—osso bucco, frozen lemon soufflé. She also provided the entertainment, for when she mentioned that one of her skills as a psychoanalyst was giving the Rorschach, Bill and Pat wanted to see it. *Rorschach* has entered the language as a metaphor for any ambiguous sign that someone reads in a characteristic way. Though it has fallen by the wayside with the advent of prescriptions and facade work, the original test, a set of inkblots, most black-and-white, some with color, can be a serious diagnostic tool. Jeanne brought out one of the colored cards. I forget what Pat saw, though I remember Bill saying, "You're wrong, duckie." He saw an oil strike, a nod to the old family business, and to his business, since he was a gusher of words. He used the white space, which Jeanne told them is the sign of an oppositional temperament. He ignored the color, which Jeanne did not tell them is a sign of being detached from one's emotions. Maybe he was, but my journalistic father had backed me up when my real one hadn't.

BILL MADE A pool for the 1980 election; he loved pools, setting the terms himself, and urging everyone on the editorial staff to place bets. I made a side bet with Priscilla, predicting that Reagan would win in a squeaker; she was more hopeful. For every electoral vote over my guess, I offered to give her a dollar. Reagan won many such electoral votes, carrying forty-four states. When I came into the office the day after election day, I wore a plastic Reagan boater I had picked up on the campaign trail, and I owed Priscilla more than two hundred dollars. She allowed me to take her to Paone's instead.

The 1980 election was like getting the keys to the kingdom. It was as thrilling as it was unbelievable. *National Review* splurged on an ad in the *New York Times*, taking credit for conservatism's victory. I came up with the tagline, over a picture of Reagan reading one of our issues in a campaign plane: "I got my job through *National Review*." This was true enough, for we had built the movement that made Reagan its champion.

One glitch disturbed the euphoria. In December the magazine would celebrate its twenty-fifth anniversary. Every five years we held a party in the Pierre or the Plaza, grand midtown hotels with ballrooms like rococo palaces. If the president-elect could come to our twenty-fifth, the prince and his adviser, the cave and the philosopher, would be in perfect alignment. Bill had invited Reagan to be there in the spring, but that was an eon ago in campaign time. He sent reminders, but they were all whimsical: "Cinderella expects Prince Charming." No one on Reagan's staff knew what he was talking about. By the time the joke finally got straightened out, the transition team told us that Reagan was already booked solid.

I was flabbergasted by both my heroes, the greater one for bungling the invitation, the lesser one for dissing us, and I took my pique to Bill Rusher. Since he couldn't do anything about Buckley's language, he didn't say anything about it. He patiently explained that Reagan was about to become the most powerful man in the world, and did not have time to turn around. Rusher was right. Because of Reagan, America, Poland, Afghanistan, Nicaragua, the Soviet Union, and the world would all change. *National Review* would have to find its place.

CHAPTER 5

"BLISS WAS IT in that dawn to be alive / But to be young was very Heaven!" So Wordsworth recalled the beginning of the French Revolution. A sense of the world coming into shape and falling into place just as you do can be a heady congruence. In the early days of what we called the Reagan Revolution many young people passed into the movement, and through *National Review*.

Hiring young writers is an economic necessity for poor magazines, but you have to have an eye for talent, even when it is half-feathered and squawking. *National Review*'s record was very good. Many of our recruits came via Jeff Hart. Alongside his sway in the lecture room, he made himself the center of gravity for conservatives at Dartmouth. His on-campus political persona was three parts Teddy Roosevelt, two parts Lord of Misrule. He loved to provoke, and he encouragèd his charges in their provocations. But his professorial eye was always sifting wheat from chaff. One of the best talents he sent us followed me as summer intern, Paul Gigot. Paul went on to be editor of the *Wall Street Journal*'s editorial page, and winner of a Pulitzer Prize. The intern after Paul was a Harvard political philosophy student, Charles Kesler. Your copy of the *Federalist Papers* is edited by him. Soon after Charles came David Brooks, a student at the University of Chicago. David came to Bill's attention by writing a mocking survey of his career in the *Maroon* when Bill came to Chicago to speak (David made Bill out to be the founder of two magazines, the *National Buckley* and the *Buckley Review*, which then combined to form the *Buckley Buckley;* he got the magazine right). Bill hired him on the spot. You read him two mornings a week in the *New York Times.*

Mona Charen, later of *Crossfire*, was as attractive as she was talented, and she played the part of aspiring young writer with flair. She met Bill by interviewing him for her yearbook when she was a student at Barnard. She had a harder time arranging to speak with Irving Kristol for her senior thesis. She managed to get him on the phone, where he made it clear he was not interested in talking with her. But the call went back to Kristol's secretary, whom Mona, unfazed, told to schedule an appointment. When she showed up for her interview, Kristol told her appreciatively that he liked how she did that.

Unlike all these collegians, Terry Teachout came to us from the real world of work, writing music criticism for the *Kansas City Star* while he clerked in a bank and played jazz bass on the side. He began reviewing books for us, specializing in omniscience. In one letter to Bill, Terry fretted over some liberal tripe that had run in his paper. Bill quoted the line in a column, which caused the *Star* to rebuke Terry; Bill, characteristically, rebuked the *Star* (I handled that correspondence). Terry came into the city, and we had lunch at the Guardsman, a bar around the corner from *National Review* that gave you free drinks if you had fought at Imjin River. Terry was a little reserved, a little anxious, bursting with attention, eager to show how much he knew. None of us ever needed persuading of that; the proof was always on the page.

WORKING FOR BILL was an endless process of catching up with his old acquaintances, who were legion. One day Bill told me he was meeting the political scientist Harry Jaffa for lunch at Paone's; would I like to come along? Jaffa has a footnote in the history of American politics for contributing the most incendiary line to Barry Goldwater's acceptance speech at the 1964 Republican convention: "Extremism in defense of liberty is no vice; moderation in pursuit of freedom is no virtue." Great speechmaking, lousy politics. The sentence added its pebble to LBJ's landslide. For years I have used it as a mike test before TV shows.

In the small world of political science Jaffa was equally famous as a disciple of Leo Strauss. Now *Straussian* is equated with *neocon*, and both terms mean little more than *Jew warmonger*. But in the early eighties, the Straussians were an aggressive and persecuted sect of political philosophers. I had encountered them at Yale, in two courses taught by Charles Fairbanks.

Strauss, a German Jewish émigré academic, died in 1973, leaving a cadre of devoted former students. The simplest version of his thought is that we should take political philosophers of the past seriously, since any one of them might be able to tell us the right way to live. The survey begins with Socrates, in Aristophanes' hostile version and Plato's admiring one. Then, after a long flight over many theists, one lands at Machiavelli who, it turns out, is more than a bookish Don Corleone but a thinker of revolutionary importance (but maybe his importance is that he is a bookish Don Corleone). A drumroll of moderns follows: Hobbes, Locke, Rousseau, Marx, Nietzsche.

Learning all this for the first time was exhilarating stuff, not least because a few of these writers (Nietzsche, Rousseau, Plato when he chose) wrote well. Soon, one noticed that the Straussians read these authors in a particular fashion. Philosophers, they claimed, never really said what they meant. In despotic ages, they had to be careful, and habits of indirection lingered. As an English major, I was fine with close reading, but their readings seemed to follow an agreed-upon script.

Harry Jaffa disagreed with his fellow Straussians, however, for he had formed his own lineage of philosophers—an American branch line off the main trunk. (Since Jaffa taught at Claremont Graduate School outside Los Angeles, his version came to be known as West Coast Straussianism.) The Jaffa Express ran from Jefferson to Lincoln and back, with no stops in between, like a shuttle. Jaffa believed in the Declaration of Independence, and in the new birth of freedom promised in the Gettysburg Address.

Few conservatives agreed with Jaffa. Russell Kirk was nostalgic for Confederates and Tories. Frank Meyer thought well of the American Revolution, but condemned Lincoln as a statist. Jaffa fought with both of them. One of Jaffa's few converts was Bill—oddly enough, considering his early support of segregation, but Bill always liked a good debater.

When I came to read the founders on my own, I saw how right Jaffa was. On July 9, 1776, George Washington had the Declaration of Independence read to his troops. Weeks later thousands of them fought in defense of it at the battle of Long Island; hundreds of them died, and thousands were thrown in prison, where many more died over seven years of brutal captivity. When you ask men to pledge their lives, fortunes, and sacred honor, you had better know why, and you had better tell them.

Bill and I got to Paone's before Harry and were at the table when he arrived. We then learned that he had come with a mission. Bill had recently written in a column that if George III had captured Washington during the Revolution, he would have been morally justified in hanging his rebellious subject. Harry had to set Bill straight. He started in before he took his seat. If Washington was rebelling against injustice, how could George III be justified in hanging him? Before the salad arrived, he had compelled Bill (and me as bystander) to agree with him. Perhaps it was with that lunch in mind that Bill said, If you think disagreeing with Harry Jaffa is tough, try agreeing with him.

BILL WAS SURROUNDED by eastern Europeans—refugees from communism, and witnesses against it. They came to us out of sympathy, appreciation, and the urge to say even more. Their lives were all somewhat disoriented, even if they had avoided jail or special suffering, for they were uprooted, unwilling Columbuses thrust into a new world. Many of them wished to show they were not as their persecutors, the socialist-realist louts, but men and women of culture. The burden of what they had been up against made others suspicious; America's many distractions—so much entertainment, so little news, even less understanding—made still others impatient.

Perhaps the happiest of the émigrés we knew was Jan Lukas, a Czech photographer who had escaped in the sixties. He was a photojournalist, a realist, who used a Leica and natural light; he had a limp, but he shuffled along tirelessly, to get the right angle, the right juxtaposition. Maybe his mobility helped him make the transition to a new continent. He loved the New York scrimmage: In one of his images, he caught a crew of workmen tearing up a city street in front of an ad for Dutch Masters cigars, Rembrandt's syndics looking between the hard hats. Bill made Jan's pictures into *National Review* covers, even if the relation to the contents was oblique to the breaking point, so long as he could use one of his images somehow.

Jan took many shots at *National Review* functions. I remember Erik von Kuehnelt-Leddihn telling him frostily at one party that the nationalism of the Czechs had helped break up the old Austrian empire. But Jan said simply that the old republic (1918–1938) had given him the best years of his life.

As difficult as the eastern Europeans were Bill's musician friends. They lived in the country of order and light, but in our world they could be demanding and peculiar. The musician I saw the most of in Bill's company was Rosalyn Tureck. He took me to her 1977 return to Carnegie Hall (she had spent twenty years performing in Europe). She played the Goldberg Variations on the harpsichord; Bill's party went to the Russian Tea Room, samovars and Christmas colors, during the intermission for a bite; then in the second half of the program, she played the Goldbergs again on the piano. She maintained that Bach had known early versions of the fortepiano, and so it was not anachronistic to play him on Steinways and even Bill's Bosendorfer now. Her attack was crisp and articulate, but she played with more obvious warmth than Glenn Gould. She had the airs of a diva, not in the sense of a supermodel talking trash on the E! Channel, but in the original sense of a temperamental musician. One addressed her as *Madame*. (She's a Jewish girl from Chicago, said Jeanne, who was allowed to say it, being a Jewish girl from Cincinnati.) Once she was to play a concert at Bill's house in Stamford. Jeanne and I arrived early, and Bill asked if I wanted to play a duet with him before his other guests arrived. We had hardly begun hacking away when the phone rang from upstairs; Mme. Tureck told us not to touch the piano. We slunk away like schoolboys. "She didn't want our cooties on the keys," said Bill.

Bill's Bosendorfer in New York was a difficult instrument, with a thunderous bass and a thin treble. Yet there were times when Tureck tamed it. One night she played Busoni's transcription of Bach's chaconne in d minor, a gift, from the late nineteenth century, to the dead master: Here, this is what pianos have become, perhaps you would have done this with them in your time. Tureck rattled dust out of that thing that must have been in there forever. Then she followed it with one of Schubert's Moments Musicaux, a little piece every beginning pianist plays, only she played it perfectly.

Bill majored in Bach, but he minored in jazz. When Bill was a boy, Fats Waller used to come up to the Buckley family's estate in Sharon in northwest Connecticut, to play for the black help. Unfortunately for the white folks in the big house, none of them knew of these performances. Bill made up for lost time via the stride pianist Dick Wellstood, who was no diva at all. Like most jazz musicians, he had a tough time making a living, and at the end of his life had to practice law. When his friend clarinetist Kenny Davern visited him in his office to see how the straight life was going, Wellstood ruefully mimed playing on the edge of his desk. Bill dragooned both him and Tureck to play at one of *National Review*'s anniversary parties. It was a bizarre programming decision; the hundreds of guests yakked happily over their dinners while the two geniuses flailed in the surf. At least Wellstood, after a lifetime of club gigs, was used to the experience. Someone told him that if you shouted, "Fuck you very much!" to a noisy audience, it sounded like "Thank you very much!" He tried it once, and found that it was not so.

THE TERSEST DEFINITION of Reaganism that I ever heard, tight enough for a business card, was made by Bob Tyrrell, editor and founder of *The Alternative*, later *The American Spectator*: "Fight Communism; cut taxes; the pieties."

Start with the last, on which Reagan did the least. "The pieties" included the ordinary rituals of civic life, so battered by the last decade. Reagan was a flag-waver, by temperament and sheer length of life; he had waved the flag when he was a New Deal liberal and all liberals did it; he kept waving the flag in his decades on the Right. Sometimes his demotic patriotism was excessive: He began the habit of snapping off salutes to military personnel (the commander in chief is supposed to be saluted, not to salute), and the custom, inflated to meaninglessness by repetition, of recognizing heroes in the balcony of the House when he delivered his State of the Union addresses. Flags became omnipresent during the Los Angeles Summer Olympics in 1984, when the very beer commercials seemed patriotic.

More seriously, "the pieties" Reagan honored referred to the structures of family life: the traditions of meeting and mating and reproducing that had not been challenged outside of problem plays and trashy novels until they became political footballs in the seventies.

Abortion was the most serious social issue—a matter of life and death. Some conservatives supported it, James J. Kilpatrick for one. Bill let him say so in *National Review*—he typically let the magazine's veterans speak their piece—though, like Samuel Johnson taking care as a young parliamentary reporter that "the Whig dogs should not have the best of it," he always gave the prolife side the last word. The doughtiest opponent of abortion in our ranks was Jim McFadden. From his eighth-floor perch he directed an unceasing campaign on all fronts, from wire-pulling to polemics. When Rep. Daniel Flood, a pork-barrel Democrat with a waxed mustache, quit Congress in the wake of a bribery scandal, McFadden said he always liked old Dan; he was reliably prolife. It was McFadden who persuaded Nat Hentoff, the civil-liberties absolutist of the *Village Voice*, that fetuses had liberties under the law.

As governor of California, Reagan signed a liberal abortion law, but he changed his views to become a rhetorically prolife politician. He promised to appoint judges who would follow the Constitution, unlike the justices of the Supreme Court who had devised *Roe v. Wade*. Many of Reagan's appointees did what he said they would do, some (Justice Sandra Day O'Connor, Justice Anthony Kennedy) didn't. In 1983 Reagan published a passionate essay in the *Human Life Review*, McFadden's monthly, "Abortion and the Conscience of a Nation," linking the fight against abortion to the fight against slavery. "Abraham Lincoln recognized that we could not survive as a free land when some men could decide that others were not fit to be free. . . . Likewise, we cannot survive as a free nation when some men decide that others are not fit to live." When abortion opponents gathered in Washington every January 22, often in snow or sleet, to deplore *Roe v. Wade* on the anniversary of its passage, Reagan sent them greetings. Abortion opponents were grateful for these gestures. And nothing changed.

What we learned is that presidents are like tribesmen whose numerals consist of "One, two, many." It is impressive to accomplish one thing in office, astonishing to accomplish two; three is in the never-never-land of many, and the pieties were Reagan's third.

HIS FIRST PRIORITY was fighting communism. He knew it was serious, and he knew it was wrong. One day he asked Tony Dolan, a former editor of *National Review* who was one of his best speech-writers, to include, in the text Dolan was working on, the passage in *Witness* when Whittaker Chambers sees, in the convolutions of his baby daughter's ear, a refutation of scientific socialism: a manifestation of intelligent design, and a victory of the meaning of life over the meaning imposed on it by history, power, and murder. Reagan did not need Tony to look the passage up; he quoted it from memory. It was the actor recalling something well put, the man reciting what he believed.

Reagan, unlike Chambers, believed communism could be beaten. But his administration began with a defeat. In December 1981 the Polish army put down the Polish labor movement. Direct action was out of the question; Reagan left the Polish unionists to the care of the Polish people, the pope, and the Virgin of Czestochowa, in addition to whatever help the AFL-CIO and the CIA could supply covertly.

The central front of the war against communism comprised two related struggles: the arms race and the contest for public opinion. They were related, because one purpose of the Soviet Union's nuclear arsenal was to terrify and demoralize the West. Our European allies, several of whom harbored powerful Communist parties, were the most vulnerable to such pressures, but America was assailed by psychological warfare too. One of Bill's many debates with former Democratic presidential candidate George McGovern concerned the arms race. They met before the Yale Political Union, and *Firing Line* taped it. Bill didn't want to surrender advantage to the enemy; McGovern was for peace at any price. McGovern at Yale rode a tide of idealism, innocence, and alarm; he hardly needed to argue, only to slip on his prairie-preacher manner (he had a degree in divinity). I had ridden up with Bill for that match, and sat on the podium behind him to his left. He was tense and high-strung; in his left hand he curled a piece of paper, wet with sweat from camera lights, heat in the room, and concentration. He tried in his summary to strike a chord by evoking a classmate of his who had served in the CIA and spent years in a communist prison, but he ran over his time and the effect fell flat. McGovern turned his upper-plains marlinespike of a voice to Deuteronomy 30:19: "I have set before you life and death. . . . Therefore choose life." The kids yelled like hell.

One of Reagan's countermeasures to such stuff—beyond his own upbeat personality—was to appoint like-minded men to key public positions. Bill's old college friend Van Galbraith was a veteran of the CIA who had spent years as a businessman in France. In an inspired move, Reagan made him ambassador. François Mitterand, the Socialist president elected in 1981, was a cynical old turtle who would do anything for or to anyone. Van was his ideal foil, sunny, fluent, combative, and ever ready to remind his hosts that there was a cold war on. The French called him *ambassadeur du choc*. Van's out-there anticommunism shocked even the State Department; that was something Reagan tolerated from time to time.

Across the board, Reagan reconfigured the arms-control debate by adding missile defense to the mix. Arms-control professionals feared missile defense as destabilizing, and skeptics mocked it as science fiction. Bill Rusher, sensitive to the latter charge, wanted to replace Star Wars, the nickname enemies had fastened on it, with his own coinage, Star Shield. When he urged the substitute phrase on us at editorial conferences, Buckley demurred: He said Star Shield sounded like a brand of condoms. Rusher should not have worried, for Star Wars was a jibe that boomeranged; in a culture obsessed with pop culture, it caught the George Lucas cycle at the peak of its early popularity, and amplified Reagan's can-do vibe. The Soviets would later admit that the computer technology that would have been necessary to replicate missile defense and, if possible, pierce it caught their command economy flatfooted.

Outside the main front, Reagan pursued a strategy of reversing communist gains. In the early days of the cold war, this approach was known as rollback. Burnham had been an early advocate of such a policy; he had called one of his books *Containment or Liberation?* favoring the second. The crushing of the Hungarian revolution of 1956, and America's acquiescence, had convinced him that the United States would do no liberating, and so it proved after the Prague Spring in 1968, and in Poland now. But the Soviet empire had put out low-hanging fruit in far-flung places: Afghanistan, Angola, Nicaragua, Grenada. Grenada fell in 1983 when the local revolutionary was murdered by cronies further to his left, allowing America to invade in the interest of restoring order. The painless victory distracted attention from the simultaneous death of 241 Americans in Lebanon, killed in their barracks by a suicide bomber while they were on another mission to impose order. In Afghanistan, Angola, and Nicaragua the United States began aiding local counter-revolutionaries.

NATIONAL REVIEW SUPPORTED Reagan's forward policy, and sometimes we got chances to see it in action. Now, when every child spends a year studying art in Florence, or building huts in Costa

Rica, world travel seems routine. But to me, whose pre–*National Review* experience of foreign countries was a few trips to Toronto and an American Express tour of Europe with my parents, this was new. *National Review*'s editors were always welcome in Taiwan. Jimmy Carter had downgraded our relations, so the Taiwanese were all the more eager to hold on to what friends they had. Bill Rusher, who loved East Asia, had been going there for years. Jeanne and I met with him in Taipei.

Economically, Taiwan was not yet a tiger, but a bustling third world country. There was only one modest skyscraper in the capital. The most impressive building was the Grand Hotel, on a hill overlooking town. Politically, Taiwan was a buttoned-up authoritarian state; there I had my first experience of having one of my books paged through by a customs official. Compared with the frantic massacres and purges of the mainland, it was the earthly paradise. There was not much to see—a few beauty spots, the tomb of Chiang Kai-shek, a performance of indigenous dancers. Our guide was a veteran of the Nationalist army, who had a knack for ordering dull dishes when everyone else in the restaurant seemed to be eating something better. He had fought in World War II and remarked once, without special emphasis, that the Japanese had killed people "like ants." There was also the National Palace Museum, the life raft of Chinese art, saved preemptively by the Nationalists from Cultural Revolution goons. China and Taiwan have both come a long way since the early '80s, but Taiwan maintains its lead in everything but GDP and force; votes there are meaningful, and prayers send no one to jail.

NATO offered tours of its bases. Bill would confer the invitations that came to him on his junior colleagues. So I got to see divided Berlin. As the air force plane that carried our batch of reporters came in to land, I was surprised to see, out the window, how many pleasure boats there were on a small East German lake. It was, of course, the Wannsee or one of the watercourses in the island of West Berlin. Free Berlin was like any European city; communist Berlin was a grim armed camp. Passing through Checkpoint Charlie was cold war ballet. The communists had no right to enter an American military vehicle in Berlin, or even to check IDs; our officers removed the name tags from their uniforms before we pulled up. We freely stopped, however, to let the communists walk around the bus and peer in the windows, to make sure we were not smuggling in John Paul II or Solzhenitsyn. Then the bus moved on.

Two-hundred-some people were killed trying to cross the Berlin Wall in the generation that it stood. Years later, when Chris Buckley was writing for Tina Brown's *New Yorker*, "The Talk of the Town" ran an item commiserating with Erich Honecker, the East German communist who had helped put the wall up, and ruled as dictator for eighteen years. The old man, involuntarily retired, was ill, yet he was to be tried for his crimes. Chris is less political than his father, and less confrontational, but he could not let that one pass. The next time he saw Tina, he said simply, "Honecker?" To her credit, she was abashed.

Taiwan and Berlin were old lava fields; one could also go to hot spots. I came to think of these trips as cold war tourism, and some of them were morally questionable. For a time in the 1980s the Unification Church sponsored junkets for journalists, in an effort to acquire prestige. The young Moonies who ran them knew very little about journalism, but they were hardworking and helpful and never offered any suggestions about what one should write. One leg of a South African trip I took went to Angola. Angola had been in the throes of a civil war since the Portuguese evacuated in 1975. The CIA had sponsored a faction in the North, which soon fell by the wayside. The Soviet-backed faction captured Luanda, the capital, with the help of Cuban troops. Jonas Savimbi had been the candidate of the Chinese, until he turned from them to the United States, as more active allies. His movement, UNITA, was headquartered in a bush village in the southeastern corner of the country called Jamba.

The junketeers, who included Bill Rusher, took off from what is now Namibia in a DC-3, workhorse of the third world, and landed on a dirt airstrip. The forms of sovereignty were scrupulously observed in Savimbi's domain. A customs official in a cap and belt, like a cop's dress uniform, greeted us in a flimsy shack and stamped our passports. We were loaded onto the beds of trucks and made a ninety-minute journey over trails in the bush. The country was overgrown, but scrubby. A portion of the ride was a loop thrown in for mystification, for we passed the same spot twice. Jamba was a collection of buildings in the trees.

In the Reagan years Savimbi stood high in the opinion of the conservative movement. He was fighting communism's puppet; he had visited Reagan in the Oval Office. His operation in Jamba seemed insubstantial, though we were clearly seeing only a staging area, without glimpses of troops or weapons. Some of what we saw was not attractive. We were treated to a calisthenics display by older boys in basic uniforms—shorts, shirts. They performed rigid exercises with complete solemnity—bare-bones Leni Riefenstahl.

Late one night we were treated to a long briefing. Two high-ranking officers in combat uniforms—no spit and polish here, but camo, boots, and pistols—brought out prisoners captured from the government side, who testified to having been trained in the Soviet Union. Nick Eberstadt, the demographer, gave one, a pilot, a detailed grilling; if he was a ringer, he had been well coached. Two older, sadder people, a man and a woman, who had been sitting quietly by now took their turn. They had been maimed by the government side, and would testify to that. The man, we now saw, had no hands. His arms ended in pointed stumps, with the skin grown over the tips in paler tones.

It was sickening to make these wretches perform. One of us—I believe it was Tom Bethell of *The American Spectator*—asked if we could wrap the evening up, so they could go to bed. The better spoken of the two officers—he was quite fluent in English, and had the jaunty manner of a time-share salesman—brushed the question aside with a wave of the hand. "No, no, we are here for you, for as long as you like!"

Savimbi himself appeared, unannounced, at some point that night. He was a forceful figure, bursting out of his uniform, but if you looked at him carefully he seemed old for this line of work (he was in his early fifties).

I never wrote about the midnight press conference. When a book by Fred Bridgland, an English journalist who had covered Savimbi extensively, appeared with some criticisms of him, I made sure to review it in *National Review*. Better than nothing, but still letting someone else do my dirty work. Never turn away from what you yourself have seen. Savimbi fought on unsuccessfully, long after the cold war ended, dying in a firefight in 2002.

CUTTING TAXES, THE second item on Tyrrell's list, and the main event of Reagan's domestic policy, was a revolution in political tactics. For years—decades—conservatives had called for smaller government and balanced budgets, to little effect: No one cared. Now, under supply-side tutelage, we worked the problem from the other end, promising to leave more money in people's pockets.

Reagan had become a supply-sider early in the 1980 election cycle—he had other political ideas, it turned out, besides tapping Richard Schweiker—and his victory put Wanniski over the moon. Jude came to editorial drinks one evening in the interval between the election and Reagan's inauguration. He was not only kibitzing economic policy but in his own mind staffing the administration, and he had the perfect slot for Jack Kemp, the eager young supply-side congressman. Reagan should make him ambassador to the United Nations. There he could lecture communists and despots on the virtue of low tax rates, and make them all feel the power of the supply side.

We were not convinced. *National Review* had been born railing at the United Nations, whose neutralism and supranationalism we found equally hateful. Add the Evelyn Waugh attitude to lesser breeds without the law (we made an exception for natives who were anticommunist), and the notion of Kemp appealing to the better angels of the nature of the General Assembly seemed insane. Jude didn't care. He would go on to have his own Oval Office meeting with President Reagan—the worst thing that ever happened to him.

The supply-side program was embodied in a bill sponsored by Kemp and Sen. William Roth. (Protocol directs that the name of the sponsoring senator go first, though the protocol of charisma directed that this bill was universally known as Kemp-Roth.) Kemp-Roth called for three income tax–rate cuts of 10 percent each, spread over three years. In the first flush of victory, Reagan got a scaled-down Kemp-Roth bill through Congress. Then a sharp, steep recession hit. Liberals who had never cared about balancing a budget in their lives wrung their hands over red ink, and Republicans who did not want to be whacked in the 1982 elections (and who were maneuvering for later advantage) joined them. The *Wall Street Journal* and *National Review* defended the tax cuts stoutly, but a deal delaying some of the cuts and raising other rates began to take shape.

The administration dispatched James Baker, Reagan's chief of staff, to New York to sell Bill and the editors on the deal. We met Baker in the suite of some midtown hotel, where we all sat on uncomfortable stuffed chairs like tuffets, ranged around a little table, too big for a nightstand, too small for poker. Baker had run Gerald Ford's campaign in 1976 and George H. W. Bush's in 1980, yet somehow he had emerged at Reagan's right hand. Like carbonation, he rose with every shake-up. Bill expressed our objections to the deal, redundantly: We had been banging away at them in issue after issue. Baker leaned forward, making a show of listening, and giving his spiel, which was the administration's talking points.

Though I had been following elections all my life, I had little experience of politics with a small *p*, one-on-one. Yet even I could see we were up against a done deal, and this was only stroking. The man I most admired in the world was performing for a functionary, a courtier, and performing in vain. Though it left an acrid taste, I was grateful for the lesson. Intellectuals who take White House jobs in the hope of belonging to a kitchen cabinet, or who imagine that, thanks to old acquaintance or ideological affinity, they have a president's ear, deceive themselves. A president's ears close the moment he lowers his hand after taking the oath of office. Maybe Martin Van Buren had time to take advice, but the pressures of the modern presidency are so all-consuming and crazy-making that the possibility of input is past; the man or woman in the top spot is strapped to a toboggan for four or eight years. Idea men have their chance in all the years the president is getting there; then they may have an impact. In that sense, we had had one on Reagan. But now the window was shut.

Reagan's political judgment in accepting the deal was superior to ours. He knew when to give, and he knew when to give a little, saving the most he could. But making political judgments was only one of our functions; we also had an obligation to say what policies were best. We made our case, then concluded our last editorial on the deal, the Tax Equity and Fairness Reform Act of 1982, with the one-sentence concession that since Reagan wanted it, it should pass, in order to preserve his political clout.

Chapter 6

Intellectuals are the Kleenex of administrations—used, then discarded. Nevertheless, dozens of us went to Washington in the Reagan years. After Wordsworth's lines on the dawn of the French Revolution, he says why it seemed blissful:

. . . the meagre, stale, forbidding ways
Of custom, law, and statute, took at once
The attraction of a country in romance!

Attractive because now one could change them. The march to Washington that I had called for in 1978 came to pass. People one knew got jobs at think tanks and on congressional staffs, and as journalists. Policy wonks had some impact, by helping to set the terms of debate; staffers could be useful technicians; journalists commented on the passing scene, though every new one diluted the impact of all. Still others flew into the White House as speechwriters.

Speechwriting was very good for many conservatives. Peggy Noonan found a voice, which she now uses as a columnist, partisan but optimistic, a Republican Oprah. Pat Buchanan ran for president. Chris Buckley wrote for Vice President Bush (it was in that capacity that he chided Garry Trudeau for his bomber jacket)—an assignment that gave him the material for his first comic novel, *The White House Mess*. He was the conduit through which I also came to write speeches.

Chris and I had overlapped two years at Yale—he was two years older—though I had not known him there; working for Bill did not make me know him any better. When Chris came to edit his own magazine, *Forbes FYI*, a lifestyle supplement for *Forbes* subscribers, I wrote for him and we became friendly, but he led a distinctly non–*National Review* life. Chris had many of his father's talents: He wrote well (his novels quickly joined, then surpassed, his father's on the best-seller lists). My favorite novel of Chris's is *Little Green Men*, in which a journalist rather like George Will comes to believe in UFOs. He immediately loses caste, and is dropped from his Sunday-morning talk show. But he finds an equally large audience in the other America, the millions who cling to unfashionable creeds. Until the plot resolution kicks in, *Little Green Men* is a very dark book about religion and class in American life. It is also very funny. I read it on a flight, and the moment when the George Will character meets his first alien made me laugh so hard that other passengers turned to stare.

Chris also had Bill's manners as an editor. Years later, in the new millennium, I did a piece for *Delta Sky*, the airline's in-flight magazine; when it appeared, the editor, Duncan Christy, sent me a three-by-five card, with a handwritten note: "Rick—Nice work." I knew all the links in this chain: Duncan was a veteran of *Forbes FYI*; he had learned the courtesy from Chris, who had learned it from Bill. So the good habit replicated itself, like DNA.

Bill's conservatism and his role in the world had not replicated themselves, however. Chris shared his father's convictions, but he did not live them in the same way. He was not on the firing line week after week, as Bill was; as we at *National Review* were; as I was. This necessarily gave his convictions a different quality. Chris was conservative from habit, more in the manner of my parents (if my parents had been raised by wealthy Yalies). Chris must have decided, very early on, not to become his father. Chris's decision to go his own way may have added a shade of urgency to Bill's efforts to find a successor.

Writing for George H. W. Bush expressed Chris's political position perfectly. The thing to do would have been to write for Reagan.

But Chris chose the less ideological running mate. Bill, of course, had wanted Bush to win the nomination, but I wrote that off as one of his quirks. For Chris, Bushism was a settled way of being.

By chance, it became my way of being too for six months in 1982. Bush was a loyal soldier in the administration, and he was given the task, assigned to vice presidents since Nixon had been one, of campaigning for his party's congressional candidates whenever and wherever help was needed. It was thought that Bush would need to take on an additional speechwriter for the campaign season. Chris knew just the man—David Frum, yet another Yalie (class of 1982). David had made a name for himself on campus as a conservative. He has written that he passed election night 1980 in a blur of champagne and alfresco singing of "Happy Days Are Here Again." Chris had spotted his writing in the *Yale Daily News* and invited him to Washington for a meeting with Pete Teeley, Bush's press secretary. All went well until David mentioned that he is Canadian. With America coming out of a recession, it was thought unwise to give a job, even one so specialized, to a foreigner. So Chris and Pete turned to me.

Since the gig was temporary, Bill was willing to spare me. I went down to Washington to meet Chris and Pete in the West Wing of the White House. The White House is a noble shell, but the inside has been so redone that it feels like a historic hotel in Ohio or Tennessee; the offices feel like cubicles in the business center. Teeley was no smart-ass kid on a holiday, but a professional—pleasant, blunt. When Chris had written a speech citing Thucydides, Teeley, spotting a tongue twister for their boss, crossed out the historian's name and substituted Plato. I asked if I would have to rent a room in Washington; so long as it wasn't in the Hay-Adams, Chris said. It proved not to be necessary; Bush needed me for one-shots and for campaign swings. Otherwise, I lived and worked in New York as before.

My first trip with Bush was to New Orleans. Vic Gold, who had been press secretary for Goldwater and was a longtime Bush friend and adviser, accompanied us. Vic was from New Orleans, and ran out of the motorcade at one stop to buy a po'boy and show it off to the Yankees. Bush had come there to address a convention of the Episcopal Church, his church.

As I sat at the back of the hall watching Bush address his coreligionists, Vic sat beside me, fuming. He was a fighter, and he could see that this crowd of WASP liberals was unsympathetic to his boy. Bush had a tropism toward such people. They were his homies; he was friends with the presiding bishop. He spoke with an evident earnestness that, I believe, won some of the audience over.

Bush on the podium was naturally stiff, but if he relaxed, that could be worse, for then he was tempted to improvise, for which he had no gift. He would find himself in a long and lengthening sentence, and I would think, You have brought no verb. He was better at the staccato rhythms of pure campaigning.

One interesting thing happened on the flight down. I was sitting in the back of Air Force Two, when word came that the vice president wanted to talk to me about the speech I had written. I put on a necktie and went to the front where he sat with the pages before him. I crouched in the aisle to listen. Bush pointed to a passage in which, cribbing from the *Wall Street Journal* quoting Hernando de Soto, I had said that capitalism could lift up the poor of Latin America. It was the one mildly edgy argument I had inserted, but he evidently felt I had not made the case. "Now this here," he pointed: "Are you comfortable with it?" Lyndon Johnson would have screamed. Richard Nixon would have told a wounding joke (anti-Semitic if I had quoted a Jew). Bush's mild question was the haute WASP way of saying, Get this crap out of here. I went back to my seat and did.

I wrote the basic stump speech that Bush used on his campaign swings, and I retooled it depending on who he was stumping for. When he went to New Jersey to support Millicent Fenwick, the liberal Republican congresswoman running for Senate, I took out the references to abortion. One morning I had the slight surprise, like glimpsing one's face in an unexpected pane of glass, of seeing a story in the *New York Times* about Bush on the campaign trail and reading my own words. I clipped the item, and boasted to my friends. But my journalistic experience inoculated me against illusions. I was proud of everything I wrote for *National Review*, but all the editorial matter was anonymous; it expressed the magazine's voice, not mine. Sometimes, I channeled the voices of my colleagues, Jeff when I wanted to be slam-bang, Burnham when I wanted to be coldly analytical, Bill when I wanted to be wistful or ornate (Joe was inimitable). Speeches were even less mine than editorials. Everyone knows that writers give politicians their words. But the effect of the words depends not on their merit but on the political profile of the person delivering them. Politicians bring their past history to the podium with them, which defines what they say. We speak rightly of Washington's Farewell Address even though Alexander Hamilton ghosted it.

I HAVE NEVER liked Washington, D.C.—something about the combination of pompous buildings and dull people. But America's capital was becoming its media capital as well. In 1983 *National Review* took an inevitable step by opening a Washington office.

Our new Washington correspondent, and point man of our heightened presence, was John McLaughlin, a laicized Jesuit and former Nixon speechwriter. His prose was off-road driving, full of rocks and craters, but energetic. He sent it in by a proto–fax machine, each page taking three minutes to print itself off a spinning drum, one of those innovations, like steam cars or Menshivism, that was quickly superseded. He filed a fair number of columns from the Arab world, giving us the sheik's-eye view, until we had to remind him of his beat. Bill and the senior editors came to the kickoff party, as did Ronald Reagan.

Reagan on-screen or on a platform was low-key yet engrossing. Reagan in person was both more potent and less satisfying. His attention was like a beam; when I shook his hand, I paused in the light of it. When he moved on to the next person, the feeling snapped off. The accounts of Reagan's most observant associates—Noonan, Buchanan—discuss the paradox of his aloof warmth; it drove Edmund Morris, his biographer, to fiction. The preparty meet and greet offered a taste of it.

Jan Lukas gave me a more tangible souvenir. McLaughlin, Bill, and Reagan were the climax of our program, but each of the senior editors gave brief remarks first. I decided to make use of my prejudices by admitting that New Yorkers had a stuck-up attitude: Washington, we thought, has "no nightlife, no restaurants. But there are many good restaurants in Washington: good Vietnamese restaurants, good Afghan restaurants. Lose a country, gain a restaurant." Jan took a picture the next moment. I see that I had outgrown the polyester; I was wearing a Prince of Wales suit and a bow tie. I also see that I snapped my mouth smugly on the punch line, a bad habit I will never outgrow. Behind me on the podium, Reagan and Bill are laughing. Years later the line came back to me when I heard Margaret Thatcher give a speech to the Heritage Foundation. Americans were in such a funk before Ronald Reagan, she said, that a cynical joke became popular: "Lose a country, gain a restaurant." John O'Sullivan, whom I did not then know, had been at the opening of our Washington office and repeated the line to her. Passing into the oral tradition was more gratifying than writing speeches.

The most important thing that McLaughlin accomplished had nothing to do with *National Review*; he transformed the medium of political talk, incidentally sounding the death knell for *Firing Line*. *The McLaughlin Group* invented the political sitcom. Each character was a personality; what they said counted for nothing. McLaughlin presided in a foghorn voice, bellowing questions and judgments. Fred Barnes and Morton Kondracke, his first name transmogrified by McLaughlin into the science fiction Mor-Tahn, were squeaking, ineffectual good scouts. Jack Germond, Bob Novak, and Pat Buchanan played the villains, glowering gigantic dwarfs. The pace was brisk, and there was a pioneering use of clips.

At some point after the McLaughlin revolution, Neal Freeman came to Bill to suggest modifications in *Firing Line*'s format. Neal had been Bill's right hand in the early sixties; he had found Warren Steibel to produce *Firing Line*, and he later became a producer himself, as well as one of the directors of the magazine. During the meeting with Bill, one of Neal's assistants, zealous for change, showed insufficient respect for the show as it was. "He put a muddy footprint in the pure classical temple," Neal recalled. He saw the visor go down over Bill's eyes, and that was that. Surely, Bill was right. What could he have added—a Ten-Worst List? Boner of the Week? But to be right meant death—lingering and mourned, but death all the same. He had given McLaughlin and the new world its chance. He had made political talk a gladiatorial contest, and he marked the advent of shtick (though his shtick was more interesting than that of any of the yak-in-the-boxes who followed him). What distinguished him from his successors was that he cared about ideas and issues. Novak and Buchanan did too, but they developed theirs in their written words; their TV appearances were mere display. The end of *Firing Line* was the end of one form of television intelligence.

A POLITICAL MAGAZINE that covers only politics is a failure, because politics is about more than politics. A magazine must find strong writers with quirky minds and let each have his head. Their obsessions give a magazine life, and the cacophony of their different obsessions gives it variety. Readers look to favorite magazines for features—elements that stand out like landmarks and that create, then fulfill, expectations. The easiest way to generate features is by using design elements and graphics—pie charts, naked women—though the best way is to build features around writers.

Keith Mano anchored the back of the book with "The Gimlet Eye." When the column debuted, Bill said his assignment was "to go about seeking strange and remarkable things." He found many, none of them related to politics. He described the scene at a screening of *The Rocky Horror Picture Show* when the cult was new; he went to a fire walk and scorched his feet; he went to a Russian Orthodox mass when the Romanovs were canonized; he wrote about phone sex. He delighted Pat by describing his problems getting outfitted for a convention of cross-dressers. "Do you know how hard it is to get size 12 pumps?" Anyone who wants to know what the seventies and eighties felt like only has to read these bulletins, traveling for twenty light-years now but still blazing.

John Simon was our movie reviewer for many years, and for most of those years someone was clamoring for him to be canned. John worked hard to show what he knew, and then he worked hard to make his showing off cool and quick, but it was easy to see why he provoked readers, for he was conservative in nothing but his taste. He praised *The China Syndrome*, the anti–nuclear power tract, because he loved Jane Fonda. A conservative reviewer might have done the same, but at least paused to note the movie's agenda.

John's special cross was his temperament. I once saw him tangle with Arianna Huffington at a conference that *National Review* sponsored in Hollywood. This was in our conference-giving phase, and Arianna's conservative phase. The two sat on the same panel, and Arianna had finished a paean to the decency of the American public, which the left-wing gloomsters of Hollywood outraged. John could not stomach her optimism. He quoted Melville, crying "No, in thunder!" to the great American yes. Then he lost everything by correcting Arianna's pronunciation. (Arianna has a thick Greek accent, but John carries trace elements of the Balkans himself.) She responded as the spunky woman standing up to a bully, and the audience whooped. I felt bad for John, who was right on the main issue, and who had been ahead on points until he let his anger get away with him.

Bill let Keith have his say, phone sex and all, and he defended John at every turn, because they were ornaments to the magazine. Bill, like time, worshiped language and forgave everyone by whom it lived.

Joe's mind was always prowling through a range of subjects. When one caught his interest, his enthusiasm could be exhausting. It struck him that liberals were like bees: No one issued them directives, or even laid out arguments, yet they always swarmed together. He called this behaving like a hive. Every group did so, he admitted, including conservatives, but we, who believed in continuity and tradition, would not be ashamed to say so; it was liberals who were always claiming to be free spirits—every one of them. For several months, Joe was quite a pain in the neck about the hive. Then Jeff, who was putting together an editorial section in Bill's absence, said,

All right, let's mention the hive in every item. A paragraph on the Fed may have escaped. This was the correct editorial decision; when someone volunteers to charge, let him go.

Joe's restlessness made him our best book reviewer, writing with equal ease about Marlon Brando or John Locke. He pitched his perfect game with Peter Singer's *Animal Liberation*, which he reviewed in the voice of archy, the cockroach who wrote on Don Marquis's typewriter. archy, as every newspaper reader once knew, was heavy enough to press the keys by jumping down on them, but not heavy enough to work the shift key that made capital letters or punctuation marks.

dear boss
well now i ve seen everything
in human effrontery
do you know of a book called animal
liberation it s by an australian
human named peter singer

i should have got suspicious
when all his examples turned out to be
mammals and a few birds and fish
and nary an insect among them
the gall boss the sheer gall
of the human no offense boss but
sometimes i think there hasn t been
an enlightened human since
shakespeare
who said quote
the poor beetle that we tread upon
in corporal sufferance finds a pang
as great
as when a giant dies unquote
he was ahead of his own time
and he s still ahead of singer s

When Joe had written good copy, he carried it, grinning, from office to office, reading his favorite bits.

Jeff was fascinated by the cultural meaning of sports. An excellent tennis player all his life, he used tennis as a prism for tracking the ups and downs of civilization. Campy women's tennis undies, Jimmy Connors's tantrums, the death of Baron von Cramm, the thirties David Cup star—all were big with portent for him. This must have been baffling to normal readers who liked baseball, but George Will wasn't on staff, Jeff was. Bill let his writers write about what they knew. Jeff also knew about Ivy League football, more precisely, about one Ivy League football player: Hobey Baker, Princeton, class of 1914. Fitzgerald had written about him, and Jeff made poetry out of his good looks, his sportsmanship, his death in World War I. Jeff's laments for Baker showed us the vein of old-school nostalgia that, for all Jeff's tormenting of his colleagues at Dartmouth, ran very deep in him.

WHAT I WANTED most to write about was politics. I got an even better assignment than covering the 1980 election—covering the 1984 election, with a campaign book at the end. The book was Bill's doing—one more favor in the string of them. It made up for my literary false starts. My college novel had been written, typed (I had written it by hand on legal pads), and sent to publishers, all of whom passed. Jeff was characteristically helpful, commending me to his editor, and to Jacques Barzun. Chris Buckley suggested his agent, a woman named Lucianne Goldberg who lived on West End Avenue; she wanted more sex.

No book had come out of my 20,000-word series in 1978. So one day Bill took me to a meeting with his longtime editor, Sam Vaughan, who was then at Doubleday. Bill said (and probably had said even more strongly by letter), This guy is good; he ought to have a book; let's do this. I said when after the election I thought I could have it done (New Year's! It actually got done four months later), and Sam gave me a $15,000 advance.

This meeting happened in the spring of 1984. But I had already been on the road for the magazine, following campaign swings, attending debates in Iowa and New Hampshire. It was the last election cycle in which reporters ran to pay phones to dictate their copy. The Democrats had the only contested race; Walter Mondale, Carter's vice president, was the front-runner, but seven other men challenged him. This forced me into alien territory, trying to understand what motivated people I disagreed with. I saw Mondale as the fulfillment of New Deal liberalism, and I concluded early on that he would win the nomination, since he best expressed his party's essence. I was right, but there were other forces stirring—racial-identity politics (Jesse Jackson), hunger for something new (Gary Hart)—that made the race interesting.

The Republicans were superficially calmer, for all of them were Reaganites, committed to his reelection and—ostensibly—to his agenda. But because ambition and disagreement never rest, there was a subterranean struggle, as among creatures in the leaf litter on the forest floor, to define what Reaganism meant and what it would become.

Covering an election thoroughly gives you material for years. On the Democratic side, Mario Cuomo, who keynoted their convention, was a major player into the nineties; Jackson and Hart lead a flickering existence even now. On the Republican side I found myself writing about Bob Dole, Jack Kemp, and Newt Gingrich, as well as my former boss, Vice President Bush.

The most memorable episode of the campaign was Jackson's Central American tour. It was Jackson's first presidential contest, and between the end of the primaries and the opening of the San Francisco convention, he decided to visit Panama, El Salvador, Nicaragua, and Cuba to establish his foreign policy bona fides. I wanted to be *National Review*'s first correspondent in Havana since John Leonard.

Havana was a tropical East Berlin. The strata of the regime were epitomized by the cars on the streets. Most were crappy-looking Soviet-made Fiats (the workers' paradise). Officials rode in Zils, Soviet knockoffs of the '56 Chrysler (the rulers' paradise). But every tenth car was some expat from prerevolutionary Detroit, carefully repainted, running no doubt on paper clips and rubber bands: Fords,

Chevies, Dodges, DeSotos, Hudsons—the lost link to America. Here and there we learned of other missed connections, like phantom limbs. The correspondent of the *Guardian* told me that his maid had been very excited to hear of Jackson's visit, until she learned that it was not Michael. We met Castro at select ceremonial moments, when he manifested himself like the Wizard of Oz. At one point he walked down the aisle of Jackson's plane, shaking hands with the press like a candidate, though he had never run for office.

Jesse Jackson is thick and slick now, a memory of his younger self, like some old Havana Chevy. But in 1984 he was thrilling. Despite every disagreement, I found myself half-liking him, because my prose liked his words, and the drama he wove around himself. The affection ended in Havana, where he capered and shouted in tableaux of Fidel Castro's devising; how could it have been otherwise when a political faith healer visited a totalitarian state? The low point was a church service, which saw Jackson hectoring a wretched congregation of Cuban Methodists, asking them to use their "moral force" to get the United States out of Central America, while Castro sat behind him on the altar, listening gravely: subjects, puppet, and puppeteer, all together. I felt like Bill covering Nixon in China, except that Jackson, unlike Nixon, was unembarrassable.

I called the book *The Outside Story*, because I could claim no insider information. I never liked interviewing (I was too shy, too know-it-all) and never built on that first batch of seventy-five. I took an inventory of my talents—noticing, describing—and made a theory of it: The most important things that happen in elections are the things that happen in public—deeds, performances, pledges. Elections are decided by the outside story, not by the frantic maneuvers that reporters (and the maneuverers themselves) love to recount.

The election was a blowout for Reagan. After his early recession, the economy was roaring; everyone liked his tax cuts. The morning after his forty-nine-state victory, Reagan said some sporting words about poor Mondale, then asked why his own campaign hadn't laid on a few more days in Minnesota. The outside story of this election was conservatism triumphant.

This book, like my novel, was written on legal pads, but it was typed on a word processor, a Kaypro, using WordStar. Bill was the in-house pioneer of the computer age, and evangelized for WordStar with the fervor of Jesse Jackson. He continued to use it till the day he died; when someone pointed out that there were better programs, he said, "I understand there are better alphabets."

Bill did three more favors for the book once I had finished writing it. The first was to insist that it have a preface. First books, he believed, like debutantes, need a formal presentation to the literary world. I asked his old friend Murray Kempton if he would write one. I had met Kempton in my small office, reading him in a volume of his old columns that was shelved there, and in person at Bill's Christmas parties. Before the Iowa caucuses of this election cycle I had given him a ride into Des Moines from the airport, during which he said how much he had liked covering Nikita Khrushchev back in the day, and disliked covering John Anderson. It was pure Kempton: Anderson the liberal Republican congressman was self-righteous, so Kempton scorned him; Khrushchev the Communist tyrant had some humanity, so Kempton liked him. Bill did not ask Kempton to honor my request for a preface, but apart from Bill's friendship I would never have known him well enough to ask. Kempton acceded to my importunity.

Bill, unasked, wrote a blurb—his second favor. It was a little late in the day to trade on my precocity—I was twenty-nine when I began writing *The Outside Story*, thirty when I finished, thirty-one when it was published—but Bill did not let the chance slip. The book, he wrote, "[is] done with the kind of maturity one simply does not expect from someone of that age who hasn't written a book before. . . . No one who reads it will write of it as other than a remarkable stylistic performance."

No one besides Bill wrote of it as a remarkable stylistic performance, but the reviewers were kind, and there were a number of them. Writers from right-world could count on reviews in right-world— *National Review*, the *American Spectator* (where Terry Teachout reviewed it). But I was reviewed in the daily *New York Times*, and the

New York Times Book Review, in both pleasantly. I am not modest about *The Outside Story*; I did a good job. But goodness itself does not guarantee notice. *National Review*'s imprimatur, which was Bill's, guaranteed that. We were wrong, from the *Times*'s perspective, but we were worthy of consideration; so much had Bill wrung from them, his third favor, to me and to all of us.

Doubleday used to have two bookstores on Fifth Avenue in midtown, a large one on the west side of the street, a smaller one on the east (the heroine of Whit Stillman's *Metropolitan* buys a book there). In a suite above the smaller store I had my first book party. Everyone on Fifth Avenue did not know my name—my sales indeed were tiny—but I had a respectable start, which was almost as good as a success.

Bill performed one more favor, for the book's author. My advance was the first fat nonpaycheck check I had ever cashed. Meanwhile, in order to write the book, I had gone part-time at *National Review* for six months. My income probably netted out, but I hadn't withheld anything for taxes. When April 15 rolled around I faced a huge (for me) shortfall. If I went to my parents, I expected I would get a lecture. I went instead to Bill, who became my banker as well as my employer and my publicist. I paid him back with weekly slices out of my paycheck. It was like doing drop sets on a leg press, increasing weariness moderated by the slightly lower financial weight I bore. Owing money is one of the most humiliating experiences on earth; no wonder so many Victorian novels were written about it.

ONE DETAIL OF the 1984 election—an inside story—did not make it into my book. There was a period in Reagan's first term when it was not clear whether he would run again; Nancy's reluctance to have her husband risk defeat fostered the uncertainty. So if not Reagan, who? We discussed this at one of the directors' dinners for the magazine. Every editorial night when Bill was in town, we had dinner at Seventy-third Street. There would be a guest or two—the famous, the would-be famous, friends of Bill's. We sat at a circular table in the dining room, with Bill praising the wine (his criteria were taste and cheapness) and leading the discussion—he threw out questions, and rapped his glass if more than one person spoke at once. A waiter in a dinner jacket took orders for after-dinner drinks and brought around cigars. There were several pitfalls here for David Klinghoffer, an Orthodox Jew, and Jay Nordlinger, a Christian Scientist, when they joined the staff, though Pat took care that they had food and beverage they could eat and drink.

But several times a year the editors were augmented by the magazine's directors—donor-advisers, who, however, had no stake in the magazine (Bill owned all the stock himself). Then two circular tables were set up for dinner; the Hispanic servants and the waiter were reinforced by additional black-tied help. At these dinners Bill would ask the editors to say a few words, before discussion became general.

So whom should we support in a Reagan-less 1984? Jack Kemp, who was thought by many to be the conservative heir apparent, successor to Reagan as Reagan had succeeded Goldwater? Were there other options? Van Galbraith, on a visit from Paris, came up with one. Van was the most ebullient person I ever met (on Bill's transoceanic sails, he woke the next watch by saying, "Good news, you don't have to sleep anymore!"). By this point he had had a fair amount to drink, which made him even more effusive. Why shouldn't Bill run?

He developed the theme. You could get kids to volunteer in New Hampshire; it would be exciting, like running for mayor of New York twenty years earlier, only better. At this point I had drunk a lot myself. I have never been able to hold my liquor; to make matters worse, I always took one of Bill's cigars, because it seemed like the sophisticated thing to do, and because I thought a cigar would cut the poire William, which I thought might cut the wine, though none of these things ever happened. The dinner was already running late, and I rose to go.

Bill shook my hand on the way out. I said it was time to leave since the discussion had taken an unserious turn. He said, Your rise would be even more meteoric.

Thinking about it a quarter century later, I marvel at my rudeness. I was reacting to an aspect of Bill's life—flattery. Bill came in for a lot of criticism—he designed his life to provoke it, the better to hit back—but he also came in for a lot of praise, most of it deserved, and a lot of flattery, which no one deserves. Much of the flattery was not ill-intentioned; it was the praise of people who didn't know how to talk or think, and so said things that were out of proportion, absurd. Van knew how to talk and think, but his campaign scenario was so unlikely—running for president was not running for mayor of New York, and Bill had gotten only 13 percent of the vote in that race—that it seemed one more roof tile in the tornado of flattery that whirled around him.

Yet Bill did think of himself in the top spot. He had his reasons. He knew he was smarter than Reagan; he knew that, in certain circumstances, he spoke as well. He had no preparation, but what preparation had Reagan had when he first ran for governor? What preparation had Jim had when he first ran for senator? These reasons were worthless; Bill lacked the instinct for popularity, the willingness to compromise, the patience, and the brutality to be a successful president. He would have made a better president than Franklin Pierce, but that's a bad test. Still, who was I to disabuse him? Reality would do it soon enough.

I was equally rude one other time, after reading four of his Blackford Oakes novels. I, along with dozens and dozens of his friends, got his new books as soon as they came out, each with the scratch of an inscription, but he wanted my reactions to the fiction. I took the first four novels on vacation one spring, and read them on the beach. There was a two-chapter flashback in the first, *Saving the Queen*, about the hero's years at an English school with a sadistic headmaster, which worked as a short story. ("Yes," Ernest van den Haag agreed with me, "zat was *belles lettres*.") The theme of the second, *Stained Glass*, which told the story of an imaginary anticommunist in postwar West Germany, had scholastic complication: When is the good better than the perfect? When is it necessary to act, even at the risk of acting wrongly (the CIA decides that the heroic German must be killed)? But the characters never came alive; the writing was functional; the sex scenes were ludicrous. The third and fourth novels seemed no good at all, and I said all this in a long memo to Bill. Chris wrote farces, but he wrote them well. Bill did not have the gift.

I was piqued, no doubt, as I wrote my memo, by the failure of my own novel—the double failure, for not only had it not been published, but it had not pleased Bill. He was the only reader who hadn't liked it. All I remember of his comments was that the descriptions weren't vivid enough. I was irked. I had wanted to write stories since my ten-pagers that began with the table of contents. It would also have been nice to write something outside Bill's shadow, in a form that he had only just begun to try.

Worst was Bill's failure to praise. He had been doing it since I was fourteen; what right did he have to change his tune now? This is what comes of praising people more than they deserve; they come to expect it. Bill wasn't the only victim of flattery.

But I also thought I was giving Bill an honest judgment (it's the judgment I still have). I thought we all belonged to the republic of writing, where only good writing counted. That is why Joe and Jeff could follow their fancy and their obsessions, why Keith and John Simon could go off on tangents, why I was the heir apparent.

What I did not realize about Bill's novels, which did not work, or his run for the White House, which never happened, was that he wanted my good opinion almost as much as I wanted his. Because he was so powerful, and because I idealized him so, I wrongly assumed that he was invulnerable. Sons misunderstand their fathers as much as fathers misunderstand their sons.

CHAPTER 7

TWO UNEQUAL CYCLES ran through my life, like a polyrhythm: presidential elections every four years, *National Review* celebrations every five. In 1985, the first year of Reagan's second term, the magazine (and I) would turn thirty. Priscilla would step down as managing editor, and I would take her place. Priscilla told Linda, who might reasonably have expected the job, given her longer in-house service, that she would be assistant managing editor. I never asked when other people learned what Bill's plans were for me; I had known them so long myself that I half expected everyone else to have figured them out. But certainly becoming managing editor was a signal.

Before then, the magazine had to plan its anniversary issue, a job that was also given to me. My idea was to give the issue over to dissidents in the Soviet empire, and ask them to write about the post-Soviet future.

There were moments when I thought of my idea as strategic. The guerrilla wars that the Reagan administration was sponsoring in Central America, southern Africa, and Afghanistan were important distractions, but how could the core of the Soviet empire be shaken? I wrote a thumb sucker for Bill suggesting that the Middle East be moved north, by stirring up central Asia's Moslems; he thought the piece was half-baked, which it was, and it never ran. (Al-Qaeda and its clones have taken on the assignment.) Encouraging the resistance of Europeans, Russian and otherwise, seemed like a better idea; Solidarity had already shown the way. But then reality would break in, and I would realize that my idea was quixotic. The Kremlin (as shorthand for the Soviet state) seemed as solid as the Kremlin (the building); I did not seriously imagine that either could be shaken. Still, why not think about it? I had come to know, by mail, a young man named Ojars Kalnins, who submitted humor pieces to *National Review*. It turned out he was a Latvian American, and we began to correspond about that. Soon I found myself on Latvian, Lithuanian, and Estonian mailing lists (the three went together, like unlucky children in a fairy tale). David Klinghoffer, a Brown graduate who worked as a summer intern for us, then stayed on, asked me once if I was Baltic. He could not understand anyone who didn't have a grandmother from one of those places caring about them. And he was right—hardly anyone did care. It was my POR fondness for lost causes, from Charles I to Lysander Spooner, coming out.

The flaw in my plan for a special issue was that I proposed to cede some editorial guidance, and the responsibility for an introductory essay, to historian John Lukacs (no relation to Jan Lukas; they were not even from the same country). John had come to America from Hungary after World War II, and I had read his magnum opus, *The Last European War*, a history of World War II up to Hitler's invasion of the Soviet Union, and Pearl Harbor. After those events, the future depicted by Orwell and Burnham—Europe divided between Eurasia and Oceania—was inevitable. John wanted to memorialize Europe's last moments of independence, horrible moments, because they saw Hitler's successes, but noble moments too, because they saw Churchill's resistance. John had a refreshing mind; I liked his distinction between popular sentiment and public opinion: Popular sentiment is what everyone thinks; public opinion is what everyone thinks everyone else thinks. The first is what is actually skulking in your mind; the second is what you tell a pollster after mentally straightening your tie. He showed me how narratives could be organized thematically; his books began with the story, then broke out particular subjects for detailed discussions. It was always good to meet him for a drink when he ventured from his kingdom, his house outside Philadelphia. He was unsuited to my project, however, for a reason that was just becoming evident. Though he knew many American conservatives, and sometimes wrote for us, he had contempt for us—not as individuals, but as a force in public life. He believed we were stupid, and prone to national socialism, if not actual Nazism. Any conservative success at the polls made him flash back to the European fascist movements of his youth. He might have understood the dissidents, but he would have had a hard time saying anything about them to us, because he wouldn't trust us to understand them. Jeff intuited John's aversion, and reacted harshly, as was his wont. After we had published one of John's pieces, on Solidarity (pro-Solidarity but anti-American in equal measure), Jeff said that he had not eaten enough beet soup in Budapest to comprehend it. After I outlined my plan for a special issue at an editorial dinner, Jeff wrote an alarmed memo, suggesting a collection of pieces asking "whither conservatism" instead. That is what we did, and some of those pieces were interesting. But the format was predictable; dissidents could have been a keeper, if I had trusted myself enough to be the editor.

Ronald Reagan came to this anniversary dinner, but I didn't get to meet him again. Security was so tight that I might as well have been watching him on television. I did get a chance to introduce Jeanne to one of her cousins. I found Mrs. Pat Buchanan sitting to my left, and on her left Morley Safer (Jeanne was at the next table). Jeanne knew, from someone in her family having looked it up, that Safer was a distant relative. He was from Canada, where part of her family had settled; moreover, his jowls looked just like her late father's. Five years earlier, at the last anniversary dinner, we had seen Safer doing a stand-up on the party for *Sixty Minutes* outside the ballroom. I had told Jeanne to introduce herself when he was done, but she didn't want to bother him. Now I would not lose the chance; breaking into his conversation, I explained that he and my wife were related, ticking off the surname and the Canadian connection as proof. "He thinks I'm Morley Safer," he said to Mrs. Buchanan, then to me,

"I'm Mike Wallace." "Perhaps you're related too" was the best I could manage.

Reagan paid Bill a handsome tribute, calling him "perhaps the most influential journalist and intellectual in our era. . . . He changed our country, indeed our century." This was high but realistic praise, worth more than a million schemes to run for president: The man who had done it was acknowledging the man who had helped educate him, and prepared his way. In the crush of that dinner, I was barely closer to Bill than I was to Reagan; I hope Bill appreciated it.

WHEN I BECAME managing editor I moved into the second-floor office that had the ringing turtle and the bottom drawer of the dumbwaiter. It was a vertiginous feeling, like first learning how to drive; you go nowhere—around the block, to a gas station—but it seems momentous. Since the key to running a magazine is finding good people, who are also your people, to do the work, I turned to friends of mine from Yale.

I suggested that Wally Olson write economic editorials for us, which he did from outside. Wally was not a pure supply-sider; he knew too much economics for that, and had opinions on such things as money supply; he presented all his opinions in a tart, nimble style. Kevin Lynch, the articles editor, left to go to Radio Free Europe, and I proposed Rich Vigilante to replace him. I had known Rich since his freshman year; the first book he bought when he had come to New Haven, even before classes began, was the Bollingen edition of Plato. For a few days he carried it around with him everywhere, like a talisman. Like Plato, he understood the value both of clashing ideas and of coming to a conclusion. He was also funnier than Plato.

To fill out my team I drew on a chain of younger friends of friends. Maggie Gallagher came as Rich's assistant, though her great gift was writing. She had one of the easiest and most flowing natural voices I had ever read. When I saw that Philmont, New York, the upstate town where Oliver North had grown up, was holding a celebration for him, I told Maggie to take the train up and write nine hundred words about it. She noted, among other things, a tipsy old lady doing her own little jig, which provoked a letter to the editor from the tipsy old lady. Later we hired Mark Cunningham, an intense young man. He was the only one on staff competent to do an obit for Robert Heinlein. I cut one graf, which quoted Heinlein abusing Samuel Johnson for calling patriotism the last refuge of a scoundrel. I told Mark that Heinlein's patriotism, and ours, was sufficiently established, and we were not in the business of taking potshots at Samuel Johnson. A non-Yalie I wished to hire was Terry Teachout, as book review editor, but the opportunity never came up.

I brought in one new columnist. When I came to the magazine the religion columnist was Malachi Martin, a former Jesuit, who struck me as dreadful. I glanced at one of his novels, which purported to be a lightly fictionalized look into the Vatican. He claimed that the Vatican was dominated by a cult of pedophiles who held Black Masses. He was replaced by Michael Novak, who is sane, but Michael did not seem to me to be suited to column writing. He expatiated on the virtues of capitalism, which we knew already, and wrote very little about religion. One day I read an essay in a newsletter by a Lutheran minister, the Reverend Richard Neuhaus, which gave a tour d'horizon of American belief. At last, I thought, someone who knows there are Protestants in this country. Reverend Neuhaus continued to know it after he became a Catholic priest. He made a good religious journalist and polemicist.

There is nothing wrong with cronyism or nepotism, so long as you have interesting friends and talented relatives. Certainly, Bill heeded this principle in drawing on his many siblings over the years; it applied equally to his use of his friends, since the first spark of so many of his relationships was perceiving someone's talent. My instincts were justified by the later careers of the people I chose. Wally is a popular law blogger and writer on legal matters, who made an original critique of his own worldview, pointing out the libertarian results that flow from the legal traditions and mores that corsair trial lawyers flout. Rich founded *City Journal*, the Manhattan Institute's urban policy quarterly, and made it stylish as well as hard-hitting, and he turned Regnery Books, a limping conservative house, into an assembly line for best-sellers that were purely hard-hitting. Mark is the editorial-page editor of the *New York Post*. Everyone knows Terry. The only friend whose evolution I regret is Maggie, whose books and columns burrow too deeply into the sociology of marriage and child rearing. Many people can summarize the results of studies; few write as well as Maggie when she is in her groove.

My new hires got used to representing the magazine in public. Rich, Maggie, and I went up to Yale one evening for a debate in the Political Union against a team led by the *Nation* columnist (as he then was) Christopher Hitchens. The topic was South Africa. The noose was tightening around the apartheid state. South Africa had lost its buffer zone of Portuguese colonies and white Rhodesia in the seventies. Its economic prowess kept its African neighbors from menacing it directly, but the Soviets backed the African National Congress, the main revolutionary movement, using them as Reagan used Jonas Savimbi in Angola, while liberals of every hue condemned Afrikanerdom. Eighty years earlier, when Britain was completing its conquest of South Africa, to be pro-Boer was a mark of moral purity; now the reverse was the case. Certainly, apartheid, the racial system on which Afrikaner rule rested, earned the scorn it got. At its best, apartheid would have created a patchwork of native puppet states, the Bantustans; in reality, it involved a diet of harassment and brutality for blacks who lived and worked in segregated slums outside the mines and major cities.

Some in the ruling Nationalist Party realized this. I was taken to lunch in New York one day by a South African diplomat. (Such occasions came to us at *National Review*, like trips to Taiwan; because South Africa was anticommunist, we were the friendliest faces a South African official could expect to see.) The diplomat was an Afrikaner; he suggested a midtown steak house, where he ordered a Scotch and his meat well done. I had him typecast before coffee arrived. Then, he said in his solemn way, when he had taken Christ into his life, he had seen that racism was wicked, and he had to cleanse his heart of it. So there had to be changes in the regime. . . . I had never changed my opinions because of my religion, or for any reason; I was abashed. Like many reforms, the ones the Nationalists proposed were small and late, not enough to satisfy justice, or their critics.

I was never a particularly good debater, and only became a good speaker after many years. In college the Party of the Right had held numerous debates, but they were a kind of antischool, encouraging such self-indulgence that one had to unlearn a host of bad habits. Hitchens on the podium was a triple threat: witty in the British university manner, insulting whenever it might shut a questioner down, and passionate—he began by evoking the tide of liberation, flowing irresistibly down the continent to its tip. We made the best defense of a bad cause, sticking to the low road of national interest, and skepticism: It could not benefit America to turn southern Africa over to Soviet clients, and there was no reason to think that they would govern South Africa better than the Afrikaners had, only differently badly. We did not suspect that Nelson Mandela might be a great man. His side had its share of thugs and ignoramuses, and Mandela himself had no solutions to poverty or crime, after *apartheid* the scourges of his country. But he had magnanimity. His supporters on the Left did not know this about him either, or care. They wanted to overthrow white racism, and would have accepted any competing form of oppression, black or communist.

Afterward, Hitchens and I exchanged a few pleasantries. He seemed to take the view that conservatives would be disposed of after the revolution, but meanwhile they were good company; the people he hated were liberals, slightly to his right. Left-wing kids took him off to a party, as I was taken by the Party of the Right. The next day I awoke with a hangover, and sat woodenly over breakfast in the Holiday Inn where the Political Union had put the speakers up. Hitchens bustled in, fresh as a daisy, and saw my condition at once. "It begins to lift with the first sherry," he assured me.

EVERY SECOND TERM of a reelected president has been worse than his first (Lincoln, McKinley—shot; Nixon—resigned; Wilson—stroke; Madison—enemies burn the White House . . . the list goes on). Reagan's troubles began three months after his reinauguration, when it turned out that a planned visit to West Germany would take him to a military cemetery in Bitburg containing the graves of dozens of SS men. Reagan's advance man had scouted the site in winter, when the graves were covered with snow, and hadn't noticed. Reagan decided to tough it out as a favor to an ally, but the purity of his antitotalitarian credentials was smirched.

In October 1986 he met with Soviet leader Mikhail Gorbachev in Reykjavik. Gorbachev was the first Soviet leader in years who did not have one foot in the grave. Reagan struck us as perilously willing to barter away America's nuclear deterrent, for the sake of an arms deal. Only his insistence on keeping missile defense wrecked the summit, and averted some grand disaster.

The next month, the storm hit, when the world learned that the administration had been secretly selling arms to Iran, and using the profits to supply arms to antileftist rebels in Nicaragua. Reagan's defense against the charge that he was a lawbreaker was that he was clueless—an argument made easier by the fact that Col. Oliver North, the National Security Council aide who managed the money switching, was in orbit around a private sun.

Conservatives reacted to these events with varying degrees of panic. Our recent migration to Washington had made us all jumpier. Tidal waves of emotion originating there would batter *National Review*, before vanishing without a trace. One directors' dinner was consumed by the urgency of replacing Donald Regan, the president's chief of staff, whom everyone in Washington had decided was incompetent, with someone better. Regan gave way to Howard Baker, and nothing important changed.

National Review inveighed against the Reykjavik summit before it happened, publishing among our attacks a critical piece coauthored by Henry Kissinger and Richard Nixon. These two, who supped with the devil many a time, now said that Reagan, uniquely, was bringing too short a spoon. Bill Rusher, scornful of what he took to be their hypocrisy, submitted a counterattack, calling Nixon and Kissinger "dime-store Machiavellis." Bill Buckley told him they were not dime-store anything, and that Rusher's piece was not fit for publication in *National Review*. Rusher removed the epithet, and we ran his riposte in slightly milder form.

THE WORST CONSEQUENCE for *National Review* of Reagan's troubles was Joe's reaction to Bitburg. Joe had found a subject that, once taken up, few people ever drop—the power of Jews. John Judis, the socialist journalist, would attribute Joe's anti-Semitism to his eastern European roots (Sobran is a Ruthenian name). Joe was outraged by this; his parents, he said, voted for Adlai Stevenson (suddenly, other people's liberalism became his shield). Norman Podhoretz said he was happy to learn that Joe believed Shakespeare was the Earl of Oxford; it comforted him to see paranoias flocking together. I think Joe took the wrong lessons from sociologist John Murray Cuddihy. Cuddihy, who was a friend of the magazine, wrote about the plight of nineteenth-century European Jews, freed from ghetto and shtetl into a world that was both alien and changing, Christian and liberal. Freud and Marx looked at the brave new world and offered scientific explanations of what Gentiles were "really" up to (sex, said Freud; money, said Marx). Cuddihy, turning the tables, argued that what Freud and Marx were "really" up to was ethnic self-defense. Cuddihy's work is witty and subtle, but it can be easily vulgarized. H. L. Mencken is a good writer, and Henry Adams is a great one, but I know several writers whose uncritical love of one or the other ruined them. Cuddihy had a baleful effect on Joe.

Tom Bethell, Joe's dear friend, told me that after Bitburg, Jews "moved to the front of his mind" (moving his hands from his ears to his temples, as if describing the progress of a migraine or a tumor). Joe started calling the *New York Times* the *Holocaust Update*. He discovered that *goyisher kop*, a Yiddish expression for a stupid person, means Gentile head (he should have read more Philip Roth, he would not have been so surprised). Everything fed the flames; humor and curiosity became his own enemies.

Midge Decter, Norman Podhoretz's wife, sent a letter to Bill and various other people who employed Joe, including the head of the syndicate that ran his column, collating and denouncing his new opinions. She wanted him muzzled or fired. Before Midge's letter, Bill and Joe had conversations and exchanged memos I never heard or read. Bill's way, when a colleague was going off the rails, was to employ a combination of patience (hoping the problem would go away), denial (ignoring how serious it was), and admonitions so small and oblique as to be invisible. The baggage that Bill and Joe each brought to this problem was great. Bill's father had been an anti-Semite; early in the history of the magazine, Bill had forbidden its writers to appear in the *American Mercury*, Mencken's old journal, which had slid into Jew bashing. Bill thought those problems were behind him. Joe adored Bill, and thought he was carrying on his idol's tradition of embattled honesty, fighting Zionists as Bill once fought liberals.

Bill convened the editors for a session before an editorial dinner to have it out with our erring brother. We huddled in the library, ordinarily a forum for hospitality or routine discussion, a dark-red slipper of a room, lined with books, stuffed with odd and uncomfortable knickknacks, animated by a spaniel or two. Bill let Joe talk, then talked him down, politely but tirelessly. I was no help in the situation. I was angry with Joe for being wrong, and exasperated with him for becoming an embarrassment. The first sentiment was just, but the second adulterated it with vanity and concern for my own comfort.

The session ended with Joe's promise to run anything he might want to write on the *judenfrage* by Bill before it was published. When you tell a boy to stay out of a neighbor's yard, he wants nothing more than to go there. The solution was no solution, only a recipe for ongoing tension.

THE EIGHTIES SAW one more flock of problems, settling on Bill personally. He had been famous for more than thirty years, a TV star for twenty. The fizz and the shock of youth had been his qualities and his tools, but in 1985 he turned sixty. He had assailed a slower-footed establishment, but he had long been part of it, by virtue of lifestyle, friendship, and ideological assignment: The adversary who compelled liberals to respect him had become the respectable adversary. For the first time, his act, the public performance of his life, was getting not opposition but bad reviews.

The reception of *Overdrive*, his second book detailing a week in his life, published in 1981 (a decade after *Cruising Speed*) was a harbinger. *Cruising Speed* had been a delight, with all the freshness of pulling off a new trick, and Bill's own freshness in the media-god life he lived. In *Overdrive* he repeated himself. The writing, the speaking, the friends, the rivals: He had done it all before.

Bill's take on his life had also grown darker. At the beginning of the book, he looks out the window of his study, a converted garage at the Stamford house, and sees a pheasant. He reflects that as he has been seeing this pheasant for years, it can not be the same pheasant, but the latest in a series whose predecessors have all died. The deaths of friends permeate the book. Over the years Bill had written many of *National Review*'s obituaries, but all the dead he had sent off, whether he loved them (Chambers) or disliked them (Winston Churchill), had been older. Now he was beginning to note the passing of peers. Shades of the prison house closed 'round the growing boy.

The reviewers harped on his car. The limo naturally figured in the book, and they loved to hate it—its size, its cost, its aura of enclosure. The *New York Review of Books* imagined Bill cruising into the city on the Bruckner Expressway, and asking himself, as he glanced out the window, "Was Bach less deserving?" Nora Ephron in the *New York Times Book Review* said that an Irishman turned Tory as soon as he got a horse, and so it was with Bill and his limo. (Joe noted that the *Times* would not run such comments "about just *any* ethnic group.")

The chorus of boos gave Bill the pretext for reviewing his reviewers: hand-to-hand combat, his favorite sport. Norman Podhoretz, in a favorable notice, attributed the criticisms to envy. There was something to that. But critics hit the moving target because they began to know its moves.

Spy magazine took Bill on. *Spy* was a chronicler of the rich and famous—a dog in a penthouse who chews its master's furniture. It was successful for a time because ad buyers, who are all twenty, read it and assumed that everyone else did. *Spy*'s first target was Pat. One Halloween issue they ran a cardboard insert, a mascaraed-eye cover they labeled a Mrs. William F. Buckley Jr. mask. With sure instinct they picked the moment when Pat was passing from the status of beauty to that of grande dame. "Did you see the latest issue of *Spy*?" she declared—even her questions were commanding—before one editorial dinner. I did not know what to say. I did not understand—thirty years old: When will you start learning?—that someone so well armored might be vulnerable.

Spy's next shot was aimed at Bill, and it was fired by a former employee. Bob Mack worked for us as an editorial assistant during the mideighties. He was a Randian, though pleasant. After he left, he wrote a hatchet job on his former employer and place of work. The illustration said it all: It showed Bill in Mortimer's, a clubby Upper East Side restaurant, a yachting cap askew on his head, his belly stouter than it was (though it was stouter than it had been), a glass of red wine tipped in his hand. Outside the window stood the next generation of would-be conservative leaders, noses pressed vainly against the glass (among them was me). Bill, said Mack, was tired, old, lazy, burned out. The truly consequential right-wing thinker of our time was the late Ayn Rand.

People sell out for all kinds of reasons: to make money; to get on television. Getting a byline in *Spy* is low even on this list. I wrote Bob, whom I had hired, and said my best hope for him was that he would come to understand what a horse's-ass thing he had done.

Another young man made a more serious criticism of Bill's lifework. Greg Fossedal was one of Jeff's many Dartmouth protégés. He had worked in the Reagan White House, writing in support of missile defense. He had a big ego, made of solid brass, but he was smart and full of energy. He wrote a column on *National Review*, which he described as being in a rut, populated by writers who were in ruts (he had zero use for Erik von Kuehnelt-Leddihn). Where was the new blood? He threw out some names, all of them bright.

I wrote Greg a long letter of rebuttal; I spent some time explaining what nutrients Erik added to the average conservative's diet. Jeff wrote "Fuck you" on top of a copy of Greg's piece, and got him booted from every conservative Dartmouth organization on which they both sat. Bill adopted none of Greg's personnel suggestions.

But Greg was right. Rich and Maggie were bringing in a high quality of content in the article section. Our format, however, needed a kick. The big tent held up by a handful of columnists had been standing, in the same place, since 1955. Bill Rusher put it well a few years later—we were saying "the jewel is in the eye of the lotus," the prayer that Buddhists inscribe on flags and wheels so that every flap and spin may send it heavenward. Bill Buckley had not given the kick, and neither had I. Of course, Bill had not asked me to do such a thing, but maybe he was waiting for it to be done.

CHAPTER 8

ONE SUMMER DAY in 1987 I came back to my desk after lunch and found a surprising letter. It was from Bill, and the envelope was marked "Confidential." "It is by now plain to me [it began] that you are not suited to serve as editor-in-chief of NR after my retirement. This sentence will no doubt have for a while a heavy heavy effect on your morale, and therefore I must at once tell you that I have reached the conclusion irrevocably . . . ."

I have a distinct memory of taking this letter home and tearing it up. I even remember throwing the pieces into the round wooden wastebasket in our living room. Yet as I began writing this book I found it, in a bulging folder of letters, photographs, and birthday cards (my equivalent of a filing system). I know it is the original because it has a correction in Bill's red ink. Sometimes we repress memories, sometimes we create them.

The letter made three points. The first was my unfitness to be editor. "You have no executive flair. It is not, really, desirable that I should document this, and I have kept no notebooks on the subject; but it simply is not there. . . . You do not have executive habits, you do not have an executive turn of mind, and I would do you no service, nor NR, by imposing it on you."

The second point was the turn of mind Bill thought I did have. "What you have is a very rare talent, so rare that I found it not only noticeable but striking when you were very young. . . . You will go down in history as a very fine writer, perhaps even a great writer. Nothing would distract you more greatly from realizing that achievable dream than to struggle as executive director of a small, however important, magazine of opinion which you can best continue to serve as a writer."

A third point, weaving in and out of the other two, was of less interest to me at the time, though I glimpsed it even then: Bill was using the opportunity of writing to me to write to himself about himself. "Some activities one naturally inclines to, others are diversions, and some of these can become asphyxiative. [It would be wrong to regret] not having executive pizzazz when the alternative is, in your case, so much to be preferred." Had Bill found his own routine, at cruising speed and in overdrive, asphyxiative? His talents had been striking when he was very young; the world had certainly noticed them. Did he feel they had been misused?

He concluded by asking me to think about all this "for a week or so. . . . There is a lot of time. In your case, a blessed lifetime."

My first reaction, and my second, third, and fourth, was the howl of pain. But who could I talk to for actual advice?

I talked, of course, with Jeanne. "For richer, for poorer," I said brightly. I shared the news with only one of my conservative friends, Rich Vigilante. He was loyal. His wife, Susan, who is Irish, was equally loyal, with a welcome admixture of aggression. Italians are said to be good at getting even; the Irish say, The hell with that, let's get mad.

I could not have spoken to Bill immediately even if I wished because he was out of town. I went instead to see Bill Rusher. He had been told what was coming, and he was familiar with Buckley's habits when it came to lowering the boom. Buckley typically did these jobs by letter, or passed them on to his publisher. Once, in the early days of his tenure, Rusher had had to fire an accountant at Buckley's orders. Then too Buckley was out of town; the woman took it rather hard, and said through her tears that "if Mr. *Buckley* was here," it wouldn't have happened. Rusher asked me if I had thought of a response; I hadn't. He was concerned to play the endgame as best as possible for my benefit. Think of an answer soon, he advised, "before Buckley decides to consult his fifty closest friends."

I settled on a cover story for myself: Realizing that I did not have enough time to write, I had decided to step down as managing editor and work at the magazine only part-time. I peddled this story to my friends and colleagues. My supposed motive was untrue, but I carried conviction because I was accurately describing what I intended to do.

Despite Rusher's fears that Bill might be indiscreet, the secret was well kept. Jeff didn't know; Pat didn't know. My apologies to everyone, living and dead, for my deceptions. I imagined that my new plans caused some talk in right-world, but I did not want to know about it; that would have been a distraction in my present state of mind.

My state of mind was kept unsettled by one odd, but characteristic, codicil of Bill's letter. He felt some compunction about luring me from law school in 1978, he wrote, and the earthly paradise of a plump job. He tried to assuage it by proposing to guarantee the salary I had earned as managing editor for five years. His guarantee was not simple, however, because he also proposed to deduct a portion of what I might earn as a freelancer above and beyond the subsidized salary. It was peonage disguised as a payoff, or vice versa.

My eyes glaze over even now as I try to make sense of it. My counteroffer was simpler: You should feel compunction, so give me a lump sum. He wouldn't do that; I wouldn't take his tricked-out subsidy. This back-and-forth went on for a week or two, entirely by memo, even after he came back to town; I was as leery of confrontation as he was. In the end I simply went part-time and took a pay cut.

I told my brother and my parents. My father came through. He had retired from Eastman Kodak only a few years earlier. He had never talked to me or, as far as I knew, anyone about his job. He went in the morning and came home at night. I had been to his office a couple times; it was decorated with a picture of an elk in a pond that he had taken on our road trip west. Now he told me that he had once missed a promotion he felt he deserved, which went instead to the son of a director of the company. He told the man who made the pick, and the man who benefited from it, that he believed he was the better man, but that he would do his best in the new order of things regardless. He also said that if I wanted to go to law school, ten years late, he would pay for it. Economists, even those whose systems are mindful of human motivation, can write as if jobs come out of a pot labeled "Economy." They do, but they get done because people—in my father's generation, men—go to work five days a week and do them. Some of us love our jobs, but many more of us only like them well enough. My father had gone to his job for almost forty years to support himself and his wife and his sons. Now he was offering another share of those earnings (carefully, even penuriously, saved) to me. I was impressed; he was a better man than the idol I had put in his place.

I sent Bill a letter in return, after the dickering about subsidies and salaries had ended, and a few months of that blessed lifetime had elapsed. I quoted Blake:

I was angry with my friend,
I told my wrath, my wrath did end.
I was angry with my foe,
I told it not, my wrath did grow.

In the interest of ending wrath, I wanted him to know that his behavior was "contemptible."

What had Bill and I each brought to this moment, like clumsy magi?

National Review was too tiny to have anything so formal as performance reviews, but Bill could have given me more direction during the nine years of our arrangement. Yet the lack of communication was my failure too. I had seen Bill managing and mismanaging others, right on up to Joe. Bill's signals were maddeningly indirect for such a verbalist. I might have noticed them, though, if I hadn't been so gratified by my own role. Praise and the promise of power make one unobservant; they closed my eyes and stopped my ears.

On the question of executive flair, Bill was right. I had some elements of it; my eye for talent was as good as his, and good ideas came to me too. But my notion of a manager was too much like the Deist idea of a God who puts all the pieces on the board, then lets them play the game. Good editors give good writers their head. But writers are more than writers, and most of a magazine's employees don't write at all. An executive has to be willing to insert himself directly, daily, into any problem that comes up, from James Baker making a pitch to Willmoore Kendall initiating the memorial couch.

On top of everything I was too respectful of Bill and the structure he had made to play with it. To keep it fresh, I would have needed to take it on, and him on.

If I did all that, when would I do my next book? I had already written a good one; Bill wrote a book every year. But did I want to keep writing political books that were extensions of journalism, or the kind of books that Bill's schedule allowed him time to write? Maybe my novel was no better than his; was there anything else I might do instead? And if there was, how would I find the time to bear down and do it?

Ernest van den Haag had asked me to have dinner with him in the Village earlier that summer, before the confidential letters began to fly. After we finished we walked the small streets while he recalled old haunts: He had rigged one of his beds with bells and lights that went off when it jiggled during sex. He also wanted to let me know that *National Review* would be his heir when he died. Ernest was amusing, but how many other such conversations would I have to have? Considering the magazine's eternal poverty, many. Being editor in chief would mean being always on call for such conversations; it would mean seeking them out. They were the incarnation of Bill's endless correspondence.

Bill's failing (apart from cowardice) was to have made the offer he did in 1978, having wrongly decided that I, at age twenty-three, was the second coming of him. He would have written a shorter letter in

1987 if he had said, "It is now plain to me that the evidence of your name is indicative of a larger truth: You are not, in fact, me."

Bill had his own needs and assumptions that blinded and deafened him. He wanted his handiwork to go on; his own son had taken a different path, but maybe he could find another. Youth had been so good to him, and my youth might turn up the ace of spades twice.

Whether Bill had done me a favor would be shown by the future. The future would also contain a lot of him, for we were not done with each other.

At age thirty-two, I suddenly went from precocious to retarded, from out in front to lagging behind, for I now had to start a new career, that of a freelance writer.

On the *National Review* masthead I went back to being a senior editor. I continued to come in Monday and Tuesday every other week. I could have walked out on the whole crowd and swaggered the nut-strewn roads. But I didn't do those things, for one of the reasons Philip Larkin didn't do them: the need for steady income. It is especially important for a freelancer to have the anchor of a regular gig, if he can: an income stream at least, benefits if possible. Those I had for the relatively cheap investment of four days a month.

The rest of the days of the month I was in space. After ten years of even a job as varied by junkets and campaign trails as mine had been, freelancing felt like being one of those tiny sailing ships or spouting sea monsters in midocean in old maps. It was a big world out there, and none of it had anything to do with you, unless you made a connection yourself.

As a freelancer I would go anywhere, meet anyone, do anything. I would not write for free because that would have been giving it away (this was before blogging), but I would appear gratis in other media, because that was a way of getting the brand out. I was on *The Joe Franklin Show* once. Joe Franklin was an old Broadway publicist whose anticharisma had won him a cult following among New York hipsters. When I caught up with him he was doing a TV show in the wetlands of Secaucus. I went on with an unknown rock group, a city councilman from Newark, and a young black kid who did impressions (his Reagan was very good, though he said *aks* for *ask*). I wrote several pieces for Helen Gurley Brown's *Cosmopolitan*: nothing louche, how to shop with your wife (patience), how to cancel out her vote (and how she canceled out mine). I never wrote for magazines of one hand, though I did work with a former editor of *Penthouse*. He had moved on to *AARP the Magazine*; he recalled his old job fondly, though he thought *Penthouse* had fallen on evil days: "Too many pictures of women pissing." It was not a problem I would ever have encountered at *National Review*.

One category of opportunities was available to me because I was conservative. Conservatives have been complaining, since before I was born, that the major media are biased against them, and generally speaking they are right. But that very tilt means there are openings for conservatives as foils, voices of darkness, odd men out. It was our Affirmative Action. Liberal producers or executives don't have to be actually open-minded, like Warren Steibel; they simply have to see the virtue of some variety. Many do, and I had good luck being their variety.

I cycled through a number of radio and TV slots as house conservative. Living in Manhattan was like living in a media city-state: You could grab a cab or ride the subway, and then reach a million people. I learned firsthand the strange and distorting power of television. Neal Freeman told me once that savages were right to fear photography, because it does steal your soul. Being on TV makes you recognizable, and unforgettable—except that no one remembers what you said, or where. Several times I have been stopped by strangers on the street who told me how much they enjoyed some old show on which I mixed it up with Joe Klein. I know Klein, but I have never once been on the same show with him. My oddest arrangement was being in on the debut of MSNBC. The creators wanted what they now have, a 24/7 cable news network, but they thought at first they might frame it with a *Friends*-like format of forty or so rotating commentators, who would make brief appearances three at a time throughout the day. A limo would pick me up (such shows pay peanuts or nothing, but have prodigal budgets for transportation) and take me up FDR Drive and over the George Washington Bridge to Fort Lee. There I would sit in a corner of a huge empty studio, a simulacrum of a newsroom, reading the papers or trying to work. Without warning, I would be told to hop to the set, to talk for two minutes about a plane crash or a mass suicide of cultists with Eric Alterman or Ann Coulter. Behind us on our little platform sat the bagels and fruit we were supposedly noshing on—an unchanging display of plaster, like the rustic fare in a Neapolitan crèche.

Most pleasant of my peers was Laura Ingraham. The art of being Laura, or Ann, or any one of us who were naturals (I was okay) was to be able to opine firmly, plausibly, and instantly on any topic. Laura once breezed past me as the commentators were changing shifts. What was I reading? she asked. Alexander Hamilton, I said. "Madison is better!" she cried as she vanished.

MY BEST GIG as a conservative came from the *New York Observer*. Shortly after Bill wrote his letter, I saw a notice in *New York* magazine that a new weekly newspaper was starting, owned by a man named Arthur Carter. The only other information about him in the item was that he was publisher of the *Nation* (it was not possible then to Google people). This was not promising, but I decided to try my luck, and made an appointment to see him in his new publication's offices, a stout townhouse off Park Avenue. As a freelancer, I had learned an introductory spiel, but he cut me off and said that of course he was familiar with my writing from *National Review*. He added he had once given *National Review* a thousand dollars. Why was that? I asked. "Because *National Review* does a good job, and magazines that do a good job should be rewarded." I understood that his heart's desire was to publish all the journals of opinion— the *Nation*, *National Review*, *The New Republic*—but since that couldn't happen, he would do the next best thing, which was create a paper that was truly heterogeneous.

I wrote my first *Observer* column about a cocktail party on the Upper West Side attended by Jack Kemp, the supply-side congressman who had decided to run for president. It was in October 1987, just after Black Monday, when the Dow lost almost a quarter of its value in one day. This could have been a day of disaster for supply-siders, who assigned the market sibylline predictive powers. But Kemp was his usual high-spirited self. The market, he said, nothing daunted, would go back up to 2,400 points, and even higher.

I wrote every week for the *Observer* for a couple years, then every other week, for twenty years. The *Observer* went through several stylistic incarnations, from covering community boards to discovering Candace Bushnell. I once met Carter for lunch at Gino's, an Italian hole-in-the-wall favored by Upper East Siders. "Have you heard of this drink?" he asked, holding up a cosmopolitan. I said I had. "Where?" he wanted to know. "In the *New York Observer*," I told him. Two qualities always marked the paper, drunk or sober: One could write about anything, and say it any way. Both freedoms were often abused, but the result for me was that I was welcome there.

I also began to do writing that was not conservative. I wrote for the *Atlantic Monthly* about how to read poetry out loud, or what G. K. Chesterton saw in Charles Dickens (Chesterton on *David Copperfield* was much easier to take than Chesterton on Catholicism). I wrote impressionistic items about New York—sunlight at the solstice, the Tenth Street baths, why old banks projected stony solidity—for "The Talk of the Town." Under William Shawn *The New Yorker* had been the Dark Tower of journalism—no one knew how to get in, and everyone was beginning to wonder whether it was worth it. Mr. Shawn had been eased out, and Bob Gottlieb tried to carry on the formula, with adjustments—the magazine introduced color photographs, Ved Mehta ran for 5,000 words, not 10,000 or 20,000. Excerpts from Bill's sailing books had run in *The New Yorker* under Mr. Shawn—the journalistic achievement he was now proudest of. If Gottlieb now wondered why one of Bill's employees was trying, in his early thirties, to construct unsigned 500-word items for the magazine's opening pages, he was too polite to ask.

There are some journalists it is impossible to like. But most are easy to deal with, and dealing with them admits you into the freemasonry of professionals, where the main value is hitting your mark. One of Arthur Carter's editors at the *Observer* was Graydon Carter (no relation). Graydon had cofounded *Spy*, a moral failing on his part, but he left, which showed he was not wedded to it. After he left the *Observer* for *Vanity Fair*, we remained two acquaintances who could call each other with special requests: me, when he wanted a piece on Canadian politics (*The Outside Story*, northern exposure); him, when I needed to film an Oscar party for a documentary on George Washington (celebrity, now and then).

Chip McGrath edited me when I wrote for *The New Yorker*. After William Shawn died, I was reading Chip's tribute to him when I found myself suddenly in the midst of a piece on Rwanda. I told him the discussion of massacres tipped me off that I had turned too many pages. "There were massacres under Shawn," he said. "Quiet ones." I continued to write for him when he moved to the *New York Times Book Review*, even though we never agreed on anything except hitting your mark.

Everywhere I went my association with *National Review* smoothed the way. It was a jeweler's hallmark, a proof of verbal kashruth. It was assumed that there was a level below which a senior editor at Bill Buckley's magazine would not sink. I would have to make the sale for whatever I was proposing, but *National Review* opened the door. In my nonpolitical writing, I was determined to walk through that door, then shut it behind me.

FREELANCING WAS NEW and challenging, and it brought in (some) money, but I had to write another book. I thought unimaginatively of writing a second campaign book, but my agent, Lou Ann Sabatier, had a better idea. George H. W. Bush was going to be the next president; I should write a book about him. This gave me my idea: I should write a book about the type he represented—white Anglo-Saxon Protestants. She sold *The Way of the WASP* to a good editor, Erwin Glikes, then at the Free Press.

Erwin's great coup had been publishing *The Closing of the American Mind* by Allan Bloom, a Straussian at the University of Chicago.

Curiously, this best-seller had begun as an article in *National Review*. One of Ernest van den Haag's hobbyhorses was that we did not publish enough writing by academics (that is, by people with credentials like his). Ernest would get upset when Joe would review a book on, say, Marx, without knowing the secret handshakes. Ernest got some grant money to prospect for pieces by Ph.D.s. One of them was a piece on rock and roll by Bloom. I thought it was dull stuff, hostile and predictable: what my mother would say about the Rolling Stones if she had read Nietzsche. Erwin was shrewder than I was. He asked Bloom to write a book on the sad state of American thought, and persuaded him to lead with the chapter on rock, not the chapter on postmodern philosophy; he paid Bloom $10,000, and gave another thousand to Saul Bellow for a preface. The book became a huge hit. It was the ideal book for Erwin: He had shown creativity, spent almost no money, and made a packet.

Lou Ann made him spend a little more money on *The Way of the WASP*, and he made much less, but I did a good job. My hook was the inarticulacy of George H. W. Bush, something I knew firsthand. But I saw that he spoke (or failed to speak) for a whole class of inarticulate people. America's oldest and still plurality culture did not know how to explain or defend itself. It was assailed by outsiders, undermined by cranks and freaks from within (I compiled a varied enemies' list, including Ralph Waldo Emerson and Woodrow Wilson).

Despite my dislike of interviews, I did a fair number, including one with Digby Balzell, the sociologist credited with coining the insect acronym WASP. He claimed he used it because it fitted on a chart. I made a chart of my own, a circular pattern of six WASP traits—conscience, industry, success, civic-mindedness, use, antisensuality—that I called a mantra (I should have said mandala; only one reviewer, in a French right-wing journal, caught the error). I wrote about religion, Wall Street, and the music of Charles Ives, in a medley of history, reporting, lament, and polemic.

My book redefined the term in its title. In common parlance, WASP was reserved for members of the nineteenth- and twentieth-century upper crust. I said it meant white British Protestants throughout American history. By this stroke I forfeited a world of social distinctions and analysis, from Edith Wharton down the social scale to Theodore Dreiser. But I isolated common mental and moral traits that you didn't have to be a wealthy celebrity intellectual, say, to possess, and that outsiders (Catholics, for example) could enjoy only by adoption. I gave pride of place to my family, and put William F. Buckley Jr. in his place. *The Way of the WASP* was my declaration of independence.

Meanwhile, I stayed at *National Review*. I had many reasons not to walk out on the whole crowd, beyond money. Politics was still my subject and my hobby. It kept generating new contests and new statistics, and I knew how to interpret them as well as (no worse than) other professionals, conservative or mainstream.

I cared about the results of the game. The conservative movement had been successful beyond its wildest imaginings, yet the Soviet empire still glowered in place. I took a second Moonie trip, this one to the Soviet Union. Bill had taken the staff of *National Review* there in 1975, to celebrate our twentieth anniversary, a trip I experienced only in in-house lore: Keith Mano and Dan Oliver had tormented the Soviet guide by insisting that a bearded worthy whose portrait hung on the wall of some palace was Trotsky. With the Moonies I went to Leningrad, Moscow, and Tbilisi, a typical Intourist package. There was evidence even then of cracks—Tbilisi had an almost normal number of cars on its streets: corruption? buying off ethnics?—but the cracks seemed hairline. The Soviet Union was grim, haggard, and unbudgeable. What it could not do it had almost stopped trying, but what it cared about—control and power—it did with obsessive concern.

I shared a room in Moscow with Larry Moffitt, the Moonie impresario of our trip. We were given one bar of soap, which shrank away as the days passed. On day three Larry stood in front of a large, old, nonworking radio that sat on a wall shelf and said, "Your country really sucks. We can't even get a bar of soap." Next morning two new bars appeared on the sink.

The Soviets took the trouble to seduce one of our party. Their bait was a young Russian woman at a hotel bar reading James Thurber. No one in America was reading James Thurber at that moment, but the Soviets correctly calculated that a man of a certain age would think him funny, and her beguiling. I never learned if the chit they had won by this means was ever called in.

Over these maneuvers the state sat like a stone. In Leningrad a group of us went to the Winter Palace at dusk. The empty square, the statues on the neoclassical roofline, the greenish sky made a tableau of implacability. "Kerensky, that jerk," said Arnold Beichman, an old socialist. "If only he'd shot a few people, millions would be alive now." Kerensky's unsolved problem was now our problem. I could not leave it; it would not leave me.

Bill would not leave me. He did not want me as an editor, but he still very much wanted me as a writer, and as a friend. I had rejected the flytrap of the guaranteed salary, but he employed other arts to keep me close. Some of his gestures, in light of what he had just done, were laughable, offensive. I got one of his cards about some early freelance piece of mine, which declared, "You're the tops!" Jeanne sang a little song, inspired by Cole Porter.

You're the tops! That is why I canned you!
You're the tops! That's why I can't stand you!

Bill varied his diet of small, persistent praise with the big gesture. We had planned a trip to India at the end of the summer that he sent his letter, and we went despite the blow to my wallet; India was cheap then. Coming back through London, I found myself burning with fever and shaking so hard I could not walk without help. I spent several days in the Hospital for Tropical Diseases, where I proved to have nothing serious, only a bug that vanished at the first touch of antibiotics. During my extended stay I had to call Frances to let *National Review* know that I would be missing an editorial conference. When we finally got home, we found a large crate, and in the crate was a Casio electric piano, with four settings: piano, electric piano, organ, and harpsichord. When I called Bill, who was of course responsible, to thank him, he overrode the thanks, which he always did, with a technical discussion: The tone of this electric was nearly as good as that produced by hammers and strings. I had told Bill once what a shame it was that I no longer had the use of a piano: My mother had her upright at home, pianos were as common as bird feeders at college, but New York apartments smaller than East Seventy-third Street were unfriendly environments. Bill was filling a hole in my life, expressing thanks that I had not had malaria, and showing his devotion the best way he knew.

The reason I had no piano, I have realized, is that I had moved on from making music; I had become a writer. I turn the Casio on once in a great while to walk cautiously through some simple piece; the rest of the time it sits, covered, a table for bills and catalogues. But it does what it did at the time: recall the giver.

I could not give Bill anything so expensive, nor could I give him the slip. I gave him my copy every other week, and gave him (indirectly, because I was giving it to whoever read my freelancing or bought my books) what I wrote elsewhere.

CHAPTER 9

WE ATTACH EXCESSIVE importance to presidential elections. In real families you don't get to pick your father, but in American politics we do; and if we pick the right one, surely all will be well?

There were big fields in both parties in 1988. The Democratic front-runner was Gary Hart, though his weirdness had already begun to leak out during the last cycle, long before the scandal that finally drove him from the race. As a young man he had changed his last name from Hartpence—an unexceptionable act, except that his explanations, when he was asked about it, were evasive and absurd. He said that he had followed his family, though he had pushed for the change; then, that Hart was the original form of the name, though the original form was in fact Pence. He seemed to be a man uncomfortable with everything about himself except his ambition. After he formally announced his candidacy, we changed our masthead at my suggestion for one issue, adding Pence to all our surnames. This produced some wonderful results—Ed Capanopence, Jason Ngpence, Erik von Kuehnelt-Leddihnpence. The only name we left alone was Jeffrey Hart.

On the Republican side Jack Kemp had been coming up for years. I had first heard him speak a decade earlier, when Bill bucked two tickets to a Connecticut GOP fund-raiser to me and Jeanne. This was her first Republican Party function; she was amused when the other diners at our table—all men—rose until she sat. She was bemused by the food. "For five hundred dollars," she murmured, "all we get is rubber chicken?" I shushed her, embarrassed. Then the donor on my other side said, aloud, "For five hundred dollars, all we get is rubber chicken?"

Kemp at the lectern, then and every time since, bounced through his texts, often taking wide detours as passing facts or arguments caught his attention. He was like a bright boy driving the family car: "Let's go see the Petrified Lizard Farm!" He gave the impression of boundless energy, physical and mental; he had a jock's bearing, even after he began to put on weight, joined to the enthusiasm of the self-taught. In college he majored in sports; his real education came from later reading. Knowledge, he believed, had transformed him, and the same knowledge could transform Republicans into a party of opportunity and prosperity.

An important aspect of the gospel of opportunity for Kemp was that it could reach out to black voters. Here his experience as a football player was decisive. You want to help people you know. As Newt Gingrich, one of Kemp's acolytes in Congress liked to put it, "Jack has showered with people that most Republicans never meet."

Kemp had something of Reagan's star power. Kemp could project his quarterback glamour in retail politics. Jack Beatty, one of my editors at the *Atlantic*, told me about a bad day in the life of a Democratic chum of his. Beatty's friend lived in Washington, next to a prominent Republican who one night held a big fund-raiser. When Kemp arrived, he alone of the celebrity guests chatted with the cops on duty outside. Oh, no, thought the Democrat, another Republican with the common touch.

Kemp offered himself as the movement's candidate, the heir apparent, third in the line of succession after Goldwater and Reagan. *National Review* liked him early on. Yet he found himself boxed in by other conservative challengers. Pat Robertson was a Pentecostalist televangelist, founder of the Christian Broadcasting Network. Conservatives had welcomed Jerry Falwell and the Moral Majority into the movement, but now Robertson announced that he wished to run it. When I went to his Virginia Beach headquarters in the summer of 1986 to interview him, he used a favorite line: Evangelicals were like the eight-hundred-pound gorilla—they would sit where they wanted to. He delivered this and other rim shots with the smile of a man who was above disagreement.

National Review agreed with most of Robertson's issue positions, and we defended his odd religious beliefs (praying Hurricane Gloria away from the Virginia coast). Many secular intellectuals believed in socialism, which did more damage than hurricanes.

What irked me about Robertson—and through my reporting, *National Review*—was his frivolity. He seemed to think of the presidency as an entry-level position. Robertson's supposed qualifications were so wispy that his campaign literature included among them his father's senatorial career and the fact that he was related to William Henry Harrison. Robertson rejected Darwin, but he evidently believed in Lamarck and the inheritance of acquired characteristics. Jesse Jackson had been the first man to run for president with no experience whatever, and he was running again on the Democratic side. I had dismissed him as an instance of liberals letting blacks get away with anything. But now we were letting another clerical rookie campaign for the job as if he deserved it. Worse, he finished second in the Iowa caucuses, behind Senator Bob Dole of neighboring Kansas—and ahead of Vice President Bush.

The man I'd written speeches for was urging conservatives to recognize that he, not Kemp, was the heir apparent in fact. The movement and its history, its purity and perks, were all very well, but someone had been at Reagan's right hand for eight years, running errands, obeying orders, absorbing his emanations. The appeal to seniority is a powerful one for Republicans, who typically defer to the next man in line (Democrats kill him—or her). Conservatives often make the Republicans' choice, however rebellious they may also be.

Bush had taken our position on abortion, for reasons that struck me as characteristic of the man: One of his grandchildren was adopted; if the birth parents had chosen to abort, the child would not exist. That is not a logical argument for life, but it was a very

Bushian one, hanging an issue on a personal tie. Bush also claimed to have changed his mind on taxes. In the 1980 cycle he had called Reagan's tax-cut plans "voodoo economics." In 1988, after finally winning the nomination—Dole faded, Robertson fizzled, and Kemp, for all his qualities, found himself ground between the gorilla and seniority—Bush made an audacious pledge: "Read my lips: no new taxes." His use of such a pop phrase—ideal for rock songs or movies, which in fact picked it up—should have alarmed us. Reagan might have said such a thing credibly; after all, he had come out of Hollywood. In Bush's mouth it had the tinniness of pandering.

Bush made his pledge at the Republican convention in New Orleans. Even pre-Katrina the city seemed ripe for destruction—steamy, seamy, run-down. There I caught up with Jude Wanniski. Kemp's loss should have grieved him, but he had bigger fish to fry. He was taken with Mikhail Gorbachev, whom he called by the loathsome journalists' nickname, "Gorby." "We have to get behind Gorby," he said. His self-regard, never small, had crossed a line. Jude's brush with Ronald Reagan had convinced him that his life would be a series of such intimacies. When they did not recur, he looked for other leaders to influence, each one further down the great chain of being. After Gorbachev would come the Communist Chinese, then Louis Farrakhan, then worse yet. Only his curiosity (trammeled by his self-made schema) and his sweetness reminded me of the Jude that had been. In New Orleans I also met P. J. O'Rourke, a recent convert to libertarianism from hell-raising (not a big step). When Bush pledged to give drug kingpins the death penalty, O'Rourke asked me, "Even if the drugs are good, and the prices fair?"

We joked, but things were grim. The disarray of Reagan's second term—Bitburg, Iran-Contra—suggested weariness and exhaustion. Maybe the country needed a change, and maybe the Democratic nominee, Michael Dukakis, who offered himself as a technocrat, could supply it. Dukakis opened his campaign with a seventeen-point lead.

Desperation in Bill's home state drove him to his last direct intervention in politics, which was also one of his most effective. Lowell Weicker had been a Connecticut senator since 1970. He was a liberal

Republican, gassy and vain. The Senate is not a school for modesty, but Weicker took pomposity to a new level. Bill loathed being represented by such a person. The last straw for him came when Weicker hectored a company that had found the wreck of the *Titanic* and proposed to salvage artifacts. Weicker likened it to grave robbing. The salvagers, looking for friends, took Bill down in a submarine; he saw nothing, but retrieved a blackened pencil, which he showed us at an editorial conference.

Bill decided that the only way to take Weicker down was to back his Democratic opponent. The Republicans had lost the Senate in 1986, so control of a house of Congress was not an issue. The Democrats nominated Joseph Lieberman, a former state senator and attorney general. He was a liberal, of course, though not so preening as Weicker. Bill also had a Yale connection to him, since Lieberman, like Bill, had been chairman of the *Yale Daily News*. Bill founded an organization, Buckleys for Lieberman. Pat and her cook, Julian, passed out bumper stickers in the parking lot of their local supermarket. The actual votes moved were perhaps few, but Bill's efforts made a nice little splash. Lieberman won, and never forgot the favor.

Bush won too, thanks to Dukakis running one of the worst campaigns in history, and thanks to the Willie Horton ad. The ad told viewers that Horton, a convicted murderer, had committed rape while out of prison on a work furlough program that Dukakis supported. Liberals doubled the ad's effectiveness by harping on it as an instance of Republican racism (Horton was black). But average voters, when they saw the ad, or when liberals reminded them of it, thought only of Horton and liberal softness on crime.

Reagan had been succeeded by a caretaker. We hoped, with muted doubts, for a third Reagan term.

THE ELECTION TO pick Bill's successor had one voter, and he made his choice in the fall of 1987. The next editor of *National Review* would be John O'Sullivan, an English journalist. He would serve an in-house training period until the thirty-fifth anniversary in 1990 when Bill, then age sixty-five, would step down.

John had worked on both sides of the Atlantic: He had been the parliamentary correspondent for the *Daily Telegraph*, a specialized English assignment that requires a droll edge (though straight-faced naturalism in England often produces droll results). He had been the editorial-page editor of Murdoch's *New York Post*, and he was friends with Conrad Black, a Canadian press lord lesser only by comparison with Murdoch. A magazine that favored amateurs and academics looked set for a jolt of professionalism.

Lack of principle is Britain's national vice, indulged by many Tories. There were exceptions, however. Margaret Thatcher was one. John was another. He was a Catholic, a nationalist, an anticommunist, and a follower of Milton Friedman (he would have long learned disputes with Larry Kudlow, whom he brought in as an economics editor, about the money supply). John was also deeply pro-American. He loved older American culture, from movies to *New Yorker* cartoons to the hybrid P. G. Wodehouse (who could be more British?—yet Wodehouse used baskets of American slang). John saw America as a force for good in the world, and in Europe, where it could serve as a counterweight to Continental command states. A nineteenth-century American journalist of almost the same name, John L. O'Sullivan, had coined the phrase *Manifest Destiny*, the slogan of American expansionism. Twentieth-century John appreciated the coincidence.

In person John was festive. When he took over the magazine, we would lose Bill's seigneurial manner, but we would gain a gregarious one. John was a dedicated diner-out. One of his friends told me that she once looked in his kitchen cupboard and found no dishes, but twenty-four champagne glasses. John boasted that he had persuaded London restaurants to stock the gizmo that allows recorking of champagne bottles, the better to serve single glasses.

John brought us a whole new store of anecdotes that he told with great verve. One starred Michael Oakeshott. A group of young Tories had invited the philosopher to address them. He gave a dense and mumbled lecture on civil association, the ad hoc organizational impulse that best holds society together. When he finished, the chairman of the meeting, an older politician who was shadow minister for transport, asked, "Could this civil association of yours build Concorde?" In the awkward silence, Frank Johnson, one of John's journalist friends, stage-whispered: *He's found the flaw.*

Professionally, John was tolerant. Midge Decter called him the most "irenic" person she knew. One of his favorite phrases was, "We don't want rows." He reached out to penumbral figures over the movement's borders—Murray Rothbard, the crackpot libertarian, comes to mind—and tried to draw them in, or at least make them less unfriendly. Though John was a Catholic, he ran a favorable story on the emerging Protestantism of Latin America, illustrated with a cartoon of Billy Graham in a poncho. I could not see Bill having run it. John was doughty in defense of his own ideas, but he did not have the imp of controversy for its own sake that made Bill amusing and dangerous.

John's flaw was a perverse relationship to time. My own attitudes toward punctuality were punitive; it took me many years to stop arriving for concerts a half hour early. For John, a half hour late was early, and later still was all right. He once told me that he had had one of the childhood diseases that kept him out of school for a half year or more. He spent his recovery reading, and looked back on this time as paradise lost. His fond memory of this unforced ease struck me as another aspect of his lateness; it was the great good place that schedules and deadlines sought to drive him from. He wrote rapidly and well, and he could speak at the drop of a hat, in the complete sentences, bright and well balanced, of educated Englishmen. But he never wanted the hat to drop if he could help it. As our editor, he could help it.

Bill Rusher retired as John came on the scene, on a farewell cruise on a rented yacht around Manhattan. He marked his departure with poetry, reciting Tennyson's "Ulysses." "Though much is taken, much abides . . ." Rusher's Happy Isles, Ulysses' destination in the poem, would be Nob Hill in San Francisco, from where he would call, particularly during heat waves or blizzards, with gravely mocking accounts of the weather on his coast. I lost an in-house friend, and we lost a link to political history, and to our own.

John had several debuts as the next editor—a lunch at Paone's for the directors, a party at the Union League Club for donors and other big-deal friends of the magazine. At that party I was seated in the back of the room. Bill took John from table to table, like a designer squiring a hot model. There but for the bad grace of Bill went me. I was angry, envious, and humiliated, the last even though my shame was a closely kept secret. I did not know if John was Bill's first choice to replace me. I would see speculation in the right-world press from time to time, but I paid no attention. I knew my own role, which was all that mattered. I did not know whether Bill had told John of my role in his fate; I didn't want to know that either. I hope I kept my coldness and disaffection to myself, but as I am a bad actor, I probably did not. I know I developed a bumptious habit of citing American arcana, holding forth about Old Hickory or the battle of Saratoga. The demands of freelancing provided a useful distraction from bilious thoughts. In time my reserve melted before the decency of John's nature, as it would have for all but the most bigoted.

John gave the magazine the shake-up it needed. Nonjournalists might not have registered the changes consciously, but they gave us necessary new life. Out went the columns. John would start from scratch on every page, intending to fill it with content. This committed him to an ongoing search for new talent, which he performed tirelessly, and with great success. Two of his new European writers would become foreign ministers of their respective countries—Antonio Martino (Italy) and Radek Sikorski (Poland). They gave us on-the-spot reporting.

A third European was an old *National Review* hand, put to new uses. Bill's skiing buddy Taki Theodoracopulos (he used only his first name professionally) had done some reporting for us. Taki was an incorrigible playboy. His wife once told mine that she knew no one who thought less of his virtues or more of his vices. One of Taki's virtues was his ability to write a certain kind of thing. He had a column in the *Spectator* of London, called "High Life," which re-counted the escapades of his most idle and worthless friends. It needed the lightest of touches, but he had it, and made this un-promising material interesting. John got Taki to do similar pieces for us.

In Roman Genn, a Russian émigré, John found a genius. Genn, who became our caricaturist, had begun drawing back in the Soviet Union, where his politics and his Jewishness got him into trouble. Genn loved the crooked timbers of the human face. Under his hand, Charles Schumer and Yasir Arafat sprouted tubers, phalluses, pros-thetic hooks for noses. His comment before every presidential elec-tion was, May the biggest nose win. His drawing was utterly without politeness. During one of the Asian political fund-raising scandals of the nineties, he dressed Al Gore and the Clintons in the pigtails and buckteeth of a cartoon imperial China. Chinese American groups raged, but Genn, as John put it, would not kowtow.

Genn met the flak with ethnic caricatures of all the *National Re-view* staff. Ed Capano, our publisher, sat in a tight, loud suit, a plate of spaghetti on one knee and a tommy gun on the other. I am lean-ing, huge-headed, in an old uniform with a sash and crosshatches, on a bust of George Washington, who squints as if I have not washed in two centuries. The original hangs over my desk.

John thought of holding annual contests to find young talent. He held only one, but it found Rich Lowry and Ramesh Ponnuru, who have been our mainstays ever since. Rich is now also a mainstay of Fox, Ramesh of *Time* and the *Washington Post*. Each has written the first of many books. Genn's rogues' gallery depicted Ramesh, born and raised in Kansas, as a smiling fakir sitting on a bed of nails. He had trouble doing Rich, who is just too normal for the grotesque arts.

Besides Larry, our new economist, John added two senior editors. One was Bill Bennett, an academic who had been discovered by Irv-ing Kristol. Bennett's elevation to the National Endowment for the Humanities during Reagan's first term had catalyzed a reaction. The paleoconservatives, as they called themselves, had wanted Mel

Bradford, a literary critic and Confederate historian, for the job. They thought Bennett had not paid his dues. Like many fights, it grew to be about principle, but had begun with cheese parings.

At a lectern Bennett was smart, colloquial, and forceful. His anthology, *The Book of Virtues*, became a surprise best-seller. John was so impressed with him that he hoped he might run for president one day. I remember one memo that floated around the office (not by John, to judge from the clumsy style), which argued that one benefit of a Bennett administration would be that, as an ex-president, he would command a larger audience. There was a thought: Give a man the football to increase his gate. The Bennett campaign never materialized.

Bennett contributed little to the magazine, but John's other senior editor, Peter Brimelow, played an important role. Born in England, Brimelow had worked for an array of magazines and newspapers in Canada and the United States. When John brought him in, he already had a day job writing for *Forbes*. Peter was strikingly handsome, with light-brown hair and piercing blue eyes. He was also one of the most polite journalists I have ever met (the profession pulls for bonhomie, not civility). He had attractive graces and countenance bright. His manner was at odds with his temperament (saturnine, hopeless) and his polemical style (unrelenting).

BILL CLOSED HIS last editorial section on the eve of the thirty-fifth-anniversary banquet. Once more the spread-out pages, the adding, the arranging. I would not see anything like it again. When Bill was done he handed his black Swiss calculator to Linda—his thanks for years of devoted work. The banquet itself was somewhat of an anti-climax—I knew the ropes and pulleys; this was show—but moving all the same. There was a show of slides presenting the *National Review* Authorized Version of the magazine's and the movement's history, narrated by Keith Mano. In the beginning was the word, then came the campaigns, then the victories. Afterward, Bill spoke, ending with thanks for the chance *National Review* had given him to do his job. It was heartfelt, and his voice broke.

I was moved—moved, and bitter. I endorsed every point in our slide show, and all the applause Bill was now getting. But precisely because I understood the value of what he had done, I felt the value of what I would not do. Bill had ascended, trailing clouds of glory, John was coming into his own glory, and I was a thirty-five-year-old middling writer and former heir apparent. Two dear friends, Kenneth and Harriet Wald, not subscribers, attended in solidarity with me (I had told them my own special story). Rich and Susan Vigilante were also there. Rich and I sat together during the slide show, and drank. When Joe McCarthy flashed on the screen—Bill had not airbrushed that episode of his past—Rich murmured to me, "You know, he died of a broken heart." This was an ancient conservative fairy tale; McCarthy had died of a broken liver. Dear Rich—the air-quote *mot juste*. It seemed hilarious.

OUTSIDE THE ROUND of our lives, the world was bursting. One of George Orwell's verses has a line, referring to 1940, year of the Blitz, "There was a time when empires crashed like houses." The time had come again.

In the summer of 1989 the Soviet empire in Eastern Europe simply ended. It lived so long as its rulers were willing to kill. Once they faltered, it was over. Only in Romania was the changeover marked by violence as Nicolae Ceauşescu and his wife were penned in a courtyard and shot. Ceauşescu had made himself a cold war diplomatic broker, passing on démarches from Nixon and Kissinger. But at home he was an ugly brute; it was hard to feel sorry for him. The Berlin Wall, the icon of imprisonment, was hammered to pieces. A few months later I attended a function at the German consulate in New York—no *West* or *East* modified the adjective any longer. The guests were given party favors of Lucite cubes, with little chunks of wall embedded in them. Unlike the Bastille keys that floated around Paris after July 1789, these did not promise to be unique. There had been plenty of wall to go around.

It seemed as if the tide would sweep all the way to China, where throngs of students occupied Tiananmen Square in Beijing. During this interval a young Washington writer named Francis Fukuyama published an essay for the *National Interest*, exciting and foolish, called "The End of History." Hegel had seen freedom as the destiny of mankind, Fukuyama wrote, and the day foretold was now at hand. Irving Kristol, the *National Interest*'s publisher, wrote drily that he welcomed Hegel to Washington, and hoped he would enjoy himself. But history would not go quietly. The Chinese Communists called in the army, as the Soviets and their satraps had failed to do, and the blood flowed. A friend of mine, Claudia Rosett of the *Wall Street Journal*, was in Tiananmen Square the night of the debacle. The story she filed was the bravest, noblest reporting I have ever seen. Idealists were murdered before her eyes, but she stuck to her post. As Whitman would have said, She was the woman, she saw the suffering, she was there.

At home, Reaganism ended in the fall of 1990 when President Bush decided that there would be new taxes after all. With the brusqueness of a traveler waving off a tout, he dismissed twelve years of conservative economic arguments. Some demon inspired him to call out to reporters while jogging, "Read my hips." Breaking promises was bad enough, but a politician who had such scant respect for his own words was not long for this world. I wrote a piece in *Time* warning he could only go down, an opinion all conservatives not actually in the administration, and many in it, shared.

Bush gained a momentary bounce from the greatest challenge of his life. It seems blasphemous to couple poll talk with war, and though everyone did it, they did it guiltily, for the situation was extraordinary. In August 1990 Saddam Hussein, dictator of Iraq, invaded and annexed Kuwait. The two countries had been feuding over an oil field, and Saddam felt strong enough to eliminate the competition. Kuwait had the slightly bogus quality of most Middle Eastern countries. It was not China, or France, or even Egypt, a place inhabited by a people. Yet the ruling family had been in some sort of power there for two centuries; they were internationally recognized; they were filthy rich. For Saddam simply to swallow them was astonishing. Perhaps he would move on to Saudi Arabia.

Anxious and earnest, drained and strained, George H. W. Bush showed himself at his best. The WASP virtues I had catalogued came to his aid. James Baker, back like the bad penny as secretary of state, assembled a vast coalition of allies. Meanwhile, Bush told Dick Cheney, his secretary of defense, and Colin Powell, his chairman of the Joint Chiefs, to prepare to force the Iraqis out if diplomacy failed. The military had never fought on the North German plain, the projected Armageddon of World War III. Now they were to move their whole show to the Persian Gulf.

The war, if it happened, would be post–cold war. There had already been wars during but outside the cold war, notably the 1982 Falklands War between Britain and Argentina. A few conservatives had counseled neutrality in that conflict, including Pat Buchanan. At the time, it seemed like Irish Anglophobia. *National Review* did not share it. We had supported a feisty Britain, going back to the Suez crisis, and we celebrated Britain's victory now by slapping a yellow smiley face on our cover.

The antiwarriors included Joe. For him, the fall of the Berlin Wall heralded the libertarian end of history. Joe accepted the military-industrial complex as a means of fighting communism. But now that communism was (partly) gone, he decided that it was time to dismantle it. He joined the antiwar libertarians who had been complaining about American power for years.

The Jewish question was also involved in Joe's new pacifism. He had warned that Israel's supporters would seek to involve us in Middle Eastern wars. Israel was not the casus belli here, yet here we now were, about to plunge into a Middle Eastern war.

One of the preliminary functions for the thirty-fifth-anniversary banquet was a panel discussion among the magazine's editors, held for an audience of donors at the Union League Club. There Bill let Joe say his antiwar piece. Joe sat sadly, a small picture of a granddaughter on the table before him to give him courage. It was a brave moment for him. He was bucking his mentor, his colleagues, and most of his readers. He was not concerned, he told one questioner, with America's power; he was most concerned for its liberty. Noble words—noble, and as foolish, in their opposite way, as Fukuyama's. One said history was going our way, the other that the demands of history and politics were distractions from our own holiness. Joe's ideal world was a cloister surrounded by gangsters. The brave are not always wise or good.

Desert Shield, the buildup phase, turned into Desert Storm in mid-January 1991. I was supposed to have dinner with Terry Teachout the night the shooting started; instead, we joined millions of other Americans, and glued ourselves to CNN. The Gulf War was a real-time spectacle of late-twentieth-century high-tech craft versus third world totalitarian ineptitude.

And then it stopped. The UN resolutions, the hordes of allies, the caution of the military, and the instincts of diplomats united to push Saddam out of Kuwait, and then leave him be. Perhaps his rebellious subjects would finish him off. Prowar conservatives waited to see if that would happen. It didn't; Iraqis rebelled, and were crushed. In a speech to Congress after the war ended, Bush spoke of "the very real prospect of a new world order." Journalist Pete Hamill, writing about some slaughter of Kurds and Shiites, detected a "new world odor" instead.

IN 1991 JEANNE and I took our summer vacation in Egypt. August by tradition is shrinks' month off, and Jeanne upheld the custom. So I was in a hotel in Cairo, sleek and anonymous, when I saw the headline on a morning copy of the *International Herald Tribune*: COMMUNISM'S COLLAPSE.

Gorbachev had been in trouble as we took off from New York. He had sought to energize the Soviet system by injecting it with a dose of modernity and freedom. It had worked before: Lenin's New Economic Policy of 1921 showed the pragmatic lengths to which even one of history's monsters was willing to go. But the challenges the Soviets faced from a revived America could not be surmounted by tinkering, while even half measures alarmed party diehards. In mid-August, a gaggle of hard-liners seized the state while Gorbachev was vacationing in the Crimea. They were disobeyed by Boris

Yeltsin, a rogue Communist and self-proclaimed reformer. The Chinese had called in the army, but the Soviet army and secret police were of several minds. Yeltsin clambered atop a tank to bid the old-style Communists defiance, giving the world an image and himself a reputation. The hard-liners collapsed; Gorbachev returned to Moscow, but events had passed him by. An unwilling John the Baptist, he was shunted aside.

Jeanne and I came back to New York in time for me to write about it. John was out of town, so Bill ran the editorial conference.

Jeff wrote a thoughtful editorial about communism's origins in the "tropical growth" of nineteenth-century revolutionary impulses—"anarchism, socialism, free love . . . eccentric communities of all sorts." Even as communism surpassed and regimented many of these, its fall would leave them loose in the world. My contribution noted the technological sophistication of the rebels, who kept the whole world watching with faxes and telephones. But I was most impressed with the rebels themselves, the people who rallied with Yeltsin and the soldiers who refused to shoot them. For years, I wrote, Russians had borne the onus of a people who did not deserve freedom because they did not desire it. Their autocratic past guaranteed their communist future. August 1991 showed that Russians, like people everywhere, were capable of choosing good as well as ill.

Bill wrote a long "Notes & Asides," elated and sober at the same time, titled simply "We Won." He called the roll of the heroes of the crisis, both onstage (Yeltsin) and off (Reagan, the American who had pushed the Soviets hard, and Solzhenitsyn, the Russian who had pushed them hardest). He wrote with pride of colleagues who had "labored in this heady vineyard of anti-Communism": Burnham, Chambers, Frank Meyer. As an editor, Bill was best at conclusions; his red pen went to last grafs, most often to punch them up, sometimes to draw them deeper. His last graf now tolled like a bell. "And on bended knee, we give thanks to Providence for the transfiguration of Russia, thanks from those of us who lived to see it, and thanks to those, departed, who helped us to understand why it was right to struggle to sustain the cause of Western civilization."

In *National Review*'s statement of principles, in the first issue, Bill said the magazine would "stand athwart history, yelling stop." It did more; Whittaker Chambers reminded him that to live is to maneuver, a lesson Bill never forgot and often quoted. History, yelling, and maneuvering would all go on, but Soviet communism had stopped. Never take the victory from those who won it, including Bill and his table of cranky writers.

Sometime later I got a letter from Ojars Kalnins, my Baltic correspondent. He was now Latvia's ambassador to the United States.

CHAPTER 10

WHY WERE CONSERVATIVES sick of George H.W. Bush as his re-election approached? We pointed to specific mistakes, from raising taxes to his tied tongue, but we also judged him by the unforgiving standard of nostalgia, comparing him with the man he had replaced. Because Reagan was family, we forgave him many sideslips. Bush had come in as the executor of the estate, and no one forgives an executor even if he bungles only a few bequests.

John and I made a trip to Washington to urge Jack Kemp to revolt. Bush had made Kemp his secretary of housing and urban development. There could hardly be a less promising place for a conservative politician to spend his time. HUD was a Nixon-era creation, a gall on the tree of the Constitution. Yet Kemp's sense of mission to reach out to blacks made him eager to take the assignment. Kemp was in top form as we met—talking with the rush of a subway, noting my necktie ("That's the ugliest tie I've ever seen"), showing us his latest reading—a passage in Solzhenitsyn describing the czarist reformer Stolypin. Before he was assassinated, Stolypin had proposed giving land to peasants, to give them a stake in the country (the emancipation of the serfs had left the land they worked tied up in village communes). Privatizing housing projects, Kemp explained, could have the same effect on the urban poor now.

Kemp was eager, engaged—and unwilling to take the leap. Reagan had challenged a sitting president; Kemp wanted to keep sitting.

Talk slid from raising a standard to which the wise and good could repair to intra-administration intrigues: stuff more suited to *The McLaughlin Group* or the Yale Political Union. It is easy to sympathize with Kemp in retrospect: We must have struck him as spectators in the Colosseum, eager for blood—someone else's. He had just been in the arena himself, getting clubbed, only a few years earlier. The position of heir apparent is a demanding one, as I had discovered. It's not enough to be liked by everybody, or even only the people who count. You have to work for that glittering next job. We left without a leader.

The leader who appeared was not to our liking. Pat Buchanan had served in all the slots of a Beltway wordsmith: columnist, TV pundit, White House speechwriter. His style was bright and hard as his neatly parted hair: The speakers on the rostrum at one convention of the National Organization for Women reminded him, he wrote, of the bar scene in *Star Wars*. Colleagues and employees all liked him, which came in handy when he was being hammered for his opinions. How could he be the devil if Michael Kinsley, liberalism's canary, stuck up for him? As 1992 approached Buchanan decided he was ripe for a promotion; he would rather give presidential speeches than write them.

I went to New Hampshire to watch him announce his candidacy. On the campaign bus he mentioned that he had liked *The Way of the WASP*. He is the only presidential candidate who professed to have read one of my books, and I believed that he had. I asked him how, as an old Nixon hand, he could with consistency lead an insurgency now. (*National Review* backed John Ashbrook in 1972; Buchanan hadn't.) He easily batted the question aside: George H. W. Bush had driven him to rebellion; he was not fragmenting his party—Bush's lackadaisical performance had.

Buchanan was not simply rallying right-world. He was trying to shape it. On foreign policy he agreed with Joe: The cold war was over; make war no more. Buchanan had opposed the Gulf War until the moment the guns went off. He abandoned the free market when it came to trade, hoping to rig domestic prosperity (or at least the prosperity of established companies) by trade barriers. We disagreed on both counts. John was an activist nationalist, a believer in the English-speaking-man's burden, and a free trader. America and its natural allies had a responsibility to project their influence and, when necessary, their power, to ensure that as much of the world as possible was free and prosperous.

One of Buchanan's issues became one of ours. In the spring of 1992 we would publish an immense article by Peter Brimelow, "Time to Rethink Immigration?" The question mark was rhetorical. Peter had rethought it from a half-dozen angles, and argued, with a combination of zeal and detail, that unrestricted immigration had to be cut back. America's immigration laws had been relaxed greatly in 1965; even so, they were regularly flouted. The result had been an almost thirty-year tide of immigration, legal and illegal. (Reagan had signed an amnesty for illegal immigrants in 1986, which was supposed to clear up the problem, though it had not.)

The libertarian equated immigrants with foreign goods. A Malaysian and a Malaysian shirt were essentially the same thing—let both in so long as there was a demand. My own views were libertarian/assimilationist. I had written about the travails of immigrants fitting into American life, but the mighty paradigm of the WASP had transformed them and, I assumed, always would. Living in New York reinforced this view. The city had become noticeably more Asian and Latin American in only ten years—you did not assume, as you would have in the era of *West Side Story*, that every Hispanic was Puerto Rican—yet immigrants seemed to spare us from the depopulation on view in other cities (I was deeply impressed by my first visit to Detroit: parking lots everywhere).

Proimmigration sentiment had another source that, since I felt it, I assume motivated others: racism. Jack Kemp's mission to the blacks was morally admirable, but if they would not get with the capitalist program, we could import other minorities who would—bespectacled Asians, sturdy Mexicans.

John and Peter tirelessly pushed the new line, which brought me around; the fact that John was my boss no doubt brought me faster.

On my own I came to see that my understanding of the history of American immigration, though it was more detailed than either John's or Peter's, had ignored the element of time. The Brookhisers, Capanos, and Ngs had become Americans, but their ancestors had arrived in discrete clumps. Various factors—distance, wars, laws— had inserted pauses into the centuries-long inflow of immigrants. But that flow had now been continuous for decades with no end in sight. Time for the boa constrictor to digest the pig.

National Review laid one great bomb in the path of the Buchanan campaign, set by Bill: an essay in the last issue of 1991, titled "In Search of Anti-Semitism." Bill examined several case studies. One was novelist Gore Vidal. Bill and Vidal had an ugly run-in when they were doing political commentary for the 1968 conventions. I had missed it then—I was not yet an *NR* reader, and they were, after all, on ABC— but I had read the account Bill had written for *Esquire*, and the two fight on in the eternal present of YouTube. Clearly, they hate each other, though they process rage differently: Vidal looks like he swallowed a bad oyster; Bill grinds his jaw in fury. Bill did not revisit any of that in his article, but dissected an anti-Zionist jeremiad (Vidal should excuse the expression) that Vidal had written for the *Nation*; Bill found it "genuinely and intentionally and derisively anti-Semitic."

Bill also examined Buchanan. Buchanan's opposition to the Gulf War had other targets. Who supported the war, he had asked in one column, and came up with four names: Abe Rosenthal, Richard Perle, Charles Krauthammer, and Henry Kissinger. Who would fight it?—"kids with names like McAllister, Murphy, Gonzales, and Leroy Brown." "There is no way to read that sentence," Bill commented, "without concluding that Pat Buchanan was suggesting that American Jews manage to avoid personal military exposure even while advancing military policies they (uniquely?) engender." Buchanan's media colleagues hadn't called him on such stuff because they were pals; Jewish journalists didn't want to bring it up for fear of seeming touchy; when the Anti-Defamation League brought it up they were ignored because they brought everything up. Bill put the issue on the table.

He also began the long good-bye to Joe, who was yet another of his case studies. Joe writhed at being held up for examination like a cadaver in an anatomy class. We let him have a response in the magazine, but then the scab got repicked when Bill brought his original essay and all the reactions—there were many more besides Joe's—together in a book in 1993.

Joe finally struck back in *The Wanderer*, an old Catholic newspaper that ran him as a columnist. He wrote with the knowledge that love gives to hate. He imagined that Bill was bullied and terrorized by Jews—the "Zionist apparat" of New York, the elders of Gotham. But he was acute about aspects of Bill's personality. Bill, he thought, rejected Jew bashing because it was déclassé, and he cared above all for maintaining "*la bella figura.*" Joe reached back to Gore Vidal, saying that the 1968 fight distressed Bill so because it had shown him in an uncool light. Joe's conclusion was preposterous, but his premise was true enough: Bill cared about appearances, and had been caring about them since he used them to insert himself into the national conversation forty years earlier. Joe finished by accusing Bill of nitpicking: "Anti-Semitism just isn't a serious problem in America." Time would tell about that.

Bill sent a clumsy riposte to *The Wanderer*, speculating that Joe's problem was "perhaps medical." That was a low blow, and irrelevant. Joe's problem was moral. He indulged a vice, did not want to be criticized or punished, and grabbed any weapon that came to hand to defend himself. John fired him, in sorrow as well as anger.

Bill wrote clumsily because Joe's fall was personal. Joe was his discovery, his protégé, his failure. But another reason for Bill's clumsiness was that his style was going slack. The collage techniques that had been so crisp in *Up from Liberalism* were now diffuse and unfocused. Bill let everyone have his say in "In Search of Anti-Semitism," both an article and a book, and the result was a duffel bag stuffed with odds and ends. As life span lengthens, we imagine that productivity will keep pace, and enough writers march on into their golden years—Saul Bellow writing *Ravelstein.* in his mideighties, Jacques Barzun finishing *From Dawn to Decadence* in his early nineties—to sustain the illusion. But everyone ages at his own pace. In his late sixties, Bill's prose had cooled. He had to keep it marching, since his retirement was as active as the careers of three normal people, between *Firing Line*, his columns, and his books. And he still presided over *National Review*, even though John edited it.

BUCHANAN'S FIRST PRESIDENTIAL race—he would make two more—was one more episode in the revolt of the amateurs. During one of his New Hampshire press conferences, he said that he was giving up "three chairs" on national talk shows to make his run, as if America should be honored by his sacrifice. He could have sat in ten chairs and written speeches for all forty-one presidents, but he had never sponsored a bill, made a deal, broken his word, or sent men to their deaths. His only arena had been the soundstage, yet he felt ready for the Oval Office. One more reason for Bill, who had drawn the correct conclusion from his own inexperience, to resent him.

Jeff chaired Buchanan's campaign in New Hampshire, as a way of tormenting Bush. Jeff was brusque with presidents he disliked—he had called for both Carter and Reagan (in his second term) to resign—and the years had not made him more patient. Bush won a Pyrrhic victory in the New Hampshire primary—an incumbent should have done better.

———

MY COVERAGE OF the campaign was interrupted in the spring by cancer. The passage, from first puzzled visit to the internist to the operating room, was so swift that it would have been comic under other circumstances. Rapid transit meant less time to worry. I thought of death, when I thought of it, as running into a black wall.

The cancer I had—testicular—is stopped in a very high proportion of cases. Its treatment is well understood—no experimental procedures or agonizing debates among specialists. I would have to spend five days in the hospital, once a month for four months, receiving chemotherapy.

I decided never to use the word *chemo*, which sounds like a dog name: *Hey, Chemo! Good boy!* These chemicals were saving my life; a little respect was in order. Since my hair was bound to fall out, I shaved it off, then drew attention to the loss with headbands—bandannas I picked up at street fairs, or hems taken off old kimonos that my wife had bought. I noticed that I alarmed cabbies and impressed panhandlers, both giving me a wide berth. Several of my women friends thought the bald thing was hot. When my hair grew back, it came in all gray—I would never have to pine over the changing colors of age.

Three weeks a month I lived a normal life. I went to work, and I started working out at the gym (take care of that body before it's gone). I used my cancer to get an interview with President Bush. The *New York Times Magazine* asked me to do a piece, figuring I could get access, yet I encountered only stone walls from the White House press office. I then called Vic Gold, whom I knew from my speech-writing days, asking for help, and mentioning that I would have to schedule any potential interview around my chemotherapy. Fifteen minutes later, he called back to say that the president had approved the interview. The *Times* ended up turning the piece down, on the grounds that Bush hadn't said anything interesting, as if they were expecting Oscar Wilde; the *Atlantic* took it instead.

I could not find the time, however, to follow Ross Perot, the billionaire data processor who decided to run for president as an independent. To me he seemed like an angry old toddler, yet almost 20 percent of my countrymen would vote for him, so he must have projected something more. What that was had to be seen on the hoof, in him and in the reactions of his audiences; I simply cannot get from TV and speech transcripts the information I need to make a judgment, so I missed the most considerable third-party candidate since George Wallace. I did get a glimpse of Governor Bill Clinton, my first since his convention speech twelve years earlier. His speeches had gotten worse, empty and shapeless, yet nobody was better one-on-one. When he worked a subway in the D.C. suburbs, he spent up to a minute—an eternity in such situations—with a single commuter as others swarmed past. Why did he let so many go? Because he wanted to make the sale to the one he had. He did equally well in tough spots. I watched him in a Baltimore bar shaking hands around a pool table, until he came face-to-face with a ponytailed man who kept a grip on his cue. "Name's John," said John. "I'm a Vietnam vet." Clinton was still smarting from the revelation of his Vietnam-era maneuvers with his local draft board to avoid serving. John clearly hadn't liked them. Clinton did as well as he possibly could, holding eye contact, not risking a refused handshake, then moving on. He rode these skills to the Democratic nomination.

But as each three-week interval of normality ended, I would pack a bag and wait for the hospital to call me. When the phone rang with notice of an available bed, it was like the underground contacting a fugitive, yet I was being smuggled into enemy territory, not out of it. Jeanne and I would go to the hospital, one of the string that lines FDR Drive, to check in. STUDIO, RVR VUES, NO KITCH, $400/DAY. In hospital land my taste in music contracted. All I could listen to were the Goldberg Variations and Louis Armstrong. Bach said everything is in its place; Armstrong said the sun comes shining through.

I could read only the angry: John Callahan, the quadriplegic cartoonist; Samuel Johnson's review of an upbeat theodicy, "A Free Enquiry into the Nature and Origin of Evil" (he didn't like the enquiry, he didn't like evil, and he had his quarrels with nature). Words speak to one ear, music to another.

I hankered for company, which my friends kindly provided. The visitor who surprised me most was Taki, whom I barely knew. Yet he came one afternoon, in a polo shirt and chinos, and chatted pleasantly for an hour. He asked if I would like a hooker. It was his version of a corporal work of mercy.

All the chemicals that are used in chemotherapy are poisons, hence the nausea that is a common side effect. Science keeps developing better drugs to deal with nausea, and my first hospital stay was free of it. Yet the effects of chemotherapy accumulate over time, and I turned for additional help to marijuana.

When I entered college, the freak phase of the cultural revolution had ended. The midseventies were Thermidor, or perhaps the First

Empire—meaning that the revolution had been consolidated and institutionalized. My singing group had a dopemeister, an actual position like the pitch pipe or business manager. A couple members of the Party of the Right had done time for kitchen-table drug making. I smoked pot maybe ten times. I didn't particularly like or dislike it; it made me logy as often as it made music interesting, so I let it go. I disliked potheads: It is a trial to be around people who are so easily amused.

I was not inclined to support prohibition, however, in part because of my knowledge of the first go-round. My reading for *The Way of the WASP* had included *In His Steps*, an earnest novel of the early twentieth century, a time when Protestant orthodoxy and social uplift still shook hands. The story begins when the inhabitants of a midwestern town decide not to do anything in their daily lives without first asking, What would Jesus do? (This is the source of the expression.) There is a temperance subplot, which ends with a confrontation outside a saloon; how long, O Lord, the characters ask themselves, will this evil be suffered? They had their answer very soon with the Eighteenth Amendment. The supporters of alcohol prohibition were not killjoys or bigots; like antidrug warriors today, they were grappling with a real evil; alcohol was, and remains, the most dangerous drug in America. But their strategy did not work in that drug war, even as it has failed today.

Once I let it be known that I needed pot, everyone became a dealer. Thousands at my bidding sped, and posted o'er land and ocean without rest. My wife (who had smoked even less than I had) rolled joints with her trainer. I could easily tell theirs apart: Hers drew like chair legs, his like flamethrowers.

Marijuana affected my performance at *National Review* only once. One of our editorial conferences occurred a day after I came home from the hospital, a penumbra of time in which I was still warding off the heaves. The topic before us that morning was the Republican vice presidential nomination. President Bush was floundering badly, and some panicmonger had suggested that he replace Vice President Dan Quayle on his ticket as a way of reviving his fortunes. (Quayle had gotten off to a bad start four years earlier, and never quite shaken the impression that he was a boob.) I thought dumping him was an insane suggestion: The only thing worse than desperation is to seem desperate. I was in that stage of druggedness, however, in which the stoner is content to let the world pass by. I did not stick up for Quayle, and my colleagues unwisely—and vainly—called for his dismissal.

From that time on I developed a new sideline: poster boy for medical marijuana. My conservatism was an irresistible fillip, and I appeared often in the *New York Times* and the *Washington Post* as a prodrug advocate. (Ramesh Ponnuru has written wittily about the Homeric epithets that such outlets use for fence jumpers: "Devout Catholic" signals an abortion supporter, "lifelong Republican" a backer of whomever the Democrats are running for president.) Of course I was being used, but that was fine with me; I used the media in turn to make my point, which I believe is a conservative one: How does it encourage liberty for the state to come between doctors and patients? How does capricious enforcement strengthen the laws?

My independence was easy because the trail had been blazed by Bill. Bill had been calling for the decriminalization of marijuana for years, for a variety of reasons: Enforcement was futile, and the drug is less bad than other illegal ones. A few years after my cancer he took a more radical step, publishing a symposium in *National Review* titled "The Drug War Is Lost." He brought together an eclectic group, including a Democratic former mayor of Baltimore, Kurt Shmoke, and a hard-core libertarian, Thomas Szasz. This anthology worked as a polemic because each contribution was substantial, everyone sang from the same hymnal, and Bill supplied not running commentary but a compact introduction.

Supporters of the drug war sometimes tried to dismiss Bill's stand as an elitist indulgence, as if he were some gambling, whoring Whig aristocrat defending license in the name of liberty. I remember the host of one radio show I went on telling me, in an imitation of Bill's accent, that we just wanted to toke up (I hung up on him). Bill encouraged such sniping when he wrote that he had smoked a joint on his sailboat, beyond the territorial limit.

The notion of Bill-the-druggie was a fantasy, class envy fueled by his persona. Bill had alcoholic siblings, and he drank a lot, but he was no alcoholic (I have seen enough drunks, including one whose drinking killed him, to know the signs). The only drug Bill abused was the stimulant Ritalin, which he seemed to think of as a kind of No-Doz. Early in my time at the magazine, I mentioned that I was run-down from some bug. Would you like Ritalin? Bill asked. When I mentioned it to Jeanne (an MD's daughter, who keeps a *Physician's Desk Reference* and a *Merck Manual* on her shelf), she was appalled.

Bill's advocacy changed no minds. Legal medical marijuana could happen one day—it keeps winning referenda at the state level—but the baby boomers, who were supposed to change everything, have been in power for years, and drug policy has not moved an inch. Although Bill could tweak for the sake of tweaking, his position on drugs was not impudence but the result of decades of reflection: an example of his freedom of mind, and his willingness to follow his own conclusions.

It also embroiled him with my parents. I had written about my chemotherapy, my marijuana use, and the drug laws in my column in the *New York Observer*, and Bill had built a syndicated column of his own around my piece. (He had quoted me before, but now he was quoting me as a peer.)

After my last, weariest, stay in the hospital—my veins felt as if they had been flattened by tiny metal steamrollers—I came home to a letter from Bill. My parents had written him, berating him for proclaiming my drug use to the world. My parents were not whoring, gambling Whig aristocrats; my mother was a teetotaler, my father might have a beer while he watched a Yankees game on television. To them illegal drugs were one-third of the anti-Trinity of the sixties (acid, amnesty, and abortion). Cancer, barfing, every defining circumstance went out the window; they saw my pot use as a reflection on themselves, and blamed Bill for shaming them. They told him that their letter was confidential, and he did the right thing: write them a respectful brush-off, and send the whole correspondence on to me.

I have no copy of this mess, only my memories and a page in my diary; I must have been too angry with my parents to keep anything.

Their reaction was crazy, not wicked. Their default attitude toward doctors and disease was suspicion and denial; the possibility of losing a son put them over the edge. Scolding Bill for revealing my pot use made the situation more manageable: From him, they might get a response. Cancer answers no letters.

What was my own role in setting up this explosion? If I had told them all along what the world was like, and how I behaved in it, would they have been so shocked? Through a combination of good sense, sloth, and cowardice, I hadn't. So I scraped along, until I hit a rock. If I had been more honest—I would have hit some other rock.

Bill was the silver lining. He had handled their eruption with tact and loyalty. He had feet of flesh, as well as clay.

Being a good parent is such unsteady work. There is a biological basis—nine months for a woman, a moment for a man—then everything else is up for grabs, as in a game of capture the flag. Being a good son—any son, not just an heir apparent—is equally demanding.

———

THE GRIM CAMPAIGN wound to its end. Perot became the latest hero of Jude Wanniski, whom I interviewed for a piece on conservative reactions to the election; Jude assured me that he would win in a landslide, unless the upper classes of the world, fearful of his reforms, had him assassinated. Perot beat them to it, getting out of the race, then jumping back in, showing himself to be mad as well as unsuitable.

Walking through an autumn street fair, I greeted a table of beleaguered Manhattan Republicans who slapped a Bush-Quayle sticker on my motorcycle jacket. I left it there as a Rorschach. A clerk in Bloomingdale's laughed at the witty juxtaposition—hip gear, hick politics—until he realized I meant the politics. Another clerk confided that he had asked the souls in Purgatory to pray for a Bush victory. They must have been busy. Bill Clinton took 43 percent of the popular vote, but in a three-man race that was a landslide.

The sense of elation and relief among my fellow Manhattanites the morning after Clinton won was palpable. They acted as if they had been freed from communism. I love New Yorkers, but sometimes living here is like living in a zoo. I wish I could say, with Nietzsche and Arnold, that what does not destroy me makes me stronger; life in the liberal omphalos has made me quieter and more observant. I was grounded, as I so often am, by Jeanne. She had of course voted for Clinton (she is a single-issue, proabortion, voter), but she had never liked or trusted him.

The tone of the Clinton years that lay ahead was revealed very soon. *The American Spectator* held its twenty-fifth-anniversary banquet at the Capitol Hilton in Washington a month after the election. I had been writing for the magazine since it was called *The Alternative*. Bob Tyrrell was good company whenever he visited New York. He boasted, truly, that he was the first conservative to reach out to the unhappy liberals who later became neoconservatives (the issue of *The Alternative* in which my first piece appeared had a drawing of Daniel Patrick Moynihan on the cover). His signature column in the magazine, "The Continuing Crisis," is a masterpiece of timing: a recap of news items, world historical and freak show, strung together at slapstick pace—Henry Kissinger and Jackass put in a blender. The AOL start-up menu achieves a similar effect unwittingly. Bob knows what he is doing, and has been putting his grace notes together just so for forty years. I mostly reviewed books for them, or contributed to their "Saloon" series, working with Wlady Pleszczynski.

They had moved from Bloomington, Indiana, where they were founded, to D.C. in 1985. My opinion of Washington having been set by then, I thought this was a mistake. They were on the verge of another. As Bob greeted his guests in the receiving line, he pointed to a novelty-shop decoration pinned to the breast of his dinner jacket, explaining that he had earned it in the Arkansas National Guard. He gave a thoughtful speech, quoting Yeats's "Old Stone Cross," a gloomy song about politicians, journalists, and the futility of voting. But his remarks were addressed to the new president, whom he called "William Jefferson Clinton," with the odd formality of the Soviet-era *Pravda* (cf. James Carter). P. J. O'Rourke, the master of ceremonies, said that while Clinton might be bad for the country, he was "meat on our table."

National Review believed in smacking the enemy; it was mother's milk. Two weeks after Lyndon Johnson had taken the oath of office, we announced in the lead graf of the editorial section that our patience with him was exhausted. But as best as I could recall, we had not directed so much firepower at enemies during our own parties, on our own turf.

Equally revealing was what happened to the liberal journalist Sidney Blumenthal. I had reviewed his book about the 1988 election, *Pledging Allegiance: The Last Campaign of the Cold War*. Blumenthal was a sharp, sparkling stylist, with a flair for the epigram. Conservatives "loved [Nixon] for his enemies, and he loved to throw them against his enemies." Bull's-eye. But then Clinton became president, Blumenthal became the political correspondent for *The New Yorker*, and everything went to hell. The style became high, soft, bogus. I accused him, in the *Observer*, of writing the worst sentence in *New Yorker* history. This was it: "Just after noon on December 16, I was ushered into the Oval Office and guided by President Clinton to a gold-upholstered armchair in front of an unlit fireplace and facing the windows and the oak desk, made from the timbers of the *H.M.S. Resolute*, that had been used by President Kennedy."

What irked me about the sentence, apart from the funeral director's diction (ushered, guided) and the meaningless detail (the timbers of the desk) was its tone of choked-throat seriousness. Blumenthal was meeting History. What does it matter if a pundit loves a pol, or if a hack becomes a flack? Half the journalists in the world have written speeches, and all of us have our favorites. But Blumenthal was putting his name to drizzle that would be tolerated only in children's books, and that should not be excused there. The wizard in *The Firebird* keeps his soul in an egg. Writers keep their souls, or great parts of them, in their words. If they throw the words away, they destroy themselves. And what, after that sacrifice, would he and other Clintonites be willing to do for their leader?

Auden called the thirties low and dishonest. The nineties looked to be high-pitched and frantic.

CHAPTER 11

LIVING IN NEW York brought one face-to-face with New York's problems, and with certain problems of the conservative movement.

Bonfire of the Vanities, Tom Wolfe's first and best novel, came out in 1987. New Yorkers stared in fascination at Wolfe's grim portrait; believe me, things were worse. Ed Koch's years as mayor, beginning in 1977, had kept us entertained, and saw the city's finances stabilize. But the quality of life that New Yorkers led only deteriorated. Public amenities became unusable. In my neighborhood, Union Square was taken over by drug dealers, Stuyvesant Square by homosexual prostitutes, and Tompkins Square by bums who filled it with their tents and their cacophonous drumming. The city saw more than two thousand murders a year. New York's politicians and commentators called for a lot of money (the liberal solution) or Draco (the conservative solution). Since neither would be forthcoming, the city's problems seemed hopeless. David Dinkins, the city's first black mayor, who succeeded Koch in 1989, was free of the ugly racial politics of Al Sharpton, a young clerical hustler, and figures yet worse. But he did not know how to handle them, or any crisis that occurred. When a car in the entourage of the Lubavitcher rebbe struck and killed a black boy in 1991, the Crown Heights neighborhood of Brooklyn erupted in a three-day riot. I went to Crown Heights to write about the Lubavitchers, at the behest of David Klinghoffer, who was now our book editor. They had made a world of eighteenth-century mores and modern PR savvy: During Jewish holidays, they sent Mitzvah Mobiles to the streets of Manhattan, urging Jews to do good deeds. All their savvy was helpless in the riot; a young Lubavitcher man was set upon and killed. "Kill the Jew," his assailants cried, lest anyone miss the point. A pogrom, in the capital of the "Zionist apparat." Dinkins wrung his hands.

The Conservative Party had little more to offer than Mayor Dinkins. It had tied its fortunes to Al D'Amato, Republican senator since 1980. John had turned the editorial lunches at Paone's into forums for visiting bigwigs—Peter Jennings, Dick Armey—and D'Amato joined us at least once. A gross being, he could be funny. Talking about a Senate GOP effort to reform Social Security that he judged suicidal, he rasped, "Don't ask me to give blood if the patient's gonna *die*." D'Amato controlled both the Republican and the Conservative parties by the teats of patronage. He sealed the loyalty of the Conservatives by voting prolife. Yet D'Amato was simultaneously the patron of prochoice politics in the state GOP. He insisted that a gubernatorial candidate be both Catholic and proabortion. His pollsters had told him that was a winning formula, and that's what he wanted. The Conservative Party, willy-nilly, wanted it too.

There was an ambitious Republican politician in the city—former federal prosecutor Rudy Giuliani, who had made his name arresting mobsters, Democratic political bosses, and Wall Street high rollers (the high rollers turned out to be innocent, but the mobsters and the bosses were guilty as charged). He had decided that his road to power lay in an alliance with New York's Liberal Party—the Conservatives' mirror image—and indeed he espoused a number of liberal positions, including down-the-line support for abortion. Yet there was also a ferocity to him that made him credible as a crime fighter. Because D'Amato feared him as a rival, the Conservative Party feared him too.

The preliminary work of saving the city was being done in the academy and in the police department. Throughout the eighties James Q. Wilson and George Kelling had been touting a new style of law enforcement they called "broken windows" policing. The disorder of daily life, symbolized by broken windows that no one bothers to fix, shrinks public space, disheartens the law-abiding, and emboldens criminals. If cops arrested small offenders—turnstile jumpers and other urban pests—they would find among them more serious offenders too, and start reversing the cycle. Bill Bratton, chief of the transit police, had begun applying "broken windows" principles to the subways, and Jack Maple, a flamboyant detective who dressed in bowlers and spats, proposed tracking daily crime rates citywide by computer, so every precinct could see where the bad guys were operating and react immediately. I followed these developments thanks to the *City Journal*, the magazine of the Manhattan Institute, a free-market think tank that began aggressively studying urban problems. The revived Manhattan Institute was the brainchild of its director, an intense libertarian, Bill Hammett. The *City Journal* was the love child of its new editor, my friend Rich Vigilante. He knew policy had to be coated with lifestyle and culture; I helped him supply those, and learned the policy at the same time.

The new crime fighting was a way of helping the poor and struggling, overwhelmingly black and Hispanic, more potent than Jack Kemp's projects. If a man is killed, it doesn't matter what his tax rate is; fear and unease levy their own taxes. I took the subways for convenience; poorer New Yorkers had no choice. Disorder annoyed or disgusted people like me; it oppressed millions of people all around me. Wolfe presented the city as an ironic inferno in which we were all trapped. I had come to see it as my home. All of us were in the same boat, but the New Yorkers in steerage had the worst of it. By attending to details and making the right decisions, thousands of lives would be saved.

Hammett and Rich wanted to address the entire political class, not just the shrunken local remnant of right-world. (The Conservative Party's base in the city was right-leaning Irish and Italians, but as they left town, the party shriveled. Bill had gotten 13 percent of the vote in his 1965 mayoral run. In 1989 the Conservatives had not even run a candidate.) The politician who most listened to them was Giuliani. But he was more than a conveyor belt for other people's ideas, whatever I, reared in a journal of opinion, might like to think. Ideas and innovations need leaders to implement them and follow through. Leadership in New York required both nitpicking and a hide of iron. A successful mayor would have to master all the switch points of the bureaucracy, and defy the inevitable storms of protest. Most criminals were black or brown; wasn't arresting them racist? (Most victims were black or brown, but that wouldn't be held to a crime fighter's credit.) Italian journalist Luigi Barzini wrote of the tiny minority of his countrymen who defy the prevailing go-along, get-along culture, behaving as if the laws were meant to be enforced. Other Italians call them *fessi*, damned fools. Giuliani, with his grim Renaissance face, like a warlord or a centurion in a crucifixion, was such a fool.

When Giuliani ran for mayor in 1993, D'Amato backed a candidate on the Conservative line to drain votes from him and reelect Dinkins. George Marlin was a six-foot-five investment banker, whose haircut made Pat Buchanan look like Bob Marley. He knew all the low roads of local government finance and could explain and denounce them in English. He helped Ignatius Press publish the complete works of G. K. Chesterton, and was ever giving me stout volumes—*Chesterton on Shaw, Part 3* or *Collected Journalism: August–October 1909*. I had many lunches with him and Joe Mysak, a fellow contributor to the *American Spectator*'s "Saloon" series, at Harry's on Hanover Square, a den of bond traders. One day I violated the dress code by coming in a light-green summer suit. I was also sniffing Afrin for a summer cold. "Drugs too," said Mysak. "The whole *Miami Vice* look." George Marlin was smart, right on every issue, and a friend. I had to vote for him. Considering the stakes, how wrong I was.

The most important figure in the election may have been Larry Hogue, a demented bum who lived on the Upper West Side, throwing cinder blocks through windshields and people in front of buses (happily, he killed no one). Periodically, Hogue would be arrested, sent to a halfway house in Connecticut, then released, whereupon he would resume his ways. The system seemed powerless to stop him. Enough terrified middle-class liberals and conservatives put survival over even politics to give Giuliani the narrowest of margins in his rematch. Marlin pulled less than 1 percent.

Giuliani's first challenge was the squeegee men, who gathered at intersections, wiping dirty rags over car windows, then demanding handouts. If motorists didn't comply, they hurled abuse or objects. Giuliani said he would get rid of them, and he did. There was a tick up.

———

In October 1994 I got a call from Bill.

It could never be glad confident morning with him again, yet particular actions (giving the piano, forwarding my parents' letter), routine (editorial dinners were still held at East Seventy-third Street), and the passage of time had allowed a relationship to re-form. I walked along, at a distance. Sometimes I would remember the old intimacy, though I was too busy with my new second life of freelancing to reminisce much. My earnings did not quite come up to the level that Bill had proposed to guarantee. Once in a while *Vanity Fair* or *Time* or *The New Yorker* would pay a big check. The *Observer* paid peanuts, but it was regular peanuts. Thank God for Jeanne's practice.

Still, whenever Bill made any unusual communication—sending a letter, speaking from the other end of a surprise phone call: "Hiya, buddy!"—I was wary. Once burned.

This time Bill got right to the point. The editorial section of the magazine, he said, had run off the rails. The jokes weren't funny, the arguments didn't clamp shut, the style was unstylish. He said he didn't "want to die" with it in ruins. He offered me $50,000 extra—more than tripling my salary—to fix it.

I hadn't noticed such a change in the editorial section, but then I didn't read it with the attention Bill gave to it. Of all the sections of the magazine, he cared most about the editorials, because they came first, and because they were most like him. They were the edge of the blade, combative, wiseass, stentorian, melancholy by turns. Macaulay would have cared most for the articles, Edmund Wilson for the reviews. Bill's soul was in the edits. The prodigal father was asking his son to repair his creation.

He seemed surprised that I needed a few days to think about it. Least in my thoughts was the section itself. I had no doubt I could fix whatever was wrong. If I didn't know how to edit and write *National Review* editorials by this point in my life, what did I know?

John was a bigger problem. How would I deal with him? Bill was the boss of my boss, but John was still my boss. I liked him; he would have to feel a new arrangement as a rebuke. Naturally, this being *National Review*, everything was being done behind his back.

The biggest problem, as usual, was Bill. I was still in his gravitational field, out at the distance of Saturn; I didn't want to be pulled back to the orbit of Mercury or Venus. I had seen *Parsifal* often enough to compare Bill with Klingsor, the villain who tries to arrange the seduction of the hero in an enchanted garden. Would that be my fate if I came in closer again? Before the opera begins, Klingsor has, for perverse psychological reasons, castrated himself. Would *that* be my fate? Richard Lasky, a psychoanalyst who taught my wife, said that a narcissist no more considers the feelings of other people when he makes demands on them than we ask a lightbulb if it wants to be turned on. Bill assumed that his need, and *National Review*'s, would make me light up.

But of course I loved every minute. I had executive flair enough to save Bill's bacon, it seemed. I had the best of all worlds. I could avoid almost all the effort and tedium of running a magazine, while sucking on the sweet certainty that Bill knew that I knew that he knew he had made a mistake. Bill wasn't the only narcissist in the picture.

A final consideration was put best by my former agent, Lou Ann Sabatier. She had gone on to be a magazine consultant, but I still asked her advice. "He's offering you $50,000?" she said. "Let's get real."

I called Bill to tell him that I would do what he asked. In return I asked him to tell John that this had all been Bill's idea. Soon—hours later? the next day?—I got a call from John. He often used the British expression "Heigh-ho," a combination of "Oh, shit" and "All right, then," suitable for moving on from any difficulty, whether it was a movie that turned out to be dull or Operation Market Garden. The formal meaning of his call was "Heigh-ho," though he sounded depressed and upset. I told him, I hope convincingly, that this was no power play of mine.

Bill, John, and I were to see each other at the Union League Club, where Bill was throwing a party for Ernest van den Haag's eightieth birthday. The Lincoln Room had been decorated with black and orange balloons. Halloween, the new Christmas. Bill was pleased and happy. I told him, rather stiffly, that I was doing this to help *National Review*, and because he had made a generous offer.

"You've left out the most important reason," he said.

What's that? I asked.

"Your obligation to gratify me," he smiled.

"But how can I distinguish that," I smiled back, "from my ongoing obligation to gratify you?"

So we traded bullshit, only he meant his, and I meant mine more than I knew.

John was his usual self. I would owe a lot to his professionalism, his decency, and perhaps his opinion of my candor.

The next editorial section came soon after. John and I agreed that he would run the conferences, make assignments, and pick and arrange the paragraphs and editorials as usual. I would put them into *National Review* style. At the editorial dinner that Monday, Pat drew me aside and confided how glad she was that I had stepped in to help Bill out. "I hope I please him," I said, a little rattled by so many confidences. "You always do," she said. "Not always," I pointed out.

Bill had typically closed a section around five o'clock on editorial Tuesday. John and I closed our first around eight. When the printed copy of that issue came in the mail, I worried over what I had done—that could have been funnier, that tighter. But I soon got a call from Bill: It was "transformed," it was "professional journalism" again, and on and on. It was just like old times.

It did not last, at least not at that level. The editorial section became better, and Bill was mostly pleased with it. But there were unhappy memos. Once I had the satisfaction of telling him that an issue he disliked had been put together while I was in India. But sometimes he disliked an issue that had been put together by me at East Thirty-fifth Street.

As the months passed, I found myself drawn into John's time world, which was like a dimension on *Dr. Who*. With Hegel he believed that the owl of Athena flew only at nightfall. Because he would not crack the whip over himself, he could not crack it over others. Closings might drift to ten, eleven, midnight. John would happily invite anyone left standing to one of his haunts, Park Bistro perhaps, for an excellent French meal and a glass of champagne. Long hours made for less attention—flat edits were not trimmed enough, bland ones not sparked enough. Executive flair, still biting me in the tail.

What most displeased Bill about the editing, whether John or I did it, was that he was no longer doing it. There must have been times—beyond the stunt of the Swiss edition—when issues put together during his tenure by others had not entirely pleased him, and surely he let everyone know it. But he knew he would always be coming back into the fray, leading the charge against liberals, dullards, the spirit of the age. The evening of artists is an unhappy time.

———

ABOUT THIS TIME another interesting man came into my life. Though he was widely known—everyone carries his picture—no one understood him or gave him his due. I found him, and figured him out.

After Lou Ann stopped being my agent, I started working with Michael Carlisle, a classmate of mine at Yale whom, in one of the anomalies of megaversity life, I had never before met. Together we came up with a number of book ideas. After the Soviet Union fell, Michael (who is Russian on his mother's side) suggested I learn Russian, move to Moscow for a year, and be the new John Reed. I would as soon have moved to Angola. I thought of writing about midlife cancer, and we talked to a few editors. But memoir is a dubious genre; happily for me, none of them bit.

Finally, Michael said, Write me a list of ten ideas; I'll pick one and sell it. I came up with ten, and Jeanne said, You've always admired George Washington; why don't you add him to the list?

I had met Washington in Garry Wills's course in 1974. But Yale gave me another glimpse of him, for Yale owns John Trumbull's paintings of the Revolutionary War (the most famous, *The Signing of the Declaration of Independence*, is on the back of the two-dollar bill). They hang together on one wall, like an iconostasis, eight small canvasses and one large standing portrait of Washington after the battle of Trenton. Behind him in the portrait are a plunging horse, campfires, darkness. Ahead of him is America—if he can get the job done. He looks as if he will. Washington appears in four of the smaller scenes as well. Seeing them all together, it is clear that Trumbull saw Washington as the center of the story. Trumbull was both an insider and a trend follower: He was a veteran of the Revolutionary War who belonged to a prominent political family, and he aimed to make money selling reproductions of his work. He knew the history, and he knew his public. What did it mean that he gave George Washington top billing?

I had written about Washington once, in 1989, when I was doing essays for the back page of *Time*. I proposed one on the bicentennial of his first inauguration. My material was a combination of what Wills and Trumbull had shown me. My peg was the contrast between our national birth and the front page: Francis Fukuyama was saying that history had ended; could freedom building be that easy? I wrote with what Jeanne told me at the time was unusual passion. Even then I sensed it was important to get this right.

Michael looked at my list of eleven ideas and said Washington was the one he could sell. Erwin bought it for $25,000.

I now had to learn about my subject. Historian Forrest McDonald had written pieces for *National Review*, and through Charles Kesler I knew William B. Allen, a professor of political philosophy at

Michigan State. They steered me to the best standard sources, and to interesting new work. For six months I read.

I was no historian, but being an English major was a useful substitute, for I knew how to read with attention. When a man's tone of voice changes—as in Thomas Jefferson's discussion of black body odor and sexual appetites in *Notes on Virginia*—what is going on? What is he thinking—or not letting himself think? Being a political journalist was equally valuable. I knew what a stab in the back was, so when Jefferson and Alexander Hamilton did it to each other I recognized it. I had spent my professional life writing about political conflict, and I did not imagine that eighteenth-century politicians, even great men, could be free of it. This saved me from nostalgia, the conservatives' baby food (the liberals' baby food is hope). But living in the eighteenth century neutralized a conservative poison, cynicism. Life is hard—that is a conservative insight. Liberation is possible—that is a revolutionary insight, and these men, for all their shortcomings, had made their country more free.

What struck me most about my particular man was his constancy. There came a moment well into my writing when I was trying to figure out some maneuver of Washington's presidency. I did the detail work, mastering the sequence of events and the motives, when I had a sensation, almost physical, both thrilling and humbling: *Once again, he has not let me down.* He meant his life, and he did his best, from the siege of Boston, his first victory, to his last will and testament, in which he freed his slaves.

I have spent a lot of time looking for fathers, heroes, men. Testicular cancer—manhood diseased—added an edge to this task. George Washington had been dead for almost two hundred years. But I knew him, and I could explain him to others.

Bill was right: I could not have written this book while editing *National Review*. Washington and his world were just a little too strange, and, once you knew them, far too compelling, to be done after hours.

I had to fend off one distraction to tell their story. One day, when I was at *National Review* writing editorials, the phone rang. Lynn

Chu, who was the agent for Terry Teachout and many other conservatives, called with an offer: Did I want to ghost a book for Newt Gingrich? The job would be important and urgent. I said I was writing about George Washington; she did her best to shame me out of it, but I refused. After I hung up, the phone rang for Jacob Sullum, our new assistant managing editor, with whom I shared an office. From his responses, I realized Lynn had gone down her call list.

Founding Father got some early breaks. The Book of the Month Club, which still retained shreds of its old potency, made it a main selection, and the *Atlantic* bought an excerpt and ran it as a cover story.

Then, catastrophe. Michiko Kakutani in the daily *Times* gave it the worst review I ever hope to get. She thought the book was puffery for the dead. She was particularly disgusted by my emphasis on Washington's physicality: "inexplicable . . . [Brookhiser] spend[s] pages and pages singing the praises of Washington's physique." Of course I had. His presence was his primary communication tool; it helped him chair meetings, charm women, lead soldiers. It is one of the most powerful of all communication tools, certainly the most intimate. Yet since he lived before films or photographs, unless you see the paintings and think about them, it is lost.

All day friends called with their condolences. I went to a dinner that night at someone's townhouse in the Village, where strangers offered sympathy, as if I had died.

Relief came from the *Times Book Review* on Sunday. (In Trollope novels *The Times* of London is called the *Thunderer*, and wields the power of Zeus. The *Book Review* still had some of that power, and still has, though it ebbs.) *Founding Father* was one of two books on the cover, and the review was by Joseph Ellis. His John Adams book, *Passionate Sage*, had come out in 1993, and he was working on his Jefferson book, *American Sphinx*. He understood what I was trying to do with and for Washington, and he thought I had succeeded. *Founding Father*, he wrote, belongs "on the same shelf with Plutarch."

Some months later, when I met Ellis, he told me that the day after his review appeared, he was picking a kid up at school. He teaches at

Mount Holyoke, in a hub of colleges in western Massachusetts. Another academic parent told him, with pained surprise, that the author of the book he had praised wrote for *National Review*. "I know," said Ellis, a liberal Democrat. "But I liked the book."

Founding Father helped launch the founders' revival, which is still with us. It also began a trend of short biographies. It did something else, which all my freelancing had not quite done—it gave me a new career. I hope I will write for *National Review* as long as I write. But now I was something more. Bill had changed the twentieth century, as Reagan had said at our thirtieth-anniversary banquet. Washington changed the eighteenth, nineteenth, twentieth, and every century in which America exists as a republic. I wanted to understand how and why.

Chapter 12

Joe Klein called his book on Bill Clinton *The Natural*, and you knew what he meant. Clinton was the first Democrat since FDR to serve two full terms; he weathered a scandal that would have sunk a fleet; liberals recently turned on him for denying Barack Obama, but he will surely be back. At the same time, there was too much near death in this political life to make him as gifted as Klein and other reporters regularly said. Eliza gets across the Ohio River in *Uncle Tom's Cabin*, but that does not make her a natural river crosser, or ice floes a natural transportation link.

National Review greeted the Clinton years with a conference at the Mayflower hotel in Washington. It lasted several days, featured dozens of speakers on numerous panels, and drew several hundred spectators. Hosting conferences was a smart strategy for us in a post-Bill world. He used to sell the magazine by being a star. Now that he was no longer editor in chief (and no longer quite such a star), we needed new ways of making noise. Besides, John loved these bean feasts; in a crowded room he felt at the heart of things.

This particular conference had one very practical effect. One of the speakers was Newt Gingrich, the Georgia Republican (he liked to say he represented the Atlanta airport). Gingrich was glum and disheveled; he wore a sweater and no tie. Democrats controlled the White House and both branches of Congress; why dress up? Yet he said later that our conference recharged his optimism. People seemed eager to do things—not just fight Clinton, but push our agenda, whatever that might prove to be. The energy in the room made Gingrich believe that Democratic hegemony could be undone.

Less than two years later, he had undone it. In the 1994 elections the GOP picked up fifty-four House seats, and Gingrich became the first Republican Speaker in forty years (Joseph Martin had surrendered his gavel on January 3, 1955—seven weeks before I was born)—a turnover that startled everyone but Gingrich.

I had interviewed Gingrich for *The Outside Story*, when he had been Jack Kemp's right hand, the mastermind who might make him minority leader or Speaker. The trajectory of Kemp's career left Gingrich in the lead role in the House, a position he professed not to have sought, but who can study politics so minutely without seeing himself on top? Gingrich combined attention to detail and history with a fascination for grandiose ideas. When he assumed the Speaker's chair, he gave a reading list to the Republican caucus, an unprecedented act; incoming Speakers typically hand out lists of earmarks. I assigned myself to read and review Gingrich's list for *National Review*. It included some political classics—the *Federalist*, and *The Indispensable Man*, James Flexner's condensation of his multivolume biography of George Washington. But it also featured the work of Alvin and Heidi Toffler. The Tofflers were old New Age types who had a wave theory of human society. Mankind had lived successively by hunting and gathering, then agriculture, then industry, each wave accompanied by concepts and mores appropriate to it. Now we felt the surge of a new wave of high tech. This was like Fukuyama, exciting, obvious, and bogus—pseudoanthropology, rather than pseudophilosophy. But Gingrich believed that if America and the GOP caught the next wave, they could sit on top of the world. He tirelessly sifted the news and pop culture for signs of his own, and conservatism's, impending success, in any place, high or low, from the collapse of communism to the popularity of the Mighty Morphin Power Rangers.

Gingrich and his second in command in the House, Dick Armey of Texas, had agreed to be guests on *National Review*'s postelection cruise. Cruises became another feature of life after Bill. We bought blocks of discounted cabins on ships that sailed around the Caribbean or down the Alaska coast, and offered them at market rates to our readers, who would be entertained by panel discussions among our writers and big-ticket guests. Finally, after four decades of running in the red, we had hit upon something that made money. Ed Capano took to saying he ran a travel agency with a magazine attached. I stopped going after the first few cruises; I don't like boats, and our readers, though sweet, were relentless—24/7 access was indeed what they had paid for. My low moment came before one scheduled break, as I was about to debark at some lugubrious island port to look at the stores selling sunblock and Lladró figurines, when a reader demanded, "Why can't we balance the budget?" "Because we don't want to" would have been the only honest answer, but at that moment I didn't feel like giving any.

Though Gingrich and Armey had every reason to beg off our post-election cruise in the wake of their triumph—they would be insanely busy for the next few weeks, indeed years—they came through. When I told Gingrich at dinner that I was writing my own Washington biography, he did not ask me to abandon it in favor of him, but suggested I read historian Gordon Wood, and the old pop novelist Howard Fast. "Liberals hate Washington," Gingrich added, seemingly ignoring Fast's politics. I knew what he meant—Washington is the whitest, malest figure in American history, and thus an affront to liberalism's formal categories—but this was too much for Jeanne.

"No, Mr. Gingrich," she said. "Liberals esteem Washington. I do."

"Liberals hate Washington," Gingrich insisted. He had his game face on.

He also indicated how he intended to run the House: "We're saying we're modeling ourselves on Cannon, but we're really modeling ourselves on Reed." Joe Cannon (Speaker from 1903 to 1911) ran the House with a heavy hand, but Thomas "Czar" Reed (Speaker on and off from 1889 to 1899) ran it with an iron one.

The year 1995 saw another political phenomenon, potentially bigger than Gingrich. Colin Powell, who had been chairman of the Joint Chiefs during the Gulf War, resigned from the army and published his memoir, *My American Journey*. Chris Buckley went to the book party at I Trulli, a sleek Italian restaurant fashionably outside midtown, and was convinced by the celebrity voltage in the room that Powell's book tour would be a spectacle. He asked me to cover it for *Forbes FYI* as if it were a political campaign swing. So I followed Powell to a dozen cities, and every sort of book venue, from chain stores to independents to Sam's Clubs. All I did was watch, but since Powell wasn't saying or doing anything except signing books with a succession of Sharpies handed to him by brisk aides, what I did was watch the crowds. They repaid my attention. The lines of book buyers snaked through the aisles and out the doors. Every demographic was present. In Boston I chatted up a twenty-year-old girl, wearing a peace sign between her collar bone and her cleavage. She had not been conceived when peace was new, yet here she was to honor the general. In Detroit I ran into a man with his own Powell for President committee who said he was with the Michigan Militia—not the National Guard, but conspiracy-minded survivalists who spent their weekends training for Armageddon. Yet here he was supporting the lifetime servant of the state.

Powell was a screen onto which people projected their hopes. Drawing on my George Washington research, I compared Powell to the Patriot King—a fantasy figure of early-eighteenth-century English politics, the good sovereign who comes into the sad, scuffed political system from outside, purging and saving it. Centuries later and an ocean away he still stalks the American mind; Ross Perot and all the other amateur presidential candidates saw themselves as Patriot Kings. I might have compared Powell to another figure, whom I would write about in *National Review* several years later—the Numinous Negro, the holy black man who undoes, by his mere presence, colored-only drinking fountains, the Ku Klux Klan, the Middle Passage, all of it.

Blacks liked Powell, with all the usual in-group envy that afflicts minorities: His family was Jamaican; maybe he is Republican; isn't he a little too white? Whites ached to vote for him. I felt the tug. So did Bill Rusher, who told me after hearing Powell speak that he was as good on his feet as Reagan. He added, as a cautionary note, that he was no conservative.

Both Powell and Gingrich petered out, Powell first. In November, when his tour was done, he announced he would give a press conference at noon on a Wednesday, which happened to be the final deadline for our editorial copy. We got the printing plant to hold off until one o'clock. John asked me if Powell was punctual. I said indeed he was. Powell announced that he lacked the "passion and commitment" to make a run. He spoke for about twenty minutes, we chatted a bit, then John sat down to write, Linda and I tossing sentences at him. At 12:58 John was finished, except for a last bit of bunting. I came up with "America is proud to have him as one of its sons." Off to the printer.

Gingrich, it turned out, had charisma problems. Americans can like self-conscious intelligence in gadflies (Bill, for example), but not in their leaders. Worse, he chose to pick his first big fight as Speaker on balancing the budget. Polls showed that voters cared about the issue, and Gingrich thought he could impose spending discipline on the White House. Clinton pushed back, Gingrich pushed harder; in their deadlock, the federal government technically shut down. The mail got delivered, of course; some federal employees missed some paychecks.

In midshowdown Dick Armey came to *National Review* to explain the Republican game plan. The poor man was frazzled, barely coherent. Gingrich and the GOP were being depicted as villains, reckless, heartless. They had miscalculated. Americans say they worry about the budget, just like my questioner on the cruise, but practically speaking they do not care. Peter saw the flaw in the strategy instantly: "Imagine asking congressmen to stick their heads up over the parapet on an issue like that."

Gingrich stayed on, a marooned figure, until 1998, when he resigned his congressional seat. The Republican House majority, which had come to be about maintaining itself, lasted another eight years.

Gingrich and Powell had their day because the Right was trying to find what it should be post-Reagan, but they were not the solution. The Right was having trouble finding a leader because it was having trouble defining its mission. The communist threat was gone. Saddam was not gone, but seemed contained. Many of the things we had always said were still worth saying: Government was too big, and ordinary social life seemed under threat in the postmodern world. But how could we make these ideas compelling, and who would do the job?

Perhaps a new round of tax cuts was the solution. Steve Forbes, publisher of *Forbes* magazine, decided to run for president in 1996. I have made my thoughts on entry-level presidential candidates pretty clear, but everyone allows himself one exception, and Steve Forbes was mine. He threw the best parties in the business, after Bill's, either at the Forbes Building on lower Fifth Avenue, in the museum devoted to the family collection of toy soldiers and Fabergé eggs, or on the company yacht, the *Highlander*, which would cruise down the Hudson, around the Battery, up under the East River parade of bridges, then back. One night, thanks to crosstown traffic, Jeanne and I got to the pier only after the *Highlander* had cast off. My wife shouted for it to come back; back it came, and picked us up.

What I liked about Forbes as a candidate was his ideological passion, in his case a passion for tax cuts. I had breakfast with him at the Coffee Shop on Union Square, some years before the 1996 election. He talked of the prospects of Jack Kemp making another campaign when I pointed out to him that he was the leader of the supply-siders now. He seemed to take me seriously. Yet my conscience is clear, for he had a far more compelling reason than any urging of mine to go into politics himself. He was the eldest son of Malcolm Forbes: motorcyclist, balloonist, walking ad for the Forbes brand. When Malcolm gave himself a birthday party, he threw it in Tangier (Bill and Pat made the trek). How do you follow an act like that? By doing the one thing your father never did—run for president.

Forbes's charm as a candidate was his painful shyness; only someone who means it, you felt, would make himself jump through such uncongenial hoops. Rich wrote a profile comparing him to Buzz Lightyear, the earnest astronaut in *Toy Story*; Roman did a cover sketch of Forbes as Buzz, declaring, "To the flat tax—and beyond!"

He did surprisingly well, but not as well as Pat Buchanan, who won the New Hampshire primary. The party, taking alarm, rallied 'round the oldest of old shoes, Bob Dole. *National Review* liked Dole well enough. He tapped Jack Kemp as his running mate, for tax cuts and hope, and he appealed to our cynical impulses with his bleak sense of humor. We needed all our humor, for Dole was buried in November.

A YEAR INTO Clinton's second term, I ran into someone I had not seen for a long time, at a right-world lunch in midtown: Lucianne Goldberg, the agent who hadn't liked my novel. She was happy to see me, and seemed happy in general.

I will not reprise the Monica Lewinsky story, which broke in January 1998, except to ask why conservatives bewitched themselves so, with this and other Clinton scandals. Part of the reason was Clinton's personality. He certainly had a way of getting under our skin. His glib intelligence; his deep-down shallowness; his oscillation between self-pity and bullying; his slightly greasy charm, and the disproportionate effect it had on others (no, he was nothing like Elvis Presley, and if he had been, who would want someone like Elvis Presley in the White House?); and, most of all, his resilience and resourcefulness drove us nuts.

One consequence of our absorption was our sudden discovery of the police blotter. The *New York Times* told the world about Whitewater, a Clinton real estate deal, and other shady money stories followed him throughout his presidency and beyond. But there was always more, or possibly more, if you looked for it. The tales of alleged Clinton misdeeds bled into the fantasies of Skousenites. Anti-Clinton craziness made the craziness of the early conservative movement look respectable by comparison. The John Birch Society had contended (idiotically) with communism. The new paranoids were in a lather about a corner cutter from Arkansas.

National Review actually had the materials of a correct stance on the Lewinsky affair. We criticized the courts' decision to let Paula Jones, an Arkansas woman who said that Clinton had sexually harassed her, sue him while he was in the White House, and we opposed renewing the independent-counsel law, which we considered a deformation of the balance of power (if Congress wants to take down a president, let them slug it out). If there had been no Jones trial, Clinton would not have perjured himself testifying about his sex life. If there had been no independent counsel, there would have been no sclerotic investigation. Yet once the wheels began moving, we too helped them spin.

I did my bad bit in the *New York Times Book Review*. Two Clinton-demon books appeared from right and left. Christopher Ruddy argued that Vince Foster, a White House counsel who committed suicide, had been whacked, while Roger Morris discussed all manner of skullduggery, including the charge that Clinton as governor of Arkansas had helped the CIA smuggle cocaine into the United States. The *Book Review*, not knowing quite what to do with these productions—they came from mainline houses—gave them to me. Without endorsing their theses, I was entirely too polite. If I were Bill, or some other Latin-mass Catholic, I would say *mea culpa*.

The paranoid style in American politics goes back long before the Clinton years, or even the periods discussed by Richard Hofstadter in his famous essay (he traced it to Populist money cranks of the 1890s). The founders were prey to it—Jefferson thought Alexander Hamilton was a monarchist; Hamilton thought Jefferson would set up guillotines. It goes back beyond the founders to the Englishmen who wanted the Patriot King to save them from politicians they saw as monsters of corruption. Our paranoid episode wasted time, distracting us from constructive thought on issues of the day, and distracting a president who in the best of circumstances was not firm of purpose in fulfilling his duties.

The only conservative I remember wanting no part of the show was Christopher Caldwell. In "Hill of Beans," a Beltway column he wrote for the *New York Press*, he said the whole thing should be dismissed with a Roman thought, *De minimus non curat lex*, The law does not care about trifles.

THE NINETIES WERE more than depositions and dress stains. Rupert Murdoch had been losing $50 million a year on the *New York Post* in order to have a populist presence in the city. But he wanted to lose money on a journal of opinion too. I heard, from John and Ed

Capano, that he offered to buy *National Review*, and they said that Bill was dismayingly willing to consider his bid. *National Review* was Bill's child. Would he have sold Chris to Murdoch? Maybe, if he had felt that Chris was irrevocably out of his life. He still owned *National Review*, of course, and fussed over every issue, but he had given the management of the estate to agents, and thereby lost some of his joy in it.

Unable to buy an existing journal, Murdoch started his own, *The Weekly Standard*. One heard tales of their D.C. headquarters: Every computer had Nexis, an online article search. *National Review* had finally graduated from our Royals and our Connecticut Linotype machines to the computer age—hence the ability to send in the Powell edit instantly; we had also moved to a new building, a characterless seventies slab on Lexington Avenue, with no grime, but also no dumbwaiter. Still, a Nexis at every desk seemed grand. Everyone worried about the competition; I decided that there had to be one person at *National Review* who did not read *The Weekly Standard*, and I nominated myself to be that person. My model was Grant after he took over the Army of the Potomac. Lee made some attack, and a Union officer burst into Grant's tent to offer his opinion, based on long experience, of what Lee would do next. Grant said, Let's think what we will do next. *The Weekly Standard* found its niche, powerful but different from ours—a force in the Beltway, unknown outside it.

In 1995, the *New York Times Magazine* ran a cover story on young conservatives, and I appeared in the role for the last time. I had decided a decade earlier to stop thinking of myself as a young conservative, or a young writer; it is important to stop calling yourself young before other people stop saying it of you. So in my own opinion I did not belong in the piece, though of course I was glad to appear.

James Atlas, the author, asked me to introduce him to some of my kind. I got together a great group—Rich, Maggie, Terry Teachout, magazine publisher Sam Schulman, the darkest man I know. We met for dinner at Danal, my favorite East Village restaurant. Rich was flying. Beavis and Butthead, he declared, referring to two then-popular cartoon louts, were like Socrates. How are they like Socrates?

I demanded, perfect straight man. "Because they make the weaker argument the stronger, and they corrupt youth." Atlas wrote it all down, and used none of it.

I had better luck with the photographer, who wanted edgy. David Brooks told me how the photographer kept asking him to cross his arms. After an hour of shooting, David finally let him take one such shot, which was of course the shot they used. It made David look like a hit man. I decided to play along. When the photographer came to our apartment, I was wearing a black shirt, black jeans, and black leather boots. Delighted, he seated me in the black leather armchair in the living room, atop a striped Turkish rug. John told me, when the issue came out, that all I needed was a white Persian cat in my lap to stroke.

At the other end of the age scale, Bill's reputation changed once more. For a decade he had taken tomatoes from those who decided that he no longer enthralled them. Now there came a decision, universal, simultaneous, to treat him as a lion (in 1995 he turned seventy). Once everyone had said, How he excites us. Now they said, He still goes on. His merits, those he had had, and those he retained, were all acknowledged, but he had become emeritus.

In October 1997 he published his best late book, *Nearer My God*. It was not a defense of his faith, even at the pop level of Chesterton or C. S. Lewis, but a testimony of what his faith had meant to him. Shortly before Bill died, his priest, Fr. Kevin Fitzpatrick, asked him if he had ever doubted. "No," said Bill. How could that be, given the strangeness of his faith, and the equally baffling strangeness of the world? How could that be, of a religion loaded with famous converts, spectacular defectors, saints with dark nights of the soul, and bad boys who, as George Orwell said of Graham Greene, thought of hell as an exclusive club whose membership is reserved for Catholics? How, unless his faith was so bound to his family and his childhood, which he had chosen as a young man to employ his rebellious energies defending rather than attacking? But I doubt my own suggestion. I cannot understand the satisfactions that Catholicism gives any more than I can grasp the burdens it imposes.

The book party for *Nearer My God* was held in a small room at the Union League Club. John Cardinal O'Connor, New York's populist prelate, said a few words. The clergy were out in force: Fr. Richard Neuhaus, recently acquired from the Lutherans, Fr. George Rutler, recently acquired from the Anglicans. Sometimes the Catholic Church seems like a mob of everybody, and the two converts showed the extremes. Father Neuhaus was preachy in the best sense: articulate, earnest, intelligent. Father Rutler, who possessed equal seriousness, carried it through the world in a lockbox of whimsy, as striking as his great bald head. Another guest was Jim McFadden. Jim had been sorely tried. His son Robert had died of cancer, after writing a noble appeal to prolifers to reject violence, whether real or rhetorical—bombing abortion clinics, murdering abortionists, excusing such deeds. Jim's pipe habit had given him his own cancer, of the tongue. He bore it gallantly, writing humorous Christmas carols appropriate to his condition. The one I remember is "The Holly and the I.V."

Jim had one reservation about *Nearer My God*. Bill had read a vision of Jesus' sufferings on the cross by an Italian mystic, Maria Valtorta. The Catholic Church honors such things when it believes them to be authentically saintly, but is wary of frauds and delusions; Valtorta's visions were put on the Index of Forbidden Books. Bill, while noting the controversy, printed the vision, which moved him. It piled Pelion on Ossa, it was Mel Gibson without a camera. It pained me when Bill's literary judgment, so keen in some areas, went off.

McFadden was concerned not with Valtorta's prose style, but with her bona fides. He disliked any supplement to the orthodoxy of his Irish American Catholic experience. He joked about Opus Dei, the Spanish layman's order: "I'm already Catholic," he would say, or he would call it "Octopus Dei." I asked him now if he liked Bill's book. His affliction had left him unable to speak. He wrote on a card, EXCEPT THE SEER. Defender of the faith. I honored it in a sonless man with a destroyed tongue.

BILL WAS NOT quite emeritus, it turned out. The day after the book party, Linda called me at home. John was in Rome, but he wanted me to know that he would be leaving *National Review* soon. Bill called shortly thereafter to say that John wanted the freedom to travel and write books. He would step down after New Year's, and stay on as a contributing editor. Bill added that he wanted my suggestions for a successor.

I am too slow, and too polite, to give people the third degree on the spot, but it was hardly necessary in this case. Linda's manner, glum and clipped, betrayed her. Even if it had not, I recognized the cover story, having used it myself. The *New York Times* ran an item once about a family in Connecticut whose house had just been struck by a second meteorite; the first had hit some years before (both were tiny, and did little damage). The odds against two hits in the same spot were I forget how many -illions to one, but then meteorites are generated by the random debris of the cosmos, not by Bill.

The foreground problem was what would happen next. A new editor would have to be mindful of the unusual positions we had staked out—anti-immigration, prodrug. Wanted: a libertarian nativist, a druggie America Firster. More pressing, to me at any rate, was what would a new editor think of me? There are no guaranteed berths, even at magazines you love and that have loved you. Bill and I spoke again, two days later. In passing, he asked if my "arrangements" were what they were ten years ago.

"How do you mean?" I asked.

"You still want to write books and things," he explained (I liked the "things").

"Yes, I do," I said.

"I wanted to hear that from you formally," he said.

We said good-bye, and hung up.

Jeanne told me I owed her a dollar—after the first phone call, she had bet that Bill would offer the job to me. He hadn't, but ten years after saying he didn't want me, he did want me to say that I didn't want it.

The next day was editorial Monday. John would be in Rome until the weekend, so it fell to me to run the meeting, and incidentally announce that he would be stepping down. Karina Rollins, a young associate, gasped. Did I come across like some heavy from corporate headquarters? John himself gave me a call that morning. The crisp tenor voice, armored in Englishness. He would say only that it was "a complicated story, which I would like to tell you when I return."

When John got back he and I met, finally, for a late-night drink at L'Express, a bistro on Park Avenue South, and he told the whole complicated story. Bill's MO had not changed. He had sent John a letter, to be delivered when he himself was out of town. The editor who will lead *National Review* into the twenty-first century, Bill wrote, cannot be its first editor, or its second editor. Periphrasis, the language of crime. He gave John no more reasons than he had given me. Once again, there were financial complications. He had hired John with an offer of x dollars for ten years. Since John would not reach the decade mark, Bill proposed to deduct a prorated amount as a remainder. Bill shot first, and dickered later. John wisely suggested that their lawyers hash this out, lest he and Bill become embroiled. Dear John—irenic, even on his way out the door.

If all this had happened a year or two after my own demotion, I would have been pleased. Now I was relieved to be no longer in the arena. I was also moved by John's frankness in telling me. He was more honest with me than I had ever been with him. My great secret, so tattered after all these years, like some heirloom of the shabby genteel.

My main emotion, as we spoke across the round marble-topped table, was to be irked with Bill. I had been working for the past three years at the worst intersection of John's habits and his duties—putting the editorial section to bed. But measured against John's accomplishments—the new talent, the new high profile of conferences and cruises—his lateness was small beer. Magazines have accommodated a lot more eccentricity in editors: Hugh Hefner never got out of his pajamas; William Shawn never got out of the office or his two apartments. Bill's problem was not with John but with time, which was taking him from his lifework, and to the grave.

The only public clue John ever gave of his fate was in the valedictory letter he published in the last issue he edited, addressed to

Bill (it ran in "Notes & Asides"). He recited what he had done, and maintained the cover story with aplomb—except that he illustrated the pleasure he had taken from his years at *National Review* with a line of poetry: "It was roses, roses all the way." This is the first line of "The Patriot," by Robert Browning, and it describes the rapture that greeted the patriot when he first took power. But by the time he utters the poem, he has lost popular favor: "They fling, whoever has a mind, / Stones at me for my year's misdeeds." Indeed, the patriot is about to be executed. John was too well read never to have read the whole poem, not malicious enough to have consciously planted the reference.

Meanwhile, I had to figure out what to advise Bill. I briefly considered playing a wild card of my own. If the functions of the editor were split between a prime mover and a workhorse managing editor, could I be the former? I talked it over with Terry Teachout, always patient, always sensible, and decided that it would not be possible. Editors have made such arrangements, but they still have all of the responsibility, and much of the work. You would never write another biography, said Terry. You might write other things, and they might be your best, but they would always be written in the margins.

At the end of the month Jeanne and I went to the Virgin Islands for five nights, for a long-planned vacation; Bill said he would inform me of any developments. We came back on Halloween, to streets full of witches and cats, and found that Bill had chosen Rich Lowry to be his next successor. Bill told me that he thought it would be, I forget the exact word, but it was either *neat* or *cool*, to promote someone from within. He had also picked a man who was the same age, twenty-nine, he had been when he launched *National Review*. Rich has lasted more than ten years, and is now in danger only from actual meteorites.

CHAPTER 13

RETIREMENT REQUIRES YOU to pack your bags. Some accompany you for the remainder of the trip, some are left behind to be picked up by others. Bill had packed all his *National Review* bags once, then repacked them.

His relations with Rich were better than his relations with me or John, at least judging by the result, though I am sure Rich has his own stories to tell. One would involve his name. He has been Rich Lowry all the years I have known him, but Bill decided that this was too informal for our masthead, where he became "Richard Lowry, Editor." No one ever called him that, including Bill (though Bill occasionally, absentmindedly, called him "Chris").

I tried to tamp down whatever friction I became aware of. Elder statesman at age forty-two—precocious in all things. Bill asked Rich, as he had asked John, to write a personal column in the front of the magazine (Bill had scarcely needed one, since he was so all-pervasive). Rich produced, among other things, this vignette of the Reverend Al Sharpton: "'Sure I know Bill Buckley,' Sharpton says. '*God and the Man at Yale.*'" But then one day Bill announced that Rich should discontinue the column. I called Rich to tell him I had heard Bill was being a pita. He asked what that was, and I explained it was a pain in the ass.

I advised him that if Bill was looking cross-eyed at the column for whatever reason, let it go. Points of friction would inevitably arise; better to keep them to a minimum.

The points of friction were few, because as Bill aged he had less energy to find them, and because the gap in age between him and Rich was so great: Bill was thirty years older than me, seventeen years older than John; forty-three years older than Rich. It is human to resent the next generation, harder to resent all futurity.

Rich put his mark on the magazine immediately. His first obit was for Harry Caray, the boisterous Chicago Cubs announcer. John had not followed American sports, and Bill had ceded them to Jeff and the tennis court. Finally, *National Review* took note of the national game. The Caray obit bumped one for Ernst Junger, the anti-Nazi national socialist, by Erik von Kuehnelt-Leddihn. It ran later, Erik's last piece for us; he died in 1999.

Rich poached Jay Nordlinger from *The Weekly Standard* to be managing editor. One day when I went into Jay's office he told me, with an air of bemusement, that he was just then editing a piece by Dave Shiflett in praise of smoking, which Jay, as a Christian Scientist, believed to be a vicious addiction. But he did his duty. He would never have accepted a duty that required him to ignore political prisoners in communist countries. After the collapses of 1989 and 1991, we spoke of communism in the past tense, and intellectually its time had passed: The seal of rebuke had been added to the seals of blood and failure. But communist regimes still hung on, from Havana to Pyongyang, and since one of them was China, more people still lived under communism than had been freed from it. Jay remembered them all, from black Cubans to the Falun Gong, and wanted the world to know their stories, and to share his indignation over their oppression.

Rich tapped Michael Potemra to edit the back of the book. Except for a few points here and there, Mike is a liberal, but he has been an excellent back-of-the-book editor, curious and quirky. A book editor should want to know everything, and especially want to know a few favorite things, to give his section personality. Mike saw every new movie not in English, and he bought Jeff's Ph.D. thesis from a used-book service, where the title, *Viscount Bolingbroke: Tory Humanist*, was mistakenly listed as *Viscount Bolingbroke: Tory Humorist*.

Mike saw the possibilities at once. "Sir Roger de Coverly: 'How many wenches does it take to screw in a sconce?' Lady de Coverly: *'That's not funny!'*"

The most important innovation at the magazine was its online incarnation, edited by Jonah Goldberg, Lucianne's son, later with the help of Kathryn Lopez. High tech might not change human nature, as the Tofflers proclaimed, but the Internet had changed journalism. The Monica Lewinsky story was broken by Matt Drudge. The old guard huffed and puffed, but soon everything was everywhere. *National Review* had experimented with the Internet years before, on a site run by the Heritage Foundation. I was loaned a primitive dial-up portable computer, shaped like a small bread loaf, on whose slowish screen a half-dozen people could type and talk simultaneously. When you lost your connection, as frequently happened, you disappeared from everyone else's screens in a flurry of punctuation. During one session, after someone vanished in this way ($%#@&*), one of the survivors remarked, "Tourette's."

National Review Online was not a replica of the magazine, but an independent entity with its own content. NRO teased the magazine by calling it NRODT—National Review Online Dead Tree. I retaliated by calling the online site NR Fleeting Pixels. Time and innovation made NRO necessary; Jonah and Kathryn made it successful. Early on Jonah proposed ten ideas for NRO to Rich. The one Rich signed off on was a collective blog, The Corner, a virtual place where ten or twenty regulars could track the news, argue, crack jokes, and waste time. Other collective sites would flourish—DailyKos, The Huffington Post, VDare (where Peter Brimelow joined in connection sweet with his soul mates). None had quite The Corner's intimacy.

There is one more essential feature of NRO and The Corner that, if they ever lose it, I quit: There are no comments. Life is full of pests, why throw them an open house?

Now that all the Sturm und Drang had passed between me and Bill, and passed over someone else's head, I could enjoy, uncluttered, what had always been enjoyable. He uncased his saber from time to time, referring in one column to Christopher Hitchens as "the exhibitionist moralist," in another to Oprah Winfrey as "the lady who is alternately fat and thin, I forget her name." The Oprah line was not old-fart cluelessness, for he remembered it years later, which showed he knew exactly what he was doing when he first tossed it off. Oprah Winfrey was the most popular woman in America, and Hitchens is always a force to be reckoned with. But the old performer knew self-dramatizers when he saw them.

I began having lunches with Pat. She had made so many dinners for all of us, it was time to explore another meal. I took her to the Coffee Shop, where she tried to guess the ingredients in the Brazilian sauces. She took me to Le Cirque and Jean Georges, but the management comped her at the first, and Bill came along to the second and paid, which amused and chagrined her: "I can't seem to take you to lunch."

One of Bill's favorite forms of hospitality was scattering concert tickets on his friends. Jeanne and I received a pair to hear Alfred Brendel play Beethoven in Carnegie Hall. Bill came with Rosalyn Tureck. The two pairs of seats were separated, but we all met in the aisle at intermission. Jeanne overheard a knowing bystander say, "That's the Buckley family." Pat, who disliked Tureck's airs—a case of colliding high-pressure systems—would have been chagrined, and not amused.

Bill's generosity took extreme forms. In 1999 my mother was diagnosed with her fatal illness. I decided to own some land before I was in it, and we bought a house in the eastern Catskills. It had a slapped-on bathroom, a leak in the roof, and a propane heater that roared like a crop duster but still could not be trusted to keep the pipes from bursting in winter. But it had a brick fireplace, a small pond, and twenty acres of woods laced with stone walls. An additional outlay would bring it up to snuff. Three months after we bought it, I got a letter from Bill (hand addressed, so as to escape even Frances's notice), with a check for ten thousand dollars: "I am very pleased for you and Jeanie that your dreamhouse is abuilding. I want to make a contribution to it—the winterization you spoke of—in memory of a long friendship, done with great affection."

Bill always had trouble with proper names, never with the big gesture. I was hardly alone in receiving these gifts—without making any effort, I learned of many: a plane ticket for Harry Jaffa so he could fly east to see his son graduate from college; help with Ed Capano's first mortgage; help with Joe's health care, despite all their bitter words. When an old friend of mine ran as a conservative sacrificial lamb for local office in Connecticut, her boss threw a backyard cocktail party, grandiosely called a "fund-raiser." The guests were me, Rich and Susan Vigilante, and Bill. It was stifling high summer; Bill wore a Yale costume circa 1950, white pants and a blazer. He handed my friend an envelope with a check for a cool thou inside. There were many more such gifts, but Bill's biographer will have to be diligent to uncover them; he did not tell disinterested parties, much less his left hand.

But nothing comes unmixed. Age brought the trials of age, to Bill and, indirectly, to his colleagues. His hearing began to go. He helped it depart by firing a pistol out his bedroom window in Stamford at the geese on his lawn. The Canada goose is a noble bird, but it has gone from being a rarity to a pest; a flock of geese is an excrement machine. Pat thinned them more effectively, and more safely, with her shotguns. Bill fired too close to his head. His appetite for intelligent conversation did not diminish; it only became harder, around a dinner table, to satisfy. When the guests—Abe Rosenthal of the *New York Times*, for instance—were equally hard of hearing, traffic jams of incomprehension resulted. Talking louder did as much good as honking your horn.

Age also brought pain. Pat suffered first. She had had a number of hip replacements over the years. Katharine Hepburn had prepped her for her first, coming to the library at East Seventy-third Street to show where her own had gone in, and to tell Pat what to expect. What to expect is a lot of grief, and knowing it didn't make it any easier to bear. Pain is like water; it finds every crack in your character, and makes it wider.

When Pat fought in her weight class, she could be splendid. Michael Bloomberg came to one editorial dinner after campaigning to drive smoking from public spaces in New York. Pat's was one of the last tables in the city to serve cigarettes, like candies, in little bowls; alongside lay matchbooks initialed PTB—Patricia Taylor Buckley. She blew a cloud of smoke in his general vicinity and asked, "May I smoke in my own house?"

But there were editorial dinners when she would simply decapitate some young associate. The evenings that had been so alluring, so exclusive, became occasions for forbearance. When Bill Rusher retired he had quoted Tennyson: "Though much is taken, much remains." Tennyson had not said how rough the taking could be.

———

After Washington I moved on to other founding fathers. *National Review* had helped lead a revolution in American politics and, indirectly, in geopolitics. It was interesting to see how, and by whom, a greater revolution had been made. Alexander Hamilton's story, besides offering an irresistible arc, from the West Indies to the ten-dollar bill to Weehawken, was a story of making a revolution real. For all the brilliance of his generation, only a handful of the founders understood modern finance; if Hamilton had not taken charge of the treasury when he did, America would have become the first banana republic, only the term, in a nod to our climate, would have been *maple republic*.

John Adams and his descendants were America's first dynasty, though far from our last, as the Kennedys, Clintons, and Bushes show. The self-appointed task of the Adamses was to keep the Revolution true to itself. Being the captious clan they were, their criticisms were often hasty, ill-judged, petulant, egotistical, or frantic. But sometimes, as when John Quincy Adams fought the slave power, they had the beast by the throat.

When I came to Gouverneur Morris, the least known of my subjects, I dealt for the first time with a man whose greatest achievement was his private life. Morris wrote the Preamble to the Constitution, and he wrote incisively about two revolutions, ours and France's (his Paris diary, 1789 to 1794, reads like Alan Furst). More compelling were his generosity and poise. He had a genius for consolation; he soothed Tory friends who were driven into exile, and he saved French friends from the guillotine. After many love affairs, he married a woman who had been accused (falsely, but the dirt still stuck) of adultery and murder. He kept his good humor despite losing one leg and much of one arm in accidents. He told one correspondent (another hard-luck case) that the cards of life were fairly dealt; our job was to play them, then to sleep.

Each man's life offered a tale of fatherhood. Hamilton's father was a deadbeat dad, Morris's a depressed eccentric. The Adamses were hands-on fathers, which was equally bad: John had three sons, two alcoholics and a president; John Quincy had three sons, two alcoholics and a candidate for president. In that family, if you weren't presidential material, you could tell it to the bartender. It is a hard job to get right, then as now.

Jeanne gave me the title of one book, *What Would the Founders Do?* playing off the evangelical bumper sticker. But audiences gave me the subject. Every time I gave a talk, someone (or two, or three) wanted to know what founder X, or all of them together, would have done about the stock market/Iraq/the politics of personal destruction. Historians smile at such questions, but I took them seriously. The founders were not so remote in time—only a few degrees of separation—and they took their lifework seriously. Most of their questions are still with us, and they thought their answers had lasting value. Why not bring them into the discussion?

Washington ran like a melody through all my books—he knew everyone, and everyone thought of him—and I finally gave him another book to himself. *George Washington on Leadership* was also someone else's suggestion: An investment fund in the Midwest asked me to give a series of talks on the subject, and the talks inspired the book. I followed Washington through problems that were well trodden (sometimes I think, the Constitutional Convention, *again?*), and I followed him through problems that were obscure (how do you work with drunks? how do you get your men to use latrines?). I was no longer in the business of executive flair, but I had learned a lot about it.

My work spilled into television. The year 1999 was the bicentennial of Washington's death, and I thought I should do a documentary about him. I went to the Olin Foundation, which gave me a first check and put me together with Michael Pack, a producer and director who lived in Washington, D.C. With beginners' luck—this was my first documentary, Michael's first historical one—we broke the iron mold of talking-head historians, slow pans over ye olde paintings and buildings, and costumed actors pretending that a camera had been smuggled into the battle of Monmouth. When we shot a reenactment of Monmouth, we showed the spectators in their shorts and billed caps—us. We brought the past into the present, or took the present back to the past. Michael also worked on my interviewing. If we ever do a show on God, he will interrupt the Big Interview to tell me to push harder. "He says He's all powerful, but there's sin and suffering. If He doesn't talk about that, we have no scene. You gotta *push* Him."

Bill liked my books but seemed to like me best on television. C-SPAN's book channel is the earthly afterlife. When we are dead, or near it—channel surfing in some Marriott on a business trip—back come the episodes of our author's Q&A. Bill saw one such segment and told me warmly how well he thought I did. There are a lot of good writers out there; serious television personalities are much rarer. Bill practically invented the type, and was nearly a unique specimen of it. This was high praise, unalloyed by any personal connection.

———

THERE WAS NO more need for me to help edit "The Week." What I asked for instead was a monthly column, "City Desk." I named it after my desk, which looks out the bedroom window at delis and restaurants, windows and roofs, J. P. Morgan's church, a park that is a fragment of Peter Stuyvesant's farm, and distant airplanes dropping into LaGuardia. I could write about piercings, snowfall, celebrity, flip-flops. "Following a woman in high heels up out of the subway is like discovering America. Following a woman in flip-flops up out of the subway is like riding the subway." Roman designed a logo that shows an old typewriter, as old as my first; next to it sits a cup of coffee whose steam sketches the skyline—Empire State, Chrysler, World Trade Towers.

My "City Desk" column was shaped by the state of the city I wrote about. The story of New York was no longer *The Bonfire of the Vanities*. Giuliani had promised to clean it up, and he had. He was resisted at every turn: Race hustlers accused him of malice; left-wing lawyers sued him for curtailing the rights of strip-club owners and bums; hipsters romanticized dirt and danger, and used a new swear word to describe their passing, *Disneyfication*. Giuliani's contentious personality gave them all extra ammunition, even as it enabled him to do the needful. Normal New Yorkers reelected him by a landslide. He governed the ungovernable city, thanks to conservative ideas and his own temperament, no thanks to conservative politics.

Conservatives seemed to be equally unable to affect the 2000 presidential race. Steve Forbes made a second run; Pat Buchanan went the third-party route. But the GOP's anointed, by a kind of stealth acclamation, appeared to be George W. Bush. Eldest son of my Bush, he had been governor of Texas since 1994. I first heard him speak at some fill-a-hotel-ballroom meeting in midtown. I sat next to Heather Mac Donald, the *City Journal*'s best writer. Heather looks like an extra in a Botticelli painting, but when she speaks she is a killer. About midtalk she leaned over to me and said, "Isn't this the worst speech you've ever heard?" Indeed it was. My estimate of George W. Bush would change, but the first impression was bad. Both he and his father mangled the language, but George H. W. Bush did so out of awkwardness and deference, as if speaking well would be an unacceptable act of self-assertion. George W. Bush spoke badly out of confidence and indifference, believing that whatever he said was said well enough, and that there was no point making the effort to say it better. He was shorter than his father; when he passed through the crowd shaking hands he moved like a lightweight heading up to the ring for an easy bout, perhaps because it was fixed.

In the early Republican presidential debates he was no more appealing. The most memorable moment came when each candidate was asked to name his favorite philosopher. Forbes, who answered first, named a philosopher—John Locke—and explained why Locke was his favorite (he had expounded a theory of political liberty, and so on). Bush, who came next, smiled and said, "Christ—because he changed my heart." Orrin Hatch, who came next, insisted that he too thought well of Christ. Bush was serious about having needed to change—he was a heavy drinker during his twenties and thirties—but the figure he cut was still grotesque.

A bitter pill, made up specially for conservatives, was that Bush had his own take on our beliefs. He and all around him were certain that we had lost our way, and that they knew a better path, which they called "compassionate conservatism." Kemp and Forbes had wanted to lift all boats with tax cuts; Gingrich had wrecked on the effort to balance the budget. Compassionate conservatives would reach out to the poor by subsidizing faith-based organizations.

When you looked at the details, compassionate conservatism looked a lot like handing walking-around money to friendly churches—the evangelicals who had become a part of the Republican base, and also black churches, which might break the lock the Democrats had on their race. We wanted conservative religious ideas to influence public policy, but we didn't want the government to look for opportunities to give away more money. The new Bush men believed in compassion, and believed in their moral superiority for advocating it, which made it even harder to take.

Bush's stately progress to the nomination was interrupted by John McCain, who trounced him in New Hampshire, 48 percent to 30 percent. McCain was a little-known Arizona senator with a fairly conservative record. He was also a hero, having endured five years of torture in communist prisons during the Vietnam War. Americans had put military men in the White House before (Taylor, Grant, Eisenhower); it is the only career, apart from professional politician, that we have ever turned to (Washington, Jackson, and William Henry Harrison had been both military men and politicians). McCain, if he won, would be the first military man from a military family—son and grandson of admirals. The sense of inherited honor had sustained him in prison, and inflected the way he campaigned now.

Whenever McCain split with conservatives—and he did on several big issues, supporting campaign-finance reform, and unrestricted immigration—he made it a matter of personal purity. He was brave and noble enough to speak the truth, but those who didn't were lost in darkness. Bush thought his rivals lacked compassion; McCain thought they were scoundrels.

McCain flattered reporters with open-ended access, and reporters flattered him in turn. His bluntness seemed to them a reflection of what they imagined their own truth telling to be. As an extra benefit, he was injecting drama into the race—and screwing the Republican front-runner.

When McCain's surge was only a tremor my wife and I had gone to a midnight Easter dinner at Milos, a Greek seafood restaurant in midtown. They had set up grills on the sidewalk, and set bowls of sand on every table so that customers coming from church would have a place to put their candles. There I met Carl Bernstein. We were the only non–Greek Orthodox in the room. As journalists will, he and I talked about the upcoming election. He asked me what I thought of McCain. "A crook and a showboat," I said. He asked if he could quote that, and I said sure; I would not back off from a quip. It ended up as a takeout—the large-type block of text that sits midpage—for a piece in *Vanity Fair*.

As a junior senator McCain had slid perilously close to crookdom when he took gifts and favors from Charles Keating, a dodgy savings-and-loan operator. This near miss—the Senate Ethics Committee found him guilty of "poor judgment"—had turned him into a zealot on the issue of campaign-finance reform. *Crook* was my way—unfair to the point of dishonesty—of evoking his reformer's roots. But *showboat* was truth in labeling. You can be a hero, and a man of honor—and also a showboat.

McCain's surge rallied conservative waverers to Bush, since anyone who is a reporter's pet can't be all good. The fighting, especially in the South Carolina primary among evangelicals, got vicious. McCain was rumored to have a black love child (he had adopted an orphan from Bangladesh in 1991). Bush prevailed, with bad feelings all around. Vice President Gore, the Democratic nominee, tapped Bill's protégé Joe Lieberman to be his running mate.

My thoughts about Bush began to change thanks to a question asked of both nominees—What is your favorite book?—a common query, and almost always a worthless one. Aides come up with titles that sound good (*Blessed Are the Poor*, by Mother Gandhi, or *Why a Strong America Needs to Be Strong*, by William Tecumseh Patton). Not only do politicians no longer write the books they say they have written, they don't even read the books they say they are reading. But in this election cycle, both candidates gave interesting answers. Al Gore picked *The Red and the Black*, Stendhal's novel of the inauthentic life (Julien Sorel, born too late to be a Napoleonic officer, chooses a career in the clergy instead, with disastrous results). Perhaps this was Gore's effort to explain to himself and the world his own out-of-body affect. Bush had an unpleasant personality; Gore had no personality at all, rather a set of operating instructions. Bush picked *The Raven*, a 1929 biography of Sam Houston, widely available in Texas, which I went to the library to read. Although it suffers from the overstuffed prose of an earlier era, I could see why Bush was taken with it. Like Bush, Houston had been an alcoholic, throwing over a successful life in Tennessee to move to Indian Territory (now Arkansas) and drink. But chance took him to Texas, where he found his destiny. You could turn yourself around; you could even become a great man. George W. Bush's father had led a worthy life, but it had a very different shape; Houston was an example the son could profit from. Bush had given thought to his own life, and his thoughts were cast in historic terms.

I SPENT ELECTION night 2000 at a party of Bill's at East Seventy-third Street, where the mood was glum: Florida was soon called for Gore. I held out hope for an inside straight that would allow Bush to win with a handful of small states, even if he lost Florida; Taki chided me for my folly. Late in the evening Florida was moved back into the undecided column, but there seemed to be no prospect of a quick decision. I left at midnight, and got stuck in a traffic jam caused by the victory party for Hillary Clinton's maiden Senate race.

Next morning when I awoke, I found that Bush had been given Florida and the election, then that Gore had withdrawn his concession. So began the five-week overtime that placed 2000 along with 1800, 1824, and 1876 in the Valhalla of screwed-up presidential elections. I noticed a curious split in judgment among my friends: Everyone who followed the election casually, and many who followed it closely (Terry Golway, my editor at the *New York Observer*, for instance), assumed that Bush's slim lead in Florida, ratified by the state government, would hold, giving him the electoral college and the presidency. But everyone at *National Review* feared that Florida's courts would find a formula for interpreting disputed votes that would give the game to Gore. We had been fighting the judiciary for so long that we ascribed to it malefic powers. In the end, Florida's courts were stopped by an even greater force, the U.S. Supreme Court, which made Bush the second second-generation president, after John Quincy Adams.

The 2000 election was one for the history books, but nail-biting contests are no predictor of history-making administrations. The year 1800 marked the first transfer of power from one party to another, 1876 the end of Reconstruction. But 1824 was followed by a mere hiatus, as the victor—John Quincy Adams, as it happened—failed to accomplish much of anything in the single term that he served. Dull times can be time wasted; they can also be times of prosperity and peace.

Late in the summer of 2001 Bill held a dinner at Paone's, in a private room behind the bar, to honor Van Galbraith as he stepped down as chairman of our board of directors, and Van told an apposite story. The last time he had been in Paris, he ran into a former prime minister, a socialist, whom he knew well from his days of stirring the pot as Reagan's representative. "Monsieur l'Ambassadeur," the man greeted him, "vous avez gagné! C'est le marché qui compte" (Mr. Ambassador, you won! The market rules). The 2000 election, like the Clinton scandals, seemed like the self-generated distractions of an Antonine age.

A tremendous thunderstorm broke as Van's party ended, the gutters running with water, and the next day was mild and clear. Jeanne and I went around the corner for a croissant and coffee before I went to *National Review*, where I had editorials and paragraphs to write. New Yorkers cherish these European affectations because we do feel somewhat transnational, and because if we stayed in our apartments for every possible meal we'd go stir-crazy. Someone came in to say that an airplane had crashed in Union Square, a block away. This was absurd; there would have been noise, chaos. Nevertheless, I took a quick look. In the square was nothing but trees and statuary—thoughtful Lincoln, ardent Lafayette, an equestrian Washington. But three miles to the south one of the World Trade Towers was streaming with smoke. Like thousands of other New Yorkers, I thought of the small plane (a B-25) that flew into the Empire State Building in the forties; small planes were always zipping around the harbor now. I went back to finish breakfast. As Jeanne and I left someone else walked in and said a second plane had hit.

So it was intentional. My initial reaction was to feel agitated and detached. Before going to·*National Review* I went to vote (September 11 was a Tuesday, and there was a primary for the next mayoral election). People on the street were listening to car radios and repeating equal parts information and misinformation: A plane had hit the Pentagon; there were twelve airliners unaccounted for. My polling place was in a high school across from a hospital; little EMS vans were already pulling in.

I was trying to hold off, for as long as possible, the moment of media immersion that would begin as soon as I arrived at *National Review*. That would also be the moment of reality. All my life, from Bobby Kennedy's assassination, even from the race riot in my hometown, reality had come to me through the media (I had seen the damage caused by the Rochester riot with my own eyes, but that was after the fact). Even when I became part of the media, fashioning other people's perceptions, my own were so often ratified by the media's frame.

Yet even at the office, the new reality had a frozen quality. I supplied the freeze, because the reality was so terrible. Someone had set up a television. One tower fell, then another. On-screen it looked cheesy, like a low-budget special effect. I said, obtusely, that maybe everyone below the level of the strikes had gotten out. Lyuba Kolomytseva, our art director, wept. First guesses of possible death tolls ranged as high as ten thousand.

After an hour or so of this it was time to get to work. Rich sat Jay, Ramesh, and me down. We would start the lead editorial on the cover, and follow with eight one-page essays, by staff and contributors. I would do the lead edit and one of the essays. "City Desk" in that issue had been about a visit to the tomb of Gouverneur Morris. Though he was no bad companion for disaster, I put him aside.

Communications went down erratically; we got a call from David Pryce-Jones, one of our contributors, from London, but our production staff labored to get our copy to the printer in Virginia. They managed it by sending our files via a fax line to a friend in Wisconsin, who had functioning T1 service. Taxis disappeared; the sidewalks filled with pedestrians. On the way home I ran into my oncologist. I asked where I could give blood. He said with my medical history mine would not be wanted.

Before I went home I had to do my job. That day we hardly knew anything, not even al-Qaeda's name. But we knew we had been hit, and all of us at *National Review* agreed what the response should be. AT WAR our cover said, followed by the first sentences of the lead edit. "The first great war of the 21st century began September 11." So we scooped the *New York Times*, whose headline the next morning said U.S. UNDER ATTACK.

My edit made three points. The causes of the attack, at least as far as they had to do with us, were not something we could do much about. America was the status quo superpower, so anyone who had a quarrel with the status quo would find us, somehow, ranged on the other side; our headquarters and our totems were natural targets. War had to be met with war. In those early hours, the administration had talked of "hunting down" the perpetrators. That sounded too mild. We were not looking for traffic violators to be given a desk ticket at the night court of The Hague. War should be a straight-up military proposition. Once we discovered who had ordered the attacks, they and their allies and patrons should be paved over. The purpose of the American military was to punish offenses and intimidate enemies, not to run elections and perform social work in the slums of the world. The first two points were right and, in the immediate aftermath, almost uncontested; the third point, I would come to see, was half wrong.

But this wasn't war anywhere; it was war on New York. I tried to respond to that in a new "City Desk." The purpose of terrorism is not just to murder the victims but to terrorize the survivors: to instill confusion and fear. To a degree I succumbed. I borrowed Mike's Bible, and found myself brooding over the fall of Babylon in Revelation 18. I quoted a long passage: "For in one hour so great riches is come to nought. . . . And the fruits that thy soul lusted after are departed from thee, and all things which were dainty and goodly are departed from thee, and thou shalt find them no more at all. The merchants of these things, which were made rich by her, shall stand afar off for the fear of her torment, weeping and wailing, and saying, 'Alas, alas that great city, that was clothed in fine linen, and purple, and scarlet, and decked with gold, and precious stones, and pearls!'" Picking those words at that moment was as bad a reaction as any Frenchified theorist's or left-wing moviemaker's: We had it coming, we asked for it; we have been too happy, punish us.

But knowing my city's history, and loving what I knew, I tried to come up for air. Great cities, I wrote—Babylon, Rome, London— had always excited the envy and resentment of rubes and poets. "Of all the cities of the New World, Nieuw Amsterdam was most likely to take their place. Boston, Philadelphia were holy experiments. This city was always about trade, from beaver pelts to derivatives." I conceded all the worst things New Yorkers had traded, from slaves to sex workers to stolen goods. "But, men being men," I went on, "most of [New York's] traffic was daily and just, cleansed by their honest effort." I called on one of my subjects, Henry Adams, John's great-grandson. In his introduction to *The History of the Administration of Thomas Jefferson*, he had argued that Americans were motivated not, as Europeans often said, by greed but by hope. The "contact of a moral atmosphere" made them work and plan. In hovels and wilderness, they saw instead "a glowing continent." The same, I said, was true of Americans in New York. "The workers of the world, once they came [here], could have a vision of tomorrow, a little better than the day before. . . . The world is full of devils, the hopped-up and the sickly holy. But New York still has business to attend to."

After the attack, Manhattan was locked down below Fourteenth Street. Union Square, which sits just above that wide cross street, became the anteroom of the disaster area. Every night it filled with people—there were a lot of New York University dorms in the area—trying to make sense of what had happened. They set out votive candles, meditated, prayed to a variety of gods. But they also talked. Much of what I overheard them saying was nonsense; sometimes voices were raised. But no one pushed or shoved, everyone took his turn. This too showed the contact of a moral atmosphere.

My greatest subject, George Washington, sat on a bronze horse at the southern edge of the park, facing downtown. His statue became the focal point of all this activity. Peace flags and American flags were draped over his horse's croup, and hung from his outstretched arm; a poster of the Trade Towers was fixed to his plinth. The father of his country became the father of the discussion. A line from "America the Beautiful"—it is a quirk of writers' minds to experience everything as words—rang in my head, as if asking to be made true again: "Thine alabaster cities gleam, undimmed by human tears." The line had never been true; Americans cities have been dimmed by fires, earthquakes, hurricanes, and epidemics throughout history. Atlanta and Richmond were burned in the Civil War, Washington in the War of 1812. The last time New York had been attacked had been the summer of 1776. George Washington, the man on horseback, had been in charge of the defense that time, and he had failed miserably. The British chased him out; a quarter of the city burned; the occupation lasted more than seven years; 11,000 Americans soldiers would die in British prisons and ships moored in the East River. We had our problems, Washington had his. He had come through them; so could we.

CHAPTER 14

THE DAY OF 9/11 had passed without Bill's guidance. I'm sure Rich called him, but I don't remember being told what he said. Bill filed a column on the attack, as he would file his columns, on time, up to the week he died. But we did not look to him for leadership. I was grateful to him for having left us *National Review*, as a medium for thinking and a platform for speaking. Now we were on our own.

Characters far more important than we were gave their own command performances. On the afternoon of the attack, members of Congress sang "God Bless America" on the Capitol steps. They meant well, but it did nothing for anyone's morale. President Bush stumbled out of the gate. His television address from the inauspiciously named Barksdale Air Force Base looked like outtakes from late-night 2000 election footage; it had been better left undone. Naturally, he had other things to think about, but one of the things a president must always think about is how he appears. Bush would not begin to find his footing until he spoke from a heap of rubble at Ground Zero on September 14, and would not speak with complete confidence until his address to Congress on the twentieth.

It may seem picayune to microanalyze politicians' responses, but the modern media age requires it. When the telegraph was invented, some journalist wrote, "There is no elsewhere; everything is here." There is no later; everything is now. The only leader who was right from the curtain riser was Mayor Giuliani, who was due to leave office in less than four months. The end of his second term had been a lurid diminuendo: He came down with prostate cancer, his marriage blew up, he backed out of a Senate race with Hillary Clinton. But once the towers were struck, his aggressive personality, his mania for detail, his power of concentration, and his abhorrence of a vacuum joined with a gravity and a dolor to make him the guide through this inferno. He was the on-screen presence who told us what was being done, what he knew and didn't know, that we were right to feel overwhelmed, and that we were brave despite it all (telling us how brave we were helped make us so). For three days he was effectively the president of the United States; he was a stronger moral force than the pope, who issued some charitable boilerplate, less felt than an appeal for the life of a condemned murderer. Giuliani made one mistake, as election day drew near, angling for a third term (the state would have had to override the city's term-limits law). He made no others.

I mention this because it is so hard to recapture. Giuliani became a brand of himself, a slogan—America's Mayor—and raked in speaking fees and consultancies, but when an open presidential nomination came up in 2008, conservatives realized that he would not make a phone call to the annual prolife march, and decided that it was pointless to ask presidential candidates in wartime whether they had ever done anything. Our faith in our issue positions was mystical and childish; they were self-enacting; one had only to espouse them to guarantee victory, then fulfillment. Giuliani assisted at his own demise by running a terrible campaign. Maybe he shone only in catastrophe.

Few of my friends had been downtown. In the midnineties George Marlin had an office in the World Trade Towers, as executive director of the Port Authority, though by 9/11 he was running an investment bank in Philadelphia. The *New York Post* had moved its offices from South Street to midtown, miles away from Ground Zero. But you didn't have to be downtown to be in danger. In October Mark Cunningham learned that he had been infected by one of the anthrax letters mailed to the *Post* and other media outlets. I told him that cigarettes and booze kill anthrax, so he would be okay. He bore his ordeal and his recovery with great gallantry. In a terror war, everyone is a combatant. The sense of it fades, as it humanly must, until the attack around the corner. But it should be kept in mind as a fact of life and death.

WE TOOK THE war to our enemies. The fall of the Taliban in Afghanistan, apparently accomplished by Predator drones and CIA agents on horseback, was amazingly swift, over by Christmas. The aftermath of men shaving the beards they had been forced to wear and women enrolling their daughters in schools impressed all but the crackpot Left.

The run-up to the Iraq War lasted fourteen months, and struck us as achingly slow. Saddam Hussein had been an active brute, even in his prison of sanctions, harboring terrorists, conniving in an earlier failed plot on the World Trade Towers in 1993, refusing to come clean about his WMD programs, and of course oppressing his people. After the shooting began in March 2003, his military collapsed more quickly than the Taliban's. Shortly after the fall of Baghdad, I ran into Ann Curry's husband, Brian Ross, in a coffeehouse on Irving Place. I had known Ann since our days at MSNBC, and she and Brian lived in the neighborhood. He gave me, from her, an Iraqi 250-dinar note with Saddam's picture on it, worth about eight cents while he still reigned, Confederate money now. Uday and Qusay, his feral sons, were killed in July, and Saddam himself was captured in December. No WMD had been found, but he had used them in the past, and would have built or bought them given the chance. His fate reminded me of the refrain of "Duncan and Brady," an old American ballad about the shooting of a crooked cop: "He been on the job too long."

But the war was not over. Saddam had counted on a rope-a-dope, guerrilla resistance; al-Qaeda and Iran poured resources into it. The Confederate analogy was apt. The Union broke the Confederacy's armies in 1865, but white insurgents (the Klan and other groups) fought on, murdering freed blacks and carpetbaggers, and hoping to wear the federal government and the Northern public out. In 2004 insurgents in Fallujah killed four American contractors and hung their burned bodies from the town bridge like decorations; they did it because it was the kind of thing they enjoyed doing, but it was also a media event, for Moslem and American consumption. It took the marines two battles to clear the town.

The administration put its hopes in a two-pronged political and military strategy. Iraq held its first free election in January 2005; the spectacle of Iraqis displaying their purple fingers, dyed to show that they had gone to the polls, moved those still willing to be moved. Meanwhile, the American military planned to work with a newly re-built Iraqi army, taking on the particularly hard jobs itself. Van Galbraith, whose last job was to be the defense secretary's representative to NATO, would give us pep talks whenever he came home from Brussels, telling us that he had been meeting in Amman with Sunni sheikhs who, although they were unhappy with the new state of things, would swallow it if there was law and order, and the chance for them to make money.

But this strategy failed. The Iraqi army was too new; our supporting operations became like a game of whack-a-mole. Iraqi politicians wrangled and waited to see which way the wind blew. In February 2006 the al-Askari Mosque, a Shiite holy site, was bombed by insurgents, in hopes of provoking a religious civil war. At the end of the year the Iraq Study Group, a blue-ribbon commission appointed by a restive Congress and cochaired by James Baker in his latest manifestation, suggested a gracious American surrender.

Bush's attitudes were easy to read, but increasingly hard, as things worsened, to understand. He never lost confidence in America's ideals or in his own ability. After he was reelected in 2004, he met with *National Review*'s editors in the Oval Office (I was not asked). Ramesh told me afterward that if he had to characterize Bush's mood, he would say, "Bush in charge." Bush's second inaugural was a sweeping statement about human nature. "Americans, of all people, should never be surprised by the power of our ideals. Eventually, the call of freedom comes to every mind and every soul." Rich wrote in his syndicated column that Bush had determination "in buckets."

But that was not enough in the current state of the war on the ground. John McCain had been calling for a "surge" in American troops; it was a perfect role for him, drawing on his military knowledge, his dislike of Bush, and his complete self-assurance. A surge would not only increase our forces but use them differently. We had to fight a counterinsurgency war, neighborhood by neighborhood, town by town. This meant not just clearing and holding territory but also politicking with local figures and providing social services. The skepticism I had expressed about such measures in our postwar editorial was wrong, at least in this instance; Iraq would be won this way or not at all.

Bush green-lighted the surge, which began in January 2007. Over twenty months of hard work, hard fighting, and more dying, the surge succeeded. The Sunni sheikhs Van and others had been talking to came on board; insurgents were driven from Baghdad and most of the countryside. The war went from the number-one issue in American politics to almost no issue at all. In our post–Civil War insurgency, the original victors eventually lost heart, and minority rule was restored in the South for ninety years. In this insurgency, the Klan lost.

The commanders and their troops made the surge happen; McCain could also take credit. But so could Bush. Correcting a mistake is harder than steering out of a skid. You have to fight both the inertia of error and everyone's default response, which is simply to quit. You have to fight, most of all perhaps, your own pride and stubbornness. Bush came to see the need for a new strategy, and pushed it through. He never lost his conviction that success mattered. His second inaugural was essential to him here. The second inaugural was easy to mock: The call of freedom may come to every mind and soul, but do they listen when it calls? So often men don't, for there are other competing calls: the need to get through the day, the desire to be recognized and esteemed. Men will enslave themselves to eat, and to make a mark in the world. But Bush was also partly right:

Men want not to be bossed around, kicked in the head. The shaving Afghans and the voting Iraqis are proof—and his legacy.

———

RICH STEERED THE magazine through this bewildering time. There is a fog of war, and a fog of war reporting. Both are by turns dark with ignorance, bright with too many plausible explanations. Rich joined Bill Kristol of the *Weekly Standard* in calling for the surge in September 2006. He called it before I did, because he followed the news more closely and judged it more honestly. He avoided the opposing errors of rigidity and panic. After the fact everyone claims to know what the right course should have been, but everyone does not agree even years later, as the debates of historians prove. You have to ask questions, feel your way, avoid the madness of crowds and the certainties of cliques.

Not all of us in right-world behaved as well as Rich, not nearly. When I had been researching my first long piece for *National Review*, on why Washington doesn't work, I interviewed some veteran of the Ford administration who had trouble recalling the name of a conservative congressman whom he thought was too pure for this world. "White shoes," he said. "Ron Paul?" I suggested. In the mid-seventies Ron Paul was a doughty Reaganite; the Ford supporter may have been right to mock his shoes, but Paul backed the better man. Thirty years later he became the leader of his very own antiwar movement, a children's crusade of libertarians, leftists, and 9/11 conspiracy theorists (e.g., Giuliani stole gold that was stored in the World Trade Center).

Taki bankrolled the *American Conservative*, a semiweekly organ for Pat Buchanan, and came to believe that our problems in the Middle East and with radical Islam could be solved by pitching Israel off the sled. Taki had no love for Arabs. In his youth he had lost a huge sum gambling in London with a Saudi (was he a prince? they all seem to be). The winner offered to forgive the debt. Taki refused, though doing so made him vomit in the bathroom afterward, for he knew that if he agreed he would be forever under the man's thumb. Yet he liked Israelis and their supporters here even less. Maybe he should have gambled with some of them.

But war resistance, tinged with Israel bashing, was by no means only a phenomenon of the Right. Anti-Jewish language and presumptions, lightly coded, became a feature of ordinary liberal thought. A key term, and concept, was *neocon*. Neocons became, in ordinary usage, those who had arranged the war in Iraq and hoped to arrange one with Iran, and the important neocons were Jews. Bush, Dick Cheney, and Donald Rumsfeld were not Jews, of course, but the men who filled their ears with lies—Paul Wolfowitz, Scooter Libby, Doug Feith—were. Another term of art was *Straussian*, since Wolfowitz had been a student of Allan Bloom; surely, the two Jews had laid deep plots together. Skousenism jumped the aisle and up the social scale, to land in the copy of learned journals and mainstream pundits. You would think the Trade Towers had been leveled and Kuwait occupied by the Mossad. It was an extraordinary development.

Hatred of George W. Bush became a kind of madness. All the bad habits of the Clinton years returned, made worse by the pressure of war. For years I had been telling audiences that the politics of the founding fathers, from the 1790s to the War of 1812, was worse than ours: more crazy, more dishonest, more vile. I still said so, but the gap had shrunk. At least no politicians were killed in duels, as happened to two signers of the Constitution and one signer of the Declaration of Independence, but 2006 saw a British-made mockumentary about Bush's assassination. The film's supporters defended it as art, which it was. Goebbels was an artist too.

BETWEEN THE SUPPORTERS of Bush and the war, enthusiastic or sober, and the critics, polite or demented, stood Bill. His views on the wars and their opponents fluctuated during the last years of his life, right to the end.

Early in 2003 Bill asked David Frum to do a long essay for *National Review*, titled "Unpatriotic Conservatives." It was "In Search of Anti-Semitism 2.0," except Jew-bashing was only one item in the indictment. The writers and pundits David discussed—many, though not all of them, antiwar libertarians—thought America was sunk in imperialism and dysfunction. All during the writing and editing Bill urged David to pile it on and punch it up. Yet as soon as the article appeared, he backpedaled, in a vain effort to placate one of the targets. David had slammed columnist Robert Novak for arguing that 9/11 was not nearly as bad as Pearl Harbor, since Japan and the Nazis had aimed at world domination, whereas the jihadist hijackers were motivated merely by "hatred of Israel." (They missed their target by six thousand miles then.) Novak maintained a pantomime of outrage for years.

Bill's syndicated column also tacked from month to month. In May 2005 he wrote that it was time to choose exit strategies in Iraq. "Our part of the job is done as well as it can be done, given limitations on our will and our strength." In July, he wrote that the sort of people who planned and applauded 9/11 (he coined a new name for them, "the Talibanate") were "most heavily concentrated in—Iraq." I read the column when it appeared, and I have reread it several times now, and it is still not clear to me whether he meant to argue that we should kill the Talibanate where it now was, or that our invasion of Iraq had caused a resurrection of it there. In November he was back where he had been in May: "We are now very close to that point of general agreement" that the Iraq war should end. In 2006, Joe Lieberman was defeated in the Democratic primary for his Senate seat by an antiwar challenger, Ned Lamont. Bill supported Lieberman, who won the November election running as an independent, but that was for auld lang syne; if Bill had voted strictly on the issues, he should have backed Lamont. During these years, on this issue, Christopher Hitchens was a better guide than the man who had called him an exhibitionist moralist.

Bill was trying to think through the war, as Rich was, as any serious person must. But no one thinks in a void; our thoughts climb particular trellises. As always, Bill placed great store by the views of his friends. But because his friends now disagreed more sharply among themselves than they had in the days of the cold war, he veered between their opinions. At one editorial dinner—more and more Bill was hosting them at Paone's as Pat's health and spirits deteriorated—he repeated something he said he had heard from the English historian Alistair Horne. Horne was Bill's friend of longest standing; they had gone to the same prep school, Millbrook Academy in Dutchess County, Bill as a bright rich kid from nearby Connecticut, Horne as an evacuee from World War II Britain. It is impossible now, Bill reported, to say anything critical of Israel in the British press. The statement implied a world of judgment: Neocons held public opinion in thrall in England, even as they did here. The alleged fact was incredible—England has never been a blessed plot of Zionists. Very likely, Bill had simply misunderstood whatever Horne told him. But he offered it, uncritically, as gospel—that moment's gospel.

At other times, Norman Podhoretz would send him an e-mail or the manuscript of a book, and Bill would write a gung-ho column in response. Bill was aware of this pattern: "You haven't sent me any critical e-mails," he greeted Norman at one party. "I've been blocked," said Norman.

Long-standing assumptions of Bill's inclined him to think the Iraq war had failed. His father had been an America Firster before Pearl Harbor, and so had Bill; he named his first boat *Sweet Isolation*, a two-word poem about sailing, and a policy statement. One of his favorite quotations was a declaration by John Quincy Adams, during his tenure as James Monroe's secretary of state, that the United States "goes not abroad, in search of monsters to destroy. She is the well-wisher to the freedom and independence of all. She is the champion and vindicator only of her own." Bill himself had put isolationism in abeyance during the cold war, when the struggle against communism entailed wars and coups from Vietnam to Chile. Once communism shriveled, give or take a billion Chinese, an aspect of Bill's nature reappeared, like a rock in a dry river.

There was one more return of the repressed, which concerned the people in whose countries we were fighting. Throughout the cold war, Bill and *National Review* had sympathized with the victims of communism. The victims closest to us socially and culturally were

Eastern Europeans, many of them Catholic—the Hungarians who fought in the 1956 revolution, the Poles of Solidarity. But our fellow feeling was universal; we memorialized the sufferings of subject peoples around the world, whether they were Catholic or not—Cubans, Vietnamese, Chinese. Yet this impulse cut against the skepticism with which we viewed the political skills of most societies. One of the easiest ways to raise a laugh in our editorial section was to refer to democracy in Africa or South America (the Buckley family's experience of Mexico disposed Bill to expect little there). Once the goal of the Iraq war shifted from toppling Saddam to erecting democratic or constitutional government in his place, these doubts surfaced. On even-numbered days Bill supported smiting our enemies, and he admired plucky Israel except when its supporters were stifling discussion in Britain, but he saw nothing inspiring about making Iraq safe for poll watchers.

I knew Bill's last doubt well; I had grown up laughing at those jibes at third world elections, before writing them myself. Since college I had been reading and rereading Evelyn Waugh's global dystopias. In 2005, in our fiftieth-anniversary issue, I bade farewell to them, and the view of the world they expressed.

Waugh the anthropologist, I wrote, had taught me, or confirmed in me, a belief in "happy darkies." This was my term, not his, for the subjects of his exotic writing: people with dark skins who lived in Africa, Asia, and much of the Americas. It was ironic to call them happy, since their lives were blighted by poverty and pathology. Yet, Waugh believed, their lives could be worse. That happened whenever someone tried to transform them. Various characters in Waugh's novels—assorted black totalitarians in *Scoop*, a reforming African emperor and his English sidekick in *Black Mischief*—caused real mischief by wanting to make the darkie modern and better. They only vexed him, until their inevitable failure, when things returned to their grim but natural course.

9/11 had shown the problem in a new light. "The world of the happy darkies," I wrote, "was not in equilibrium, but in flux, and the flux could come here." Millions of Africans and Asians had moved to Europe and America; the millions more who stayed home learned of us, not always inaccurately, from news and entertainment; and it took only a few box cutters to bring down skyscrapers. In such a world we could not play defense, and the offensive would have to be more than military. It would have to involve doing, wisely and better, what Waugh's rabid or rascally characters tried: transforming the world. Doing it wisely, I added, would mean "not doing most of it ourselves, but helping other people—the other no more—do so."

What reason was there to think that anyone wanted help? The flux of civilizations created frustration and rage, but it also stimulated hope for something better. All men had such hopes, along with their many vices, because all men are created equal. I moved my chips from Waugh to Jefferson (and, with reservations, to Bush's second inaugural). Somewhat to my surprise, Bill liked the piece.

But this was all on the level of analysis and ideas. Bill was not some unknown holder-forth in *Foreign Affairs*. On this matter, he was my leader, even now that he was emeritus. Our lives and personalities had ground against each other from time to time, but for the first time in my life I disagreed with him.

He was my lost leader. I thought of Robert Browning's poem, a ferocious attack on William Wordsworth. Browning was in his thirties when he wrote it, Wordsworth in his seventies. The older man, the inspiration of every English poet, had just accepted a government pension and the post of laureate. Browning began:

Just for a handful of silver he left us,
Just for a riband to stick in his coat.

No one had offered Bill handfuls of silver to blow hot and cold on the Iraq war; he had enough silver of his own, and more than enough ribands (honors). The lines that most struck me came later on.

He alone breaks from the van and the freemen,
—He alone sinks to the rear and the slaves!

Bill had not done that, quite, either; he had never praised slavery, in the manner of the worst opponents of the Iraq war (Michael Moore depicting Baathist Iraq as a land of happy kite flyers). But he was too often indifferent to it.

The fact is he was weary. He had his own poet, Whittaker Chambers, whose words were ever at his fingertips, and some of the words he most liked to quote were from the last letter Chambers ever wrote him. "Weariness, Bill—you cannot yet know literally what it means. I wish no time would come when you do know, but the balance of experience is against it. One day, long hence, you will know true weariness and will say: 'That was it.'" Chambers's weariness was the residue of years of spying for the Soviet Union, turning on the Soviet Union, going through the mill of hearings and trials. But age happens to everybody, not just figures in the headlines.

How I hated that Chambers quotation, and Bill's love of it. It was lodged in his mind like a computer virus. Bill got Chambers's last letter in April 1961, when he was thirty-five years old, long before the age of weariness, yet his fascination with it showed something about his own attitude toward activity. He had to be in constant motion, at cruising speed. When things stopped clicking, he could see no alternative to giving them up altogether. He had given up his last boat, stopped renting his ski house in Switzerland. There comes a time when we can't handle heavy machinery, can't walk. But short of that, there are lesser regimens, shorter routines. Maybe you keep going to Switzerland because you just like the place. This didn't strike Bill as sensible, or even conceivable.

For my part, I did not want to conceive of life without him, and all his peculiarities and habits. Even the ones I never shared were part of my image of him, and thus of me. I had never been to his ski house, but it mattered that he go. He should be like a figure in a clock, changeless and punctual.

I was angry with Bill, with time, and with his attitude toward time.

CHAPTER 15

BILL HAD BEEN *National Review*'s star obituarist from the beginning. The graceful farewell, the dying fall, suited his melancholy (years ago Norman Mailer had written in the *Village Voice* that one of Bill's personae was "the snows of yesteryear"). Now the obituaries were coming thick and fast. Ernest van den Haag died in the spring of 2002. Bill led the memorial service, in the library of the Union League Club. John Simon gave the most gracious tribute, saying that Ernest, after his eyesight failed, would accompany him to plays and ask if the actresses were pretty; John always answered that they were.

That spring Jeff narrowly escaped joining the cortege. For years he drank too much; then he drank much too much; finally the bill came. I visited him in St. Vincent's hospital in New York (he had collapsed during a magazine week), before he was released to go home to Hanover. He still had his good spirits, thank God. He was reading *Commentary* when I came in, and he described a procedure during which a yellow liquid had been drained from him. "It was rather pretty," he said, the sort of sharp, surprising detail that his heroes, Hemingway and Fitzgerald, might have noted.

When *National Review* turned fifty, we decided to throw ourselves two parties, one in Washington, one in New York. The first was at the National Building Museum, once the Pension Bureau, a vast Renaissance barn on F Street. Bill was at his most lugubrious; he seemed to consider himself posthumous.

The second party at the Pierre went much better. The star of the evening was Father Rutler, who gave the invocation, searching the communion of saints for Saints William who resembled Bill. It was hard to find a match. "There was a Saint William and his wife who both became hermits, dressed in rough garments, and took perpetual vows of silence. [Stage pause.] No."

It is hard to recompense hospitality as regular as Bill's and Pat's. My private celebration was to get them to come to our place in the Catskills. Bill should see the return on his investment. They were driven up one weekend, from Stamford. It's a long trip, against the flow of the highways, which pour south into New York City, and it was made longer by a wrong turn. When the limo finally came down the dirt driveway, Pat asked, from the backseat, "Are we still in the United States?" She had brought the spaniels. Bill was dressed down for Connecticut, in a yachting cap and a cashmere sweater. We grilled a salmon for them on the deck. I told them we had tapped our own sugar maples for the syrup. "Why, you live like the Amish," Pat exclaimed.

I had a purpose besides showing off the place. I knew they were both shots, Pat a serious one. In the years we had owned the house, I had seen raccoons on the edge of rabies—not rocking and drooling, but out in the daytime, moving slowly, unafraid. What should I get for varmint control? They talked about it, then recommended a shotgun. I offered to take Bill into the woods to see old stone walls, the tourist attraction of the Catskills, which, in the traditional formula, are two rocks for every clod of dirt, but at the tree line he stopped and said he had to go back; he was too winded to continue.

The following week, back in the city, I got a call from the office from Linda, who asked if I had been expecting anything from Bill. She had a package with a scrawled address that might be meant for "Rich" or "Rick." I didn't know of anything; what did it look like? "I think," Linda said, "it's a gun." I went to the office to see.

I found a bag for ski poles, which held a leather carrying case, which held a double-barreled shotgun. Next day came the explanatory letter from Bill. "Here is my little contribution to keeping the wolves at the door." He explained that it had been given to Pat, on a trip to Spain, by the American ambassador. "I don't think it has ever been shot, but it is [by] a well known maker, beautifully constructed. This is the gun Franco would have used to bring down 5,000 quail every day." It certainly looked like something Franco would have been pleased to bring to the gun club. The metal plates between the trigger and the breech were etched with pictures of ducks and retrievers. "It is 20 gauge," Bill went on, "and should be fine for the kind of things you described. Actually, it is fine for pretty much everything." He added some tips for care, some compliments to me and Jeanne on the house, and signed it XXB.

When I took it upstate, I showed it to a hunter friend, who appreciated it, but suggested I get something more utilitarian, so I bought a .410 from Gander Mountain. But the Buckleys' 20-gauge is utilitarian for memory.

PAT DIED FIRST, in the spring of 2007. The end was grim: circulation problems in her legs, an operation, sepsis. The memorial was held at the Temple of Dendur in the Metropolitan Museum. Considering all the money she had raised for them over the years, they could have renamed it the Temple of Pat. The best anecdote was told by Freddie Melhado, an investment banker who had known her since she was Bill's exotic fiancée. The phone rang at Stamford one Sunday at nine (too early for the day of rest). "The president wants to speak to Mr. Buckley." "The president of what?" Pat asked, unfazed.

When I next had lunch with Bill, he reminisced about going out to Vancouver to ask her father for her hand. Mr. Taylor was a formidable figure, a director of the Bank of Canada, but Bill felt he was also a little intimidated by Bill's being an American, and a Yalie. Bill had picked the Taylor who did her best not to be intimidated.

Bill soldiered on, hosting the editorial dinners, Linda taking Pat's place as hostess. They began earlier, to allow Bill to go back to Connecticut to sleep. He had emphysema and diabetes, which were a torment to him. A decade earlier, the magazine had run an article, at Bill's behest (it was dense and badly written), by Ernest van den

Haag, making the case for assisted suicide. I believe Bill would not consider such a thing for himself since his church prohibited it, but he knew it was permitted to ask for release. Evelyn Waugh had died after mass on Easter Sunday, after years of wretched health; his widow was convinced that he had prayed for death.

Two things gave him particular comfort. He was able to attend Latin mass, not the modern Peter, Paul, and Virgin Mary mass, at his parish church. It was a small service, for him and his servants. The Latin mass had been virtually prohibited after Vatican II, a source of aesthetic pain to Bill, but I knew that John Paul II and Benedict XVI had opened the door to it again, and I asked Bill's friend and spiritual adviser, Fr. Kevin Fitzpatrick, if he had taken advantage of the newly tolerant climate. "I told the parish priest we were going to do it," he said, "and I told him to keep his mouth shut." So Bill could worship in the words of saints and poets and his family.

His other comfort was music. Among his dead friends were musician friends—Tureck, Dick Wellstood, Fernando Valenti. But others took their place. One evening Ignat Solzhenitsyn, Aleksandr's oldest son, gave a concert at East Seventy-third Street. He gave a big, powerful performance; the bench looked like a toadstool under him, and he pulled huge sounds out of the Bosendorfer. On another night, Simone Dinnerstein came. Her recording of the Goldberg Variations, released in 2007, caused a sensation: Some said she was as good as Glenn Gould, the eccentric titan who had made these pieces a pop hit; some said she was better; more important than better or worse, she was different, having squeezed out from Gould's shadow to reinterpret the variations in her own way. She brought out details I had never heard before; at moments she was so intimate one felt almost embarrassed to be listening in a room with other people. Bill's concert setup performed its usual tricks: One of the lightbulbs in the lamp on the piano sputtered and flashed at the fortes, causing Bill to lift himself up, so slowly now, out of his chair, to tap it.

His regulars were Bruce Levingston and Larry Perelman, Bruce a concert pianist, Larry a serious student who had decided to serve mammon, but who kept the music in his fingers as an earnest amateur. Larry cut himself no slack; he played (not all on one night, to be sure) Beethoven's last three sonatas, in which modernism, postmodernism, jazz, and opera all jostle almost insanely. But the performance I remember best, because of Bill, was of the c-minor partita by Bach. After the tumultuous capriccio that ends it, Bill said that there was a passage in that movement that had made his old friend Fernando Valenti say, despite being an unbeliever, that he believed in God whenever he played it. Bill asked Larry to play the movement again, and said he would stand by the piano and indicate the passage when it came. The left hand went boom-chk, boom-chk, boom-chk, like Wellstood playing Fats Waller, and the piece spun like equations or galaxies. Bill raised his arms over his head and grinned; love and work had delivered beauty, as promised.

I doubt if politics gave him that sort of solace; it was his job. When the surge in Iraq began, he supported it, on the grounds that even an unwise or seemingly failed venture should have the chance to end in victory. At the last directors' meeting he attended—there was always business before the dinner—he said that the struggle against jihadists was our world war, our most important mission. The jihadists had made that decision for us, but I was glad to hear that he said so. He followed the punishing warm-up of the 2008 campaign; the only thing he cared about was that John Edwards—who struck him as a pretty-boy demagogue, Harry Truman with hair—lose. The voters took care of it, even before Edwards did.

I WAS IN Washington at Michael Pack's house in February 2008, working on the scene list for a new documentary, when his wife, Gina, came into the dining room to say that Bill Buckley was dead. For all his long decline, it was a shock; there had been no sudden, serious bout, no rush to the hospital. He had died in his garage office, at his desk, evidently writing the next column that was due. The next forty-eight hours were a round of death tourism; this, that, and the other one, all wanting comments. The first e-mail I got was from the woman who, as a girl, had fretted that the crowd at the college reception to which I had lured my famous boss was crowding him too closely. The memorial mass at St. Patrick's Cathedral was a tribute to Bill's life: The eulogists were Henry Kissinger and Chris (six months later, Chris honored his father again by endorsing Barack Obama, a twofer: rebelling against his politics, emulating his provocations). But the mass also seemed like a credit roll of my life. I kept seeing faces from my teens on, beginning with Gene Meyer and Greg Hyatt.

I could not grasp his death until I got, soon after, a copy of his latest book, *Flying High*. This was a volume of his memories of Barry Goldwater (it carried a blurb by, of all people, me). He would throw in little fictionalized episodes, which drove me nuts. But there were also glimpses simultaneously mellow and vivid, of a vivid man. There was a hilarious dirty joke about Goldwater and a bumptious female supporter during the 1964 New Hampshire primary, and there was a description of a visit that Bill and Goldwater made to the South Pole eight years later. This was poignant as well as vivid, for the coda of it was about transience. Bill left the pole with a chunk of 25,000-year-old ice, given to him by a scientist. On the flight to the U.S. Naval base on the Antarctic coast, the ice melted. Bill poured it into bottles for urine, borrowed from the dispensary, one of which he mailed to Goldwater when he got home. Ten years later, visiting his friend in Arizona, he and Goldwater dug out the bottle and found that half of the ice water had evaporated.

Inside the front cover, where, in all the other books that had come once a year like clockwork there had always been a bookplate with a scrawled signature, there was this time a printed note from Linda, explaining that Bill would want her and the publisher "to send out copies of this book to the people he would have sent it to." No more writing, no more giving. Then I wept.

I TOLD HIM what he meant to me once, soon after he had stepped down as editor of *National Review*. Henry Kissinger had offered to throw a dinner in his honor, and told him to make up the guest list. Bill did a very Bill-like thing, inviting all his younger colleagues. I was the oldest guest in the room, after Chris and Bob Tyrrell. Kissinger lives in River House, at the end of Fifty-second Street, with one of those power views of the East River, black at night. He gave a tour d'horizon—Bill could make people sing for their supper even when they were throwing the supper—and there was a pause. Tyrrell proposed a toast to Bill. As we hear-hear'ed, Rich Vigilante leaned over to me and told me to say something.

I had in fact been thinking of something to say. The limitation of writers is to experience the world through words; the vanity of writers is to be always playing with words to capture the world, and their own experience. I stood up and said this, more or less: "One of Yeats's last poems is called 'Beautiful Lofty Things,' and in it he remembers people who have been important to him: an old lover, waiting for a train, tall and proud as a Greek goddess; a drunken journalist, entertaining other drunks with highfalutin nonsense. The most important is his father, defying an angry crowd at a public meeting. '"This land of saints," and then as the applause died out, / "Of plaster saints"; his beautiful, mischievous head thrown back.' Bill, you are the father of the conservative movement, and so in a way of everyone in this room. It's not my place to describe your head, but I've never known anyone more respectful of real saints, or more mischievous to plaster ones—and that has been beautiful."

Bill wrote and asked me for a copy. I told him that I hadn't written it down—which was true—and left it at that. Of course, I could have reproduced it. But if I had given it to him, I know what would have become of it: He would have run it in "Notes & Asides." There were wounds, at the beginning of John's reign and my exile, which I felt were too fresh to be bandaged over in that way, just then. He had heard it, and my friends had heard it; that was enough. But time has passed, and Bill has passed, and maybe I am man enough. Here it is.

Index

Gigot, Paul, 91
Gingrich, Newt, 117, 152, 191, 193–195, 197, 216
Ginsberg, Allen, 11
Giuliani, Rudy, 182–185, 215, 226, 230
Glazer, Nathan, 76, 77
Glikes, Erwin, 146
God and Man at Yale (Buckley), 14–15, 207
Gold, Vic, 109–110, 172
Goldberg, Jonah, 209
Goldberg, Lucianne, 116, 199, 209
Goldwater, Barry, 15, 21, 27, 42, 50, 51, 92–93, 109, 121, 242
Golway, Terry, 219
Goodell, Charles, 24
GOP. *See* Republican Party, Republicans
Gorbachev, Mikhail, 29, 131, 154, 164–165
Gore, Al, 159, 218
Gore, Leslie, 29
Gottlieb, Bob, 145
Gould, Glenn, 95
Graham, Billy, 26, 157
Grateful Dead, 13
Greene, Graham, 202
Grove, Lloyd, 31
Guardian, 118
Guatemala, 43

Haag, Ernest van den, 79, 122, 141, 147, 187, 237, 239–240
Hamill, Pete, 164
Hamilton, Alexander, 111, 144, 190, 200, 212, 213
Hamlet (Shakespeare), 41
Hammett, Bill, 183
Hancock, Winfield Scott, 21
Harding, Warren, 27
Harold: The Last of the Saxon Kings (Bulwer-Lytton), 18

Harrison, William Henry, 82, 153
Hart, Gary, 117, 151
Hart, Jeffrey, 40, 45, 48, 65, 69, 70, 91, 111, 114–115, 122, 126, 135–136, 151, 237
  Brookhiser, Richard as Buckley successor and, 139
  communism, collapse of and, 165
  1976 presidential election and, 49
  1980 presidential election and, 83
  1992 presidential election and, 172
  Panama Canal treaties and, 74
  sports and, 116
Harvard University, 51
Harvey, Paul, 9
Hatch, Orrin, 216
Hawn, Goldie, 24
Heath, Aloise Buckley, 14
Hefner, Hugh, 14, 205
Heinlein, Robert, 128
Hemingway, Ernest, 40
Henry, Patrick, 85
Hentoff, Nat, 97
Heritage Foundation, 67, 112, 209
Hiss, Alger, 26, 44
Hiss, Tony, 44
Hitchens, Christopher, 2, 129, 130, 210, 232
Hitler, Adolf, 26, 125
Hobbes, Thomas, 93
Hofstadter, Richard, 200
Hogue, Larry, 184
Honecker, Eric, 102
Hook, Sidney, 79
Hooker, Brian, 18
Horne, Alistair, 233
Horton, Willie, 155
House, Edwin, 48–49
Housman, A. E., 43
Huffington, Arianna, 114
Human Life Review, 98